Clarinet

YEHUDI MENUHIN MUSIC GUIDES

Available
Violin and viola by Yehudi Menuhin and William Primrose
Piano by Louis Kentner

In preparation
contributions on
Bassoon by William Waterhouse
Double bass by John Gray
Flute and recorder by James Galway
Guitar and lute by Narciso Yepes
Harp by Sidonie Goossens
Horn by Barry Tuckwell
Oboe by Leon Goossens and Edwin Roxburgh
Organ by Simon Preston
Percussion by James Holland
Trumpet by Sidney Ellison

To follow
contributions on
'Cello
Conducting and Orchestration
Harpsichord and early keyboard instruments
Trombone and tuba
Voice

YEHUDI MENUHIN MUSIC GUIDES

Clarinet

Jack Brymer

930927 **H**

SCHIRMER BOOKS
A Division of Macmillan Publishing Co., Inc.
NEW YORK

SCHIRMER BOOKS
A Division of Macmillan Publishing Co., Inc.
866 Third Avenue, New York, N.Y. 10022

First American Edition 1977

Library of Congress Catalog Card Number: 77–275

Printed in the United States of America

hardbound printing number
1 2 3 4 5 6 7 8 9 10

paperback printing number
1 2 3 4 5 6 7 8 9 10

Library of Congress Cataloging in Publication Data

Brymer, Jack.
  Clarinet.

  (Yehudi Menuhin music guides)
  Bibliography: p.
  Discography: p.
  Includes index.
  1. Clarinet.
ML945.B8   788'.62   77-275
ISBN 0-02-871430-X
ISBN 0-02-871440-7 pbk.

Contents

List of Illustrations

ACKNOWLEDGEMENTS

Editorial board:

General editor:	Yehudi Menuhin
Coordinating editor:	Patrick Jenkins
Advisers:	Martin Cooper
	Eric Fenby
	Robert Layton
	Denis Stevens
Drawings:	Tony Matthews
Music examples:	Malcolm Lipkin

The excerpt from *La Forza del Destino* is reproduced by permission of G. Ricordi and Co., and is that from Vivaldi's *Concerto Grosso*. The illustrations from *The Compleat Book for the Mock Trumpet* are by permission of the University of Glasgow; the volume is in the Euing Music Collection in the library there, pressmark B.e.19. The author and publisher thank all those who have supplied illustrations, including Breitkopf and Hartel London Limited for permission to reproduce music examples on behalf of copyright holders, the Rychenberg-Stiftung, Winterthur and the Staatsbibliothek, Berlin. They are also grateful to Messrs Boosey and Hawkes who assisted greatly with the technical details of the modern instrument.

'He is truly a musician, who with all
reasonable consideration gains knowledge
of music, not by mechanical operation,
but by the power of thought . . .
dominated by the spirit of discovery.'

Boethius – circa 480–524

Editor's Introduction
by Yehudi Menuhin

How enlightening it is to read, at the hands of a master, of the myriad and untold complexities of clarinet playing and of their resolutions, and how important it is to be guided towards a more understanding and profound appraisal of this skill. I have always loved that dark and 'cheeky' (no pun intended!) sound which seemed to me the very breath and voice of Bartok or Brahms.

Jack Brymer has given us all – musicians and laymen, beginners and artists, composers, teachers, clarinet-makers and repairers – a book full of countless revelations and there is even some very wholesome advice to studio, concert hall and theatre designers. All this will add not a little to the admiration and delight with which we receive and 'savour', in this book, the wisdom and experience of a distinguished clarinettist. Nor is this all: for it is his own enthusiasm and sustained excitement that the author conveys to the reader, as we explore with him the still evolving cosmology of the clarinet.

Yehudi Menuhin, 1976

1

Author's Preface

In the pages which follow I hope readers may find some of my personal views and convictions about the clarinet. Some of these are unquestionably fact; others are a matter of opinion. Where these opinions diverge from those conventionally held, I make no apology, because half the fun of playing and experimenting with the clarinet is that it can and does happen in many ways, can speak with so many and varied voices, that to attempt to pin it down to any norm is unthinkable.

Presumably any reader of a book like this has a desire to *think* about the clarinet. If I can add to this process or spur it on, I shall feel that the aim of this book is achieved.

Jack Brymer

1976

Introduction

The aim of this book is two-fold. First, to take a close look at the clarinet as it is today – an instrument studied by a very great number of people who have probably regarded it always as a fact of life, as something which has arrived more or less ready-made, and which is unlikely to change much in the future. Secondly, to make a careful examination of how the instrument came to be what it is, by reviewing its rather short history and the influences of its players and the composers who have written for it.

In addition, it is important to consider the great number of different approaches now being made by players, who albeit in a shrinking world and in constant contact with one another, nonetheless strenuously maintain their own point of view as to what the clarinet should sound like. The few short miles which separate Dover from Calais bring another spoken language; but this is hardly a more dramatic contrast than the change they also bring to the sound of the clarinet. Nor does it end there. Cross any border in Europe and a similar change in style is immediately evident, even though the radio stations of the country just left are pouring out hours of examples of their own style, and this is clearly heard across the frontier. Like some quite good wines clarinet sound can be regarded as a poor traveller. The reasons for this are debatable. They may have roots in language, or in national characteristics. They also certainly have a connection with the historical aspect of the instrument; and this historical background has been so thoughtfully and ably covered by the several authorities mentioned in our bibliography that it is best to give it more slender treatment here rather than simply duplicate what has already been so well done by others. At the same time, no book on the clarinet should claim to be complete without a section dealing with this fascinating topic – the incredibly swift rise of the instrument to a position of distinction both as a solo instrument and as the completion of the orchestral wood-wind section. This development was of course very intimately bound up with the essential differences between the clarinet and the other reed members of the orchestra, the oboe and bassoon; acoustic differences which have always set it apart and made its voice unique. A short study in these differences is an essential part of this book, couched in as simple terms as can be managed. It is hoped that the inclusion of this section in what is in no way intended to be a technical treatise will help those interested in the instrument more fully to understand its unusual nature from an harmonic point of view, and its consequent stimulation of the imagination of performers and composers during the past two centuries and more.

Certainly it is intended to reveal the personal approach of one player to the ever-present problems of clarinet-playing. Many of the opinions expressed are personal and open to discussion. They are, however, the result of an approach to the instrument which has always tried to be unbiased, and which started out with the clear eyes of youth candidly testing the instrument as a play-thing, before even understanding its possibilities as an artistic vehicle. From the age of six years it was the natural companion of the writer, so that any considerations of this or that national 'school' of playing had to come much later, and then as a question of analysis rather than as facts of life. Life with the clarinet has been one of constant experiment and discovery: a process which happily still continues. Such conclusions as have revealed themselves are contained herein. The instrument remains a fascinating bundle of inconsistencies and contradictions, some of which it is good to attempt to resolve.

Obviously any book which attempts to cover all that has been mentioned – history, acoustics, approach of players, schools of playing etc., – presents a problem of selection.

No such book can be complete, and all the excellent works in our bibliography are incomplete in some ways. We can hope only to cover some aspects which have not been generally fully treated, while also covering those which have.

One
The Clarinet Today

To one reading an orchestral score, the clarinet is the third of the wood-wind instruments from the top, following the flute and the oboe. Historically it is the fourth of them, because its invention followed that of flute, oboe and bassoon. This simple fact explains one of its most important functions in the orchestra; when it arrived, in the early part of the eighteenth century, it immediately completed the orchestral wood-wind, adding a colour to the palette at the composers' disposal which filled a gap many of them had felt for a long time. Certainly one of these was the young Mozart, who wrote in a letter to his father Leopold from Mannheim 'Oh, if only we also had clarinets – you cannot imagine the splendid effect of a Symphony with flutes, oboes, and clarinets.' The fact that he seemed indifferent to the presence or absence of bassoons is neither here nor there – there were enough of them around to make them commonplace, and he certainly did not fail to use them with the other three in his future symphonies, whenever the full section presented itself.

The plain truth is that the clarinet is an instrument of greater flexibility than any of the other three. That is not to say it is their superior, because they all have their strong and weak points. Some of these, as they apply to the clarinet, are dealt with in Chapter 5: but the clarinet has the most extensive compass of them all, almost four complete octaves,

The clarinet has the greatest dynamic range, from an

inaudible *ppp* to a trumpet-like *fff*; a subtler variety of tone-quality, from velvet-soft to steely-hard – and a consequent ready ability to blend with other instruments which makes it the essential 'binding' factor of the wood-wind section. The underlying reasons for these characteristics we can examine later, in a discussion of the acoustic peculiarities of the instrument, in Chapter 3.

Meanwhile it is important simply to know what it is that makes the sound, and what we mean when we talk of a clarinet.

The first obvious fact, as we look around, is that the word means any one of a number of instruments of widely differing sizes, from the tiny E flat of about eighteen inches, to the immense coiled length of the B flat contra-bass – about ten feet. (See p. 10)

It can mean, consequently, a sound which can be the shrill altissimo in the register of a piccolo or a gruff voice in unison with the double bass of the strings. It can also mean instruments which look very different from each other because they are of different materials – wood, ebonite (hard rubber), plastics (black or coloured), glass or metal; and different because they employ different systems of key work. Yet these are all clarinets. They have some factors in common, and these are the vital factors which decide that they *are* clarinets. They all have a *generator* of vibrations – that is, a mouthpiece with a reed attached (see fig. **3**) which acts as a simple 'squeaker' when it is blown on its own, providing the raw material of the sound, and a tube with holes cut in it to act as the *resonator* and produce the typical clarinet sound when the mouthpiece is attached to it.

Leaving aside the variations mentioned above, and assuming that by 'clarinet' most of us mean the B flat soprano instrument which outnumbers the others by an overwhelming ratio, and in the Boehm system of fingering which is also very much a world majority, a glance at the picture of such an instrument in fig. **1*** reveals some of its obvious characteristics. First, it is a fairly long tube, some 26½in. in length, and it has

* Figure numbers throughout refer to the sections of photographs.

The clarinet family. Left to right: E flat soprano, B flat, E flat alto, B flat bass, B flat contra-bass. The A natural is also in common use. Others, less used, are A flat sopranino, D natural soprano, basset horn in F, and contra-alto in E flat.

an internal bore of just over $\frac{1}{2}$in. It is a fairly stout instrument, and the reason for this is that the bore is virtually the same for the greater part of its length. In other words, it is a long cylinder – a fact which makes it quite unique among reed instruments, and is responsible for all the phenomena of compass, flexibility and general usefulness already mentioned.

The next obvious feature is the large number of keys and rings which adorn the instrument. As in other wood-wind instruments, the function of these is effectively to vary the length of the tube which is in action at a given instant. The keys help the fingers to close the holes, starting at the top, and letting the air escape from the nearest hole below the lowest one closed. This alters the pitch of the sound produced – the longer the tube, the lower the note, in the simplest sense of instrumental acoustics. It is not really so simple, as Chapter 3 will reveal, but this is the fundamental underlying principle.

The key-work of a modern clarinet is of necessity a very complex piece of engineering. The aim is extremely simple: the key is an extension of the finger, presenting to it a lever which opens or closes a hole which is out of reach. The large number of keys employed in the modern clarinet have the added effect of multiplying the number of 'fingers' available. These are necessary to deal with the great number of holes now cut in the tube, and because these holes are placed in the best acoustic position which can be found for them – which is by no means necessarily where they are convenient for the hands.

The analogy of the key with the finger can be carried still further, in that the soft pad of the finger-tip is ideal for the closure of these tone-holes, and the pad of the modern clarinet, in its hollow cup poised over the hole, is an imitation of this. Sometimes it is of soft, thin leather, sometimes of the bladder-skin of an animal, and usually padded with soft felt. The method of application to the tone-hole is vital, as the seal must be instant and air-tight under pressure. To assist this, the hole is provided with a countersunk bevelled rim, which impresses the pad and resists the flow of air. A lot of ingenuity has gone into the design of keys with this in mind. A typical successful shape is shown in fig. **4**.

In addition to this problem of closure, instant and secure, it is important that the pad should clear the hole by the right distance when the key is pressed. Too close, and the note produced is masked and 'stuffy'. Too distant, and the time necessary for its movement is long and makes the playing of quick passages impossible. The key must also be made to travel the same distance as adjacent ones, for obvious reasons of comfort.

The remaining problems are those of silence, and of correct springing – the key must return to its rest position instantly and smoothly. Silence of action is more important than it might at first seem to be. With the simple instruments of the past, loaded with only the minimum of keys, and those fairly sluggish in their movement, there was no such problem. With the multiplicity of moving parts in a modern clarinet, it is obvious that the failure to damp mechanical noise can have a serious side-effect; the pure legato which is the aim of all clarinettists is often overlaid with an intrusive percussive accompaniment due to the absence of a tiny cushion of cork from a vital bearing-point, bringing sarcastic glances and tappings of pencils upon music stands from those around. The remedy is the careful application of very slender sections of cork of the finest quality, fixed with the most modern of adhesives, to each adjacent contacting metal surface. This is an extremely skilled operation and the reason why instrument repairers and makers of the highest quality are so venerated by players.

Springing of keys is of two sorts – the spring which keeps the key in the open position, ready for closure by the finger, and the one which holds it closed until required to open. Details of the operation and design of these types are given in Chapter 4.

So much for the structure of the clarinet. From this quite complicated assortment of mechanical achievement, developed over the past two and a half centuries, derive many subtle musical possibilities, and many variations in the way these can be used. These variations may be said to divide at present into two broad and quite distinct categories – the French pattern, and the German – from which we may conclude that the key arrangement of the instrument may be varied without it ceasing to be a clarinet. As Chapter 2 will reveal, there are good historical reasons for this difference of appearance, approach and even of the method of production of sound and the aim of players when they are producing it. In purely scientific terms, the two types of clarinet are virtually identical. Here the word 'virtually' is the operative one, because it is the tiny differences, from the acoustical point of view, which make the devotees of the one or the other type take issue as to what the sound of a clarinet should be. There has been a divergence of opinion, due to historical events, and this has led us to the present duality in clarinet design. This will be discussed in detail later. Meanwhile, figs 1 and 2 show some details of the instruments in question with a few of their specifications as we find them today.

Possibly the most important characteristic of both the French and German clarinets is the beauty of the expressive vocal line of which the instrument is capable – the long sustained legato; the ability of the clarinet to play comfortably with almost any combination of instruments is equalled only by its complete self-possession when it is played entirely by itself. It is moreover very easy to learn to play in the early stages, which gives it an immediate attraction. It is, however, extremely difficult to play well and musically, because of the necessity to control the equality of its tone over a wide compass, and to correct intonation – which is, in a finely-tuned sense, not always reasonably good by nature.

So much for the clarinet as we find it today; but – where did it come from?

Two
History and Development

Ancestry

It is perhaps difficult to understand why it should be important to a clarinettist to know just where and when his instrument started. Difficult to understand, but none the less true.

It may be that there is an instinctive awareness that respectable ancestry means honourable continuity, and that a line which may have begun in ancient Egypt and continued unbroken to the second part of our century must necessarily breed an artistic integrity which could not be achieved by a mere 250 years or so of frenzied progress. It may be that there is an instinctive feeling that if one knows all the processes which have gone before, it will be easier to invent the new ones which will bring one to the ultimate goal – that aim of all musicians – the fabulous point at which the instrument becomes part of the sub-conscious, and the servant not only of the brain, but of the mind and imagination as well. In any case this interest in the very beginnings of the clarinet is inherent in anyone who tries to conquer the instrument and its many complications and frustrations; and it is the more tantalizing in that this early history is shrouded in mystery and the sort of mis-statements which have always been the disguise of half-truth. While it is easily possible to state certain well-known facts about the beginnings of the clarinet, they are unprovable. They are repeated in every book on the subject, and must be briefly re-stated here, because they are both interesting and dramatic; but these facts need careful re-examination, because they can be misleading and grossly over-simplified. To appreciate fully the startling arrival of the clarinet at the very end of the seventeenth century, it is essential to look critically at its remote ancestry, thousands of years before this.

We cannot know, and it is of slight consequence, what it may have been that primitive man first used to produce sounds, other than his own vocal chords. It could be that a form of rudimentary singing actually preceded articulate speech; and it is by no means impossible that, even before *homo sapiens* was able to communicate in words, he was experimenting with the noise-making potential of natural implements to express his emotions, and possibly also to invoke magic powers to ensure good hunting and the fertility of his tribe.

The percussive side of such sounds is obviously the simplest to discover and exploit. A good hollow bone, tapped smartly by another, can be made to emit a most satisfactory note of recognisable pitch; and the effect of tapping a row of empty skull-bones was no doubt one of musical man's earliest ghoulish delights. Soon, however, his observation of the effect of 'edge-tones' of the wind, as it blew through hollow trees and branches, must have led to the invention of the simple bone or wooden whistle, to be used as a greeting or a warning signal; and possibly these were later furnished with one or two holes to be uncovered by the fingers, thus raising or lowering the fundamental pitch.

The first wood-wind instrument had arrived, though certainly nobody knows where, or when. Even so, the foundation of the rest of the family of wood-winds had not yet been laid. This occurred only when someone carelessly split a dry reed, and discovered that by blowing down it he could make a loud 'crowing' sound, probably to the dismay of all around him – the sound-generator of the oboe; a *double* reed. It seems certain that a little later, the discovery was made that if the cane was split in a different way, below a notch in the body of the tube, this could be allowed to open and shut rapidly, emitting a loud 'squawk' when totally enclosed in the mouth and blown. The first sound generator of the clarinet family – the *single* beating reed – had arrived.

The Clarinet

The Chalumeau and Denner's clarinet

From this simple pipe of pre-history it is a far cry to the year
1700 and the work of Johann Christian Denner of Nuremberg, the superb craftsman who was the inventor of the
clarinet. Perhaps the most remarkable fact is that, in all the
centuries between, this instrument of such incredible potential failed to develop of its own accord. It seems certain that
for most of this time instruments of the double and single
reed types existed side by side in many different cultures, and
over a wide geographic field. Reeds were cut from tubes of all
sizes and used either as an integral part, beating in the chamber of the mouth as in several of the Oriental instruments,
(opposite), or as a separate double reed, making a primitive
type of oboe, and controlled by the lips of the player. It is
probably for this reason (that of control) that throughout the
Middle Ages it was the *double* reed which captured the
imagination of the players. The *single* reed was usually out of
the control of the player, and thus limited in its possibilities
of expression.

Many single reed pipes had been in use for thousands of
years and these instruments would have been well-known to
Denner and his contemporaries. Among them the zummarah,
the arghoul and the pibgorn are possibly the best known, the
last named being known also as the Welsh hornpipe. It had
several forms, one of which had a pair of single reeds encased
in a tone-chamber which acted as an air reservoir, and also a
resonating bell at its end. (See opposite.)

It can be seen that this ins.rument uses a slightly more
sophisticated method of tone production, in that the resonance is in the tube and not in the mouth as in the drawing
on the opposite page.

The spread of all these different types of pipe westwards
by itinerant players, usually of eastern origin, was a phenomenon to which we owe almost all our present interest in
wood-winds.

The flute, the oboe and the oboe's big brother the bassoon
emerged in the Middle Ages as an interesting contrast to

Pibgorn, or Welsh Hornpipe (16th century). Single reed encased in primitive tone-chamber

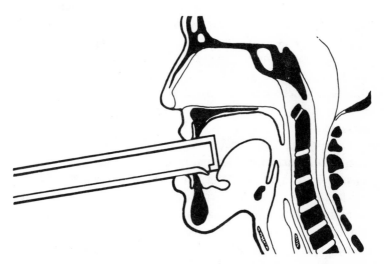

Use of mouth as resonator for pipe with integral reed

string and percussion instruments. The clarinet, for some reason, hung back. There is some mystery about the instrument which we know to have been the ancestor of the clarinet, possibly because although there are many drawings and paintings of seventeenth century origin which seem to depict such an instrument, nobody now living has ever seen one. This simple peasant pipe was the chalumeau, and it seems to have had a separate single beating reed rather than simply a sliver of cane flapping at its head. It also seems to have had a tapered mouthpiece rather than a sawn-off end section, and it is probable that the player had some sort of control of this reed in the manner of the oboe (see fig. 5). In spite of this, the chalumeau failed to develop into the clarinet. It required a push to bring this about, and this was supplied by the ingenuity and skill of J. C. Denner, in or about the year 1700. In effect the clarinet is the only wood-wind instrument which was *invented* rather than developed. This is not to say that there was not, in the case of each of the other instruments, a critical point in their history at which a sensational discovery altered their whole character and possibilities. In about 1816 all brass instruments were radically changed by the invention of the valve; the bassoon received the skilled attention of Almenräder and Heckel during the first half of the nineteenth century. Gillet (the player) and Lorée (the maker) revolutionised the oboe at the beginning of the present century: and the work of Theobald Boehm in the virtual rebirth of the flute in 1832, when a wind instrument first became a perfect mathematical creation, is too well known to need restatement.

These critical historical events were different from the creation of the clarinet by Denner, because the men who brought them about were working on instruments which already existed, having developed through the ages. The instruments were in a state of flux, but always in a form acceptable to the player, the composer and the public. Because this is so, some writers try to make a case for the same sort of smooth progression in the life of the clarinet, and to infer that Denner had at his command an instrument which was *almost* a clarinet, and which simply required improvement to transform it into one. There seems to be little evidence to support this view: in fact the chalumeau in its original form is conspicuous by its absence from any museum or private collection. We can only guess at its exact nature by making modern replicas and by studying the pictures and accounts of the day – the late seventeenth and early eighteenth centuries.

The word 'chalumeau' is derived from the Latin 'calamus' – a small reed – or from the Greek 'calane' – a pipe of reed. It was said, at the time of Denner, that it was sometimes called a 'caladrone' – a word obviously used to describe its incredibly low voice in relation to its small size. This is certainly a startling feature of the replicas we now find around us. The chalumeau plays an octave lower than a recorder of the same size, and it was to extend this low compass to a usable treble range that Denner carried out his work which ended so triumphantly.

The first reference to Denner and the clarinet is made by J. S. Doppelmeyer in his 'Historische Nachricht von den Nurburgischen Mathematicis und Künstlern' in 1730. He then wrote, 'At the beginning of the present century he [Denner] invented [*sic*] a new sort of pipe, the so-called Clarinette, to the great satisfaction of music-lovers.' A simple statement, and one which seems to be borne out by the facts, because although there seems to be no single example of a clarinet before the year 1700, there are still a great many to be seen – and heard – which date from the first three decades of the eighteenth century. However, Doppelmeyer goes on to say; 'and finally (as a result of his invention) produced chalumeaux in an improved form.'

It is this statement which seems to be ambiguous, suggesting as it does that clarinets and 'improved chalumeaux' are not one and the same. It is probably wrong to deduce this, as we shall see later. The mystery remains. Where did all the *un*-improved chalumeaux go? This is made the more puzzling by the fact that, for the first half of the eighteenth century, composers were writing for chalumeaux *and* clarinets in the same orchestra.

Several researchers are quite emphatic as to the reason for this, describing Denner's 'improved chalumeaux' of 1690 as a cylindrical tube with seven tone-holes and two diametrically opposed keys above the highest of these. This arrangement, we are assured, could not properly overblow because of the positioning of the keys, and certainly personal experiment suggests that this is all too true, so that this simple instrument had a useful compass of just a twelfth. All the same, the distinctive timbre of this little pipe – startlingly low in pitch for its short length – made it useful for operatic effects, and it was also used occasionally in concert by such composers as Telemann, who included it in his 'Carillon for two chalumeaux'. Other works of note were Ariosti's 'Marte placato' of 1707, Bonno's 'Eleazaro' of 1739, Bononcini's 'Turno Aricino', Fuchs's 'Giunone placata', the very famous example of Gluck's 'Orfeo' and Steffani's 'Il Turno', written as early as 1709.

Several of these could possibly have intended the use of the early clarinet in its lower register, but all of them used the chalumeaux simply as a pastoral sound.

The first known tutor, or instruction book, for the chalumeau is that described by the late Thurston Dart in the 1953 Journal of the Galpen Society. The complete title of the book is *The Compleat Book for the Mock Trumpet containing Plain and Easy Directions to sound ye Mock Trumpet Together with Variety of new Trumpet Tunes Aires Marches and Minuets fitted to that Instrument, and very proper for ye Brazen Trumpet, also severall First and Second Trebles for Two Trumpets the whole Fairly Engraven.* The only known copy is in the Euing collection at Glasgow University and dated 1706. The title is wrong in one detail, since the a's and b's within the stave in the examples shown here are outside the harmonic

Fig 1: *Left*: The French system.
Fig 2: The German system.

Fig 3: Mouthpiece with reed and ligature.

Fig 4: Pad in key-cup poised over countersunk tone-hole.

Fig 5: The author with his home-made reconstruction of a simple chalumeau. The little pipe is in D, and plays an octave below a fipple pipe of the same size and bore.

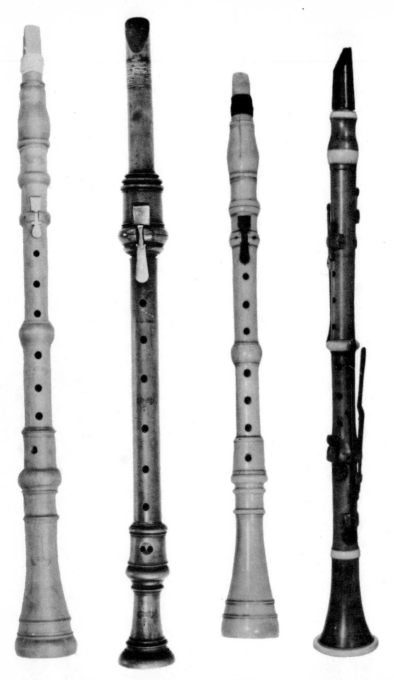

Fig 6: *From left to right:* replica of 2-key Jacob Denner clarinet, by Brian Ackerman of London. The instrument is in the four sections of a modern clarinet. The reed is shown on top, but could be played either in this position or below. J. C. Denner 2-key clarinet, probably the earliest clarinet in existence. Made of pearwood, 50 cms in length, diameter 4·5 cms (outside), 2·45 cms (bore). Both parts are stamped 'I. C. Denner' with 'D I' underneath. Superb 2-key clarinet by Scherer of London in ivory. c. 1720.
Fig 7: *Far right:* (Anon) 6-key clarinet. c. 1820.

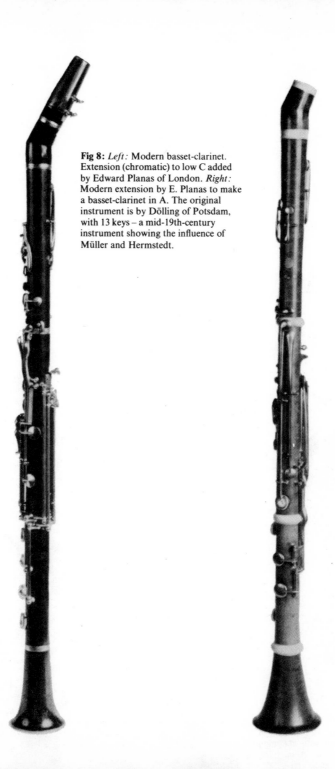

Fig 8: *Left:* Modern basset-clarinet. Extension (chromatic) to low C added by Edward Planas of London. *Right:* Modern extension by E. Planas to make a basset-clarinet in A. The original instrument is by Dölling of Potsdam, with 13 keys – a mid-19th-century instrument showing the influence of Müller and Hermstedt.

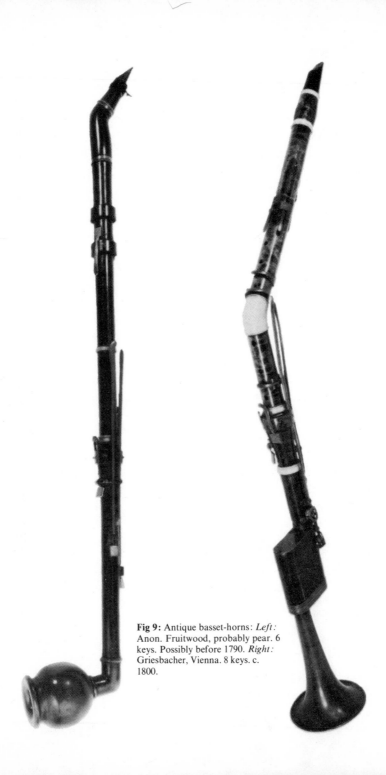

Fig 9: Antique basset-horns: *Left:* Anon. Fruitwood, probably pear. 6 keys. Possibly before 1790. *Right:* Griesbacher, Vienna. 8 keys. c. 1800.

Fig 10: Later basset-horn and lower clarinets (not to scale): *Left:* Pask, London. Cocus-wood basset-horn of unique shape; Boehm system. Late 1800s. In good playing condition. *Far left:* Key, London, 13 keys. *Right:* Uhlmann, 18 keys, mid-19th-century.

Fig 11: 13-key clarinet of German make (c. 1820) showing many of the features of Müller's 1812 clarinet – 'salt spoon' keys, countersunk holes, leather-and-felt pads and jointed levers.

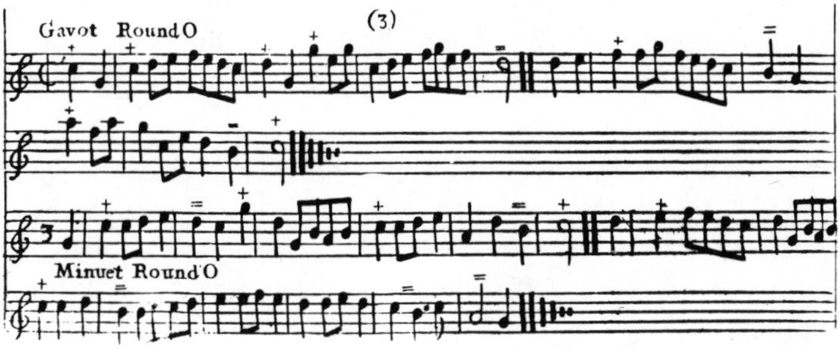

pattern of the natural trumpet, and so in no way 'very proper' for it. For the Mock Trumpet the case is different, as these examples can be easily played using the fingerings shown in the chart which was included with the book (below). This instrument, surely a chalumeau, produced

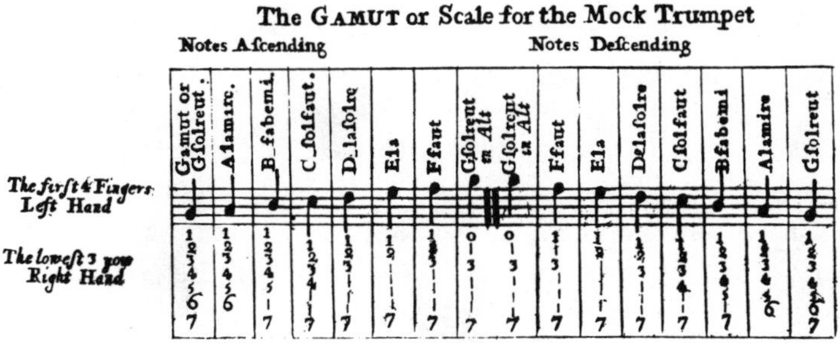

the notes in its fundamental register, fingering them like the notes of the early clarinet in its lowest register. The instrument must have been very short indeed, since experiments show that with a simple pipe of only 10ins, a scale of 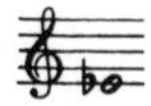 is produced, which is a third lower than that shown in the Mock Trumpet chart. This assumes that the notes were intended to be produced in concert pitch, and this is not certain. If in fact the sounds were meant to be an octave lower than shown, the instrument could have been of quite a comfortable size, say 14ins. in length. We are once again faced by the frustrating fact that no such primitive chalumeaux have survived. Certainly the clear indication that the notes *written* above the modern chalumeau register were fingered in the fundamental or un-over-blown register of the simple chalumeau is of great historical importance, however such notes may have sounded.

It is usually assumed that the clarinet, as distinguished from the chalumeau, was developed by J. C. Denner by the year 1700. The difference seems to be the disposition of the two keys, which, when properly placed, make an instrument capable of remarkable purity of sound over the whole compass of almost three octaves. The brilliant playing of a distinguished pupil of the author, Alan Hacker, upon a two key clarinet made for him by his friend Brian Ackerman, proves this point. This is no chalumeau, but a clarinet of startling purity of sound and flexibility, well able to hold its own in the woodwind section in a baroque situation. The clarinet in question is a replica of one in the Nuremberg museum, by Jacob Denner, a son of J. C., probably dating from 1710 to 1720 (see fig. 6). This may be assumed to be a 'second generation' clarinet, being made after initial experiments had been carried out by father and son to move the two key-covered tone holes in order to discover their optimum positions; as a result, both chalumeau and overblown registers can be obtained with a fair degree of accuracy. These experiments are obvious from the fact that the throat notes themselves are not perfectly placed; but such is the flexibility of that register on this clarinet that they can, with skill, be 'lipped' into pitch; and there can be no doubt that this was the approach of the players of the day. This is a most exciting instrument, and the impact upon first hearing is quite startling, because it does throw a light upon the enthusiasm of the composers of the day to introduce the clarinet into their scores.

It seems possible that his study of the two methods of resonation observed on page 17 (the mouth and the cavity of the instrument) gave Denner the idea for a third possibility. This was to combine the reed with a tone chamber inside the tube, and it brought the reed for the first time under the control of the player's lips. This gave Denner the typical shape of the clarinet mouthpiece.

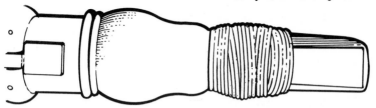

Early shape of clarinet mouthpiece with broad reed and almost square tip, with long and close facing. Jacob Denner, *c* 1720

As Denner found the chalumeau, it had a compass of only nine notes:

These could be modified by cross-fingerings to produce in addition B natural, C sharp, E flat and F sharp. With the new-found resonance of his mouthpiece, Denner must have found himself in a position to extend this compass upwards. This he did by 'over-blowing', using the same fingerings but splitting the air-column at its upper end by the introduction of a small hole, covered or uncovered at will by a closed key. This was the 'speaker-key', and from that date to this it has always been the most important one on the clarinet. There is no means of knowing what he expected to achieve when he did this. Being an experienced maker of other wood-winds, he could have been forgiven for expecting the new register produced by opening this key to be an octave higher than the original as in the case of the oboe; being the intelligent man he unquestionably was, he almost certainly did not expect this, because the odd squeak and squawk he had been able to produce without the speaker key were obviously very different from those of any other type of instrument.

Whatever he expected, what he got was a register a twelfth above the fundamental, and this meant that he had to add not one key, but two, to add the notes and thus producing a new instrument with the theoretical

compass: [musical notation] to [musical notation]

This was the clarinet; but it was obviously, at first, far from perfect, and certainly not capable of producing such a compass with any degree of accuracy.

The Bavarian National Museum in Munich proudly possesses a perfect specimen of one of J. C. Denner's earliest clarinets with only the two keys mentioned above (see fig. **6**). These are exactly opposite to each other, to be controlled by the index finger and thumb of the upper hand (either, according to choice, at that time).

The thumb key, alone, produces the A natural and the index finger, alone, gives B flat. Both keys together give a very poor B natural. This is stated to be a clarinet, but it is by no means certain that Denner's contemporaries may not have thought of it as an 'improved chalumeau'. It is possible that the two names 'clarinet' and 'chalumeau' were interchangeable for many years, while in fact the instrument was the clarinet in both cases, used in two contrasted registers – and possibly even tuned carefully so that it could present one or the other most comfortably. In the opera 'Il Turno', by Agostino Steffani, written in 1709, four chalumeaux play behind the scenes to give a pastoral effect. The parts include the notes A natural and B flat above the usual chalumeau compass, and obviously require the keys usually attributed to Denner for their production – in other words, the instrument would seem to be a clarinet. But was this in fact so?

It is significant to note the effect of trying out a most interesting instrument loaned by Mr Thomas Binkley of the USA. It is a replica of a 'chalumeau' at present in the Berlin Museum of Arts and Crafts. This instrument is pitched in C, has eight finger-holes one of which is the usual double hole for F – F sharp, and two keys for the upper index finger and thumb. It has a well defined barrel and a rudimentary bell, and very much the external appearance of a treble recorder. It is, in fact, almost identical with the Munich instrument

(fig. **6**). The mouthpiece, which the maker assures us is a replica of the original, is about the size and width of a modern E flat clarinet mouthpiece. The reed has a straight taper, without obvious 'crest' and is bound to the mouthpiece with cord. On testing, this pipe was found to have a pleasant 'pastoral' type of sound, mellow rather than penetrating, and fair intonation over this compass: 🎼 to 🎼
This was not altogether unexpected; but the instrument has the external appearance of an early Denner clarinet, and as such the upper register was the main centre of interest. This hardly existed. The two keys both gave A natural separately, and together B natural, not B flat as might have been expected. Either could be used as a speaker, and when so used the extra notes available were no more than clarinet C, D and E, after which they became wild and useless. This then, was clearly not a *clarinet*. In fact the museum authorities list it as a chalumeau, and date it as probably before 1700. The maker is unknown. Our guess is probably Denner – and that this is an instrument in a transitional stage, useful enough for works such as the Steffani opera, but not yet capable of anything using the clarinet register.

A fine example of the two-key clarinet can be seen in London at the Royal College of Music in the Donaldson collection. It is a C clarinet in ivory by a maker called Scherer, and probably dates from 1720 or so (see fig. **6**). Playing on this clarinet, which is in superb condition, is a rewarding and unforgettable experience, because it is un-questionably a clarinet in that its best sounds and truest intonation are in the overblown register. It has a clear and sweet sound – not the trumpet sound which seems to have given the instrument its name,* but with a soft and mellow vocal quality which is unobtainable on later clarinets, more burdened with dead metal. It is obvious that it can play such works as the concerto by the older Stamitz, and was the type of instrument which inspired this. Part of this work was played in an educational film, by Anvil Films Ltd ('We Make

*From *clarino*, Italian, a trumpet.

The Clarinet

Music') when it gave less trouble than many of the other later instruments which were also used. It was just such a clarinet obviously which revolutionised the wind section of the eighteenth century and inspired composers to write for it with such daring.

Both Denner and his sons were soon busy carrying out experiments with the placing and size of the thumb-key hole to improve the overblowing – that is, to correct the notes

from ![notation] upwards. This register is not easily obtained

on early two-key clarinets, and is probably imperfect in scale with the Munich arrangement of keys. In later two-key clarinets, Denner and his skilled sons placed the thumb-hole higher and narrowed it so that it approximated to the modern arrangement with the B flat produced by both keys together, and the A natural by the index finger alone. This was a great advance – but there was a serious snag. The note B natural is absent on this improved clarinet, except as produced by a grotesque flattening of the overblown C by slackening the lips. But apart from this, the two-key clarinet is an instrument of remarkable flexibility and soon 'fork' and cross fingerings made it possible to play the whole of this compass:

Denner and his sons also later inserted a small metal sleeve into the speaker hole, intruding almost to the central axis of the bore, to further improve the B flat and to prevent the collection of water in this very exposed hole. Then one or more of them increased the size of the holes previously used

to produce ![notation] and ![notation]

so that they gave ![notation] and ![notation]

The second of these changes was successful because the upper note (F sharp), was good and the F natural could be obtained by 'fork' fingering (i.e. by the use of the second finger and thumb alone). The first was a success in the chalumeau register only, because the new upper note (F sharp in the clarinet register) was dismally flat, and corrected only much later by the addition of a special 'vent' key.

Completing the compass

The missing B natural pointed the obvious next step in the clarinet's development. The way to obtain this missing note was to extend the compass downward to E natural by lengthening the instrument, and use the overblown twelfth to produce the B natural. Thus the third key in the history of the clarinet was for the fourth finger of the lower hand or for the thumb of this hand, and covered this extra bottom hole. The low E natural was simply a by-product of this improvement, but a useful one. The invention of this third key seems to have been the work of Denner's son Jacob Denner in about 1740.

There can be no doubt that this was yet another crucial turning-point in the history of the instrument, because it meant that it had a complete compass of correctly fingered notes diatonically from low E to top C – a range of almost three octaves – and a judicious selection of harmonic fingerings higher than this. There were, however, gaps in the chromatic possibilities. Some of the semitones were extremely poor when obtained by cross or forked fingerings, and some were to all intents completely unobtainable; but one feels that it had come a long way since the seventeenth-eighteenth century chronicler Mattheson said of it: 'The so-called chalumeaux may be allowed to voice their *howling symphony* of an evening in summer and from a distance, but never in January at a serenade on the water'. This statement makes one suspect that he was talking about the clarinet, since the chalumeau plays both soft and low, and to make it 'howl' is not at all easy, as it is an instrument of very slight resonance. This is yet another piece of evidence of the interchangeability of the two names at that time.

The early spread of the use of the clarinet throughout Europe in the first half of the eighteenth century indicates that it filled an important gap in the orchestral spectrum. In Italy the instrument was known as early as 1722, and was described by one Fillipo Bonnani in his *Gabinetto Armonica:* 'An instrument similar to the oboe is the clarone (sic). It is two and a half palms long and terminates in a bell like the trumpet three inches in width. It is pierced with seven holes in front and one behind. There are in addition two other holes opposite to each other, but not diametrically, which are closed and opened by two springs pressed by the finger.' Bonnani's book does not illustrate the instrument, but it was obviously the Denner two-key clarinet.

It seems likely that the addition of the third (B natural) key took place about 1740, since the arrangement seems to have been common shortly after this. The effect was probably tonally advantageous as well as valuable for intonation, because it involved a lengthening of the tube of the instrument, and the forming of a 'bell' at its end; and anyone who has removed the bell from a modern clarinet knows the immediate drop in resonance particularly in the notes emitted by the mid-section of the instrument. The clarinet had in fact reached its present shape. In contrast with oboes of the day, which were always of 'concert' pitch unless intended to have a lower voice – (the oboe d'amore, or sentimental oboe) – clarinets were made from the first in many different sizes. This gave them the facility to play in extreme keys which they would otherwise have found impossible; so the clarinet has always been a 'transposing' instrument – a feature to be discussed later.

Square brass key with felt pad over recessed tone hole

Although it seems at first puzzling that players and makers alike were reluctant to add keys to facilitate technique – and many of these keys were obvious in their design and placing – there was in fact a good reason for this. The keys were clumsy, sluggish in action owing to flabby springing and the poor bearing-surface of the securing-pins, and had for a sealing-agent nothing more efficient than a pad of thick felt (opposite). As a result there were many who believed that a clarinet of more than three keys would be impossible to play because of its lack of air-tight sealing. So it was as late as 1760 before the five-key clarinet, which was soon to be in general use, appeared. The two new keys were also on the lower part of the instrument, and were for chalumeau G sharp (clarinet D sharp) and chalumeau F sharp (clarinet C sharp). These keys seem to have been the results of experiments by several makers and players, one of whom was probably the young virtuoso Joseph Beer.

Early works for the clarinet

Even before it reached the five-key stage, the clarinet was a formidable instrument in the virtuoso field. By 1740 Antonio Vivaldi had written three charming concerti grossi which included two clarinets in C and two oboes. One of these was revived in London about thirty years ago to the delight of players and listeners alike. Here I show the sort of fanfare writing one would expect, but there are in addition many lyrical passages such as the second movement, a dialogue between oboe and clarinet. An interesting point is that the second clarinet part must have been more difficult to play on the two-key clarinet than the first, because of the wide compass. To have a clarinet acoustically sound over this range must have been rare, though the player was carefully spared the upper four notes from G to C, and could therefore concentrate upon tuning correctly the twelfth below this – the upper chalumeau.

Handel wrote an interesting little overture for two clarinets and corno di Caccia, all in D, in 1748. The writing is in the

Vivaldi: *Concerto Grosso*

fanfare manner, and breaks no new ground. There are several accounts of works played and composed by the shadowy figure 'Mr Charles', an Hungarian virtuoso who appeared in Dublin in 1742; none of these have survived. J. C. Bach used the clarinet with great freedom in the 1760s in the wind symphonies he wrote for the outdoor concerts at Vauxhall Gardens. These still sound remarkably effective, and are enjoyable to play, though the monotony of the key centres B flat and E flat suggests that they are better interspersed with other works. At about this same time, Johann Stamitz the elder wrote the concerto which was revived some thirty years ago, and which shows a fine appreciation of the possibilities of the instrument.

Possibly the very earliest concertos for the clarinet were those by Johann Melchior Molter, Kapellmeister of Durlach, dating from 1747 and written for a three key clarinet. These concertos still have the power to charm, and were written for the little D clarinet in the typical clarino manner, suggesting once more that a clarinet could be tuned for only one register or the other with much success. They have the high, clear sound of the trumpet of the day, and require nimble articulation. The same may be said of the music of C. P. E. Bach in his six sonatas for clarinet, bassoon and harpsichord. He uses the upper reaches of the instrument constantly, and hardly ever the chalumeau compass.

It seems obvious that from 1780 or so there was a change in this characteristic of the clarinet, probably due to experiments in the bore of the instrument, its diameter, its taper, and the undercutting of the tone holes. Certainly works then became common in which the chalumeau register and the upper compass were juxtaposed with complete freedom, even with obvious delight. Many of them, like the several concertos by Karl Stamitz (the younger), Ernst Eichner, and Georg Fuchs, were written for the members of the great Mannheim Orchestra – a combination usually credited (maybe incorrectly) with the first appearance of the clarinet in any orchestra. Of all the works written for these players, none are perhaps so difficult as those by Franz Tausch, who makes demands upon the technique, with huge leaps from altissimo to lowest chalumeau, which almost any player of today finds completely impossible. He was of course a virtuoso in his own right; so one can only assume that he at

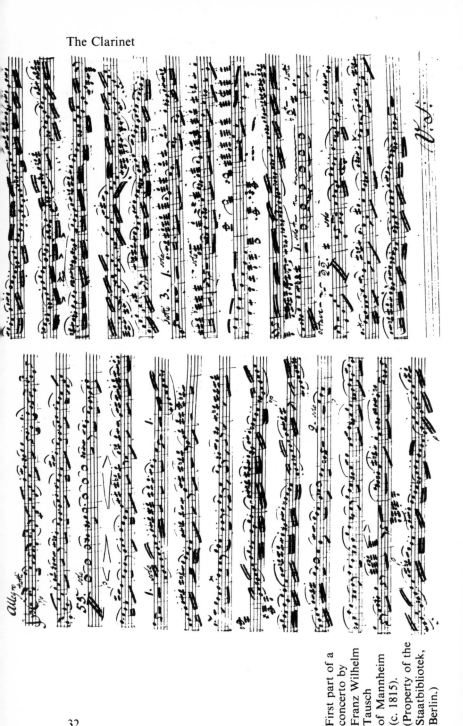

First part of a
concerto by
Franz Wilhelm
Tausch
of Mannheim
(c. 1815).
(Property of the
Staatbibliotek,
Berlin.)

least could manage to play this sort of thing upon the five-key clarinet of his day (see extract).

It must, however, be noted that this is probably exceptional. Another concerto, to be seen in the British Museum, shows him to be more staid, essentially musical and even lyrical.

It seems certain that the great Mannheim Orchestra employed two clarinettists from about 1759. They probably both played the three-key clarinet, but it is also probable that they played the oboe as well, and it seems to have been as late as 1778 that their employment was as clarinettists alone – and by that time they had almost certainly equipped themselves with five-key clarinets.

This is, of course, an exceedingly important period in the history of the instrument; the five-key instrument can be said to have been the inspiration of some of the finest classical works for the clarinet. It is worth pausing for a moment to consider the position at that time. Tausch was by no means the only virtuoso involved in exploiting the possibilities of the clarinet. There was the illustrious Joseph Beer, born in 1744, and later his pupil Michel Yost. In some ways one may regret that Mozart failed to write a concerto for Beer as he was requested, because Beer had a great international reputation and the work would have been as successful in Mozart's life-time as has been his later superb essay in that field. As it was, Mozart rejected the offer because he objected to something in the moral outlook of Beer himself. He may have been right; but in fact when we consider the personality of Anton Stadler, the dedicatee of the superb concerto Mozart penned almost on his death-bed, one can only say that Mozart left the frying-pan very much for the fire. Stadler was one of those who owed money to Mozart when he died; and it probably was not back-payment for a work commissioned from the composer, but a simple personal debt. He was it seems, a born scrounger.

To the modern listener, accustomed to the smooth and apparently effortless performance of a masterpiece of the calibre of Mozart's concerto, there is the temptation to wonder what sort of effect could have been obtained by virtuosi like Stadler and Beer upon their simple, crude clarinets. It is easy to conclude that the best they could achieve would have been miserable, and that somehow Mozart must have been looking to the future when he entrusted the clarinet with some of his most poignant and mature utterances. This is almost certainly a rash assumption: there can be no doubt that players who were capable of producing performances of real merit not only existed, but were in fact the inspiration of the composers of the masterpieces they presented to the world. It is not sufficient to conclude that the composers of these heard in their performances some hint of the possibility of future musical perfection. After all, composers like Weber, Mozart and Spohr all wrote for string instruments of a perfection which has never since been equalled. Mozart, in his incomparable G minor string quintet, wrote for the sound of the Stradivarius. How dare we assume that he wrote his equally magnificent Clarinet Quintet for an instrument incapable of the same sort of ravishing sound – a thing of dismally imperfect intonation and with mechanical defects which made many of his finest passages unlistenable? To understand the genius of a Stadler, however much we may regret his personal shortcomings, it is necessary to remember only the many fine players of our own century – many of whom, wrongly, but with a sort of God-given directness of purpose, continue to perform upon their old worn-out instruments long after these have been reduced to uselessness. Somehow they cope, compensating for the imperfections of intonation, but producing the same superb sonority as they have always done. In some ways it is this type of player, with his vision of the music he is playing, who breathes life into a masterpiece in spite of the impossibilities of his task. Present him with the perfect instrument, remove the obstacles from his path, and he may give you an interpretation of no more value than that of a well-programmed computer. Stadler must have been of that ilk – and Mozart, genius that he was, must have known this.

Certainly a really gifted modern player can make fine music upon perfectly restored instruments or new clarinets made as perfect replicas of those of the eighteenth century. The sound is both expansive and flexible, and gives one a clear insight into the inspiration of such composers as Mozart, Weber and Hummel.

The basset-horn and basset-clarinet

In recent years the history of the use of the larger clarinets – the basset-horn and the extended clarinet, now often called the basset-clarinet – has become the subject of intensive research. In the case of the basset-horn there has never been any doubt about its existence or its history. It is a clarinet pitched in F, a fourth below the B flat instrument, whose lower register is extended, usually to low C natural, by the provision of keys covering holes and actuated by the right thumb (figs **9/10**). Often the extra length of tube required for this extension was accommodated in a large box in which it turned upon itself, thus reducing the length of the instrument to manageable proportions. Sometimes, and later invariably, the instrument was a continuous extended tube, though some sort of curvature has always been essential to bring the holes and keys within reach of the player. One can but wonder at the skill and dexterity of the players of early basset-horns, whose mastery of their crude instruments was such that a host of fine players were inspired to write for the instrument. Certainly its greatest writer was Mozart, who obviously felt that the dark sound, lacking brightness or resonance, but with a misty density unmatched by any other instrument, was the perfect vehicle for dignified and sanctified utterance. His use of it in the music of the High Priest in 'Die Zauberflöte' and in the Masonic Funeral Music has certainly never been surpassed; and it is worth remembering that it was said to be his favourite instrument, so much so that he gave to it, in the part of the great Requiem which he obviously wrote himself, the most telling statement of all; the whole work starts with a subject announced by the second basset-horn. The repertoire of the basset-horn is a subject for special study, and among those who have gone into it deeply is Graham Melville Mason of Edinburgh, who has been at tremendous pains to unearth works long forgotten. There are vast numbers of such compositions, some of which are listed in our bibliography, and interest in the instrument is growing, as is the number of instruments in the hands of players. These are of course modern basset-horns, and are considered in a later chapter.

There is no such certainty about the history of the basset-clarinet, or extended clarinet, for the simple reason that, like the chalumeau, no such instrument exists in its true historical form. Like the basset-horn, there is no doubt that such a thing existed, though in what sort of number it is impossible to say. It could well be that only one player was successful in making it a practical proposition so that composers would be interested in writing for it; but since that player was Anton Stadler, the fortunate performer of the great works of Mozart as they came from his pen, the instrument, in whatever form it existed, is of crucial historical interest. The basset-clarinet was in fact simply a basset-horn in construction, but shorter and therefore higher in pitch – it was a B flat or A clarinet with basset extension. The certainty that such an instrument did exist has been established by the researches of several writers who have invariably started by examining the internal evidence of the strange shapes of phrases to be found in Mozart's great Clarinet Concerto, to a lesser extent in the Quintet, and in the obbligati from his opera 'La Clemenza di Tito'. One of the earliest of these was Oskar Kroll, who analysed this evidence in the book he wrote in 1938 or 1939 and which was published in 1948 after his death. Both he and later the American George Dazeley, without access to the text which later confirmed their findings, concluded that Mozart had originally written for a clarinet extended to low C, and that for instance the phrase which is now played:

etc.

was originally written and played:

This is merely one example. Both writers found many more, and confirmed suspicions many players had had for a long time. The text which gives confirmation to these conclusions is Mozart's autograph of 199 bars of the first movement of the concertos, obviously originally for a basset-horn in G (a scarcely known instrument) which is owned by the Rychenberg-Siftung of Wintertur, Switzerland.

It is a startling passage for any clarinettist to read, as it answers so many questions one has always had in mind when preparing this great work. Albert Einstein lists this fragment as K621b and the concerto in its final form, for clarinet in A, of which no autograph is known, as K622. Certainly the great majority of the work was conceived for a clarinet of normal compass; but by this time Mozart had had several shots at writing for the extended clarinet. The concerto dates from 1790 or 1791, and as early as 1787 he had written the first part of a quintet for B flat clarinet and strings in which basset-clarinet notes are clearly indicated. Five full pages exist of this, and the movement has been completed with great success by Robert D. Levin, so far as is known for the normal B flat clarinet only. A basset-clarinet edition would be welcomed. Also the trios K4396, usually played on two clarinets and bassoon, are now known to be written for three basset-horns (a form in which they have been frequently played in recent years) *or* three clarinets, one of which must have a basset-clarinet extension. The scholarship in this case is the work of Marius Flothius, in his edition of the work for the 'neue Mozart-Ausgabe'. This preoccupation with the lower tones of the clarinet surely accounts for Mozart's forsaking the sketch for basset horn in G for the clarinet in A with its new extended compass.

Transcription of the clarinet part of Mozart's K 612b, in the Ryshen-
berg-Stiftung, Winterthur. Originally in Mozart's hand.

An analysis of the Rychenberg manuscript, (below), shows that a very large proportion of the solo part – about one bar in every five – was found to require revision to accommodate a clarinet of normal compass, when the work was finally published in the form we now know. The first surprise is in bars 91 and 92, where the use of the bass clef in the form we now expect to find used only for the bass clarinet clearly uses the first extra semitone of the extended compass. Bar 94 descends a further semitone, and changes shape from the modern version as well. Things then progress normally for some time, until bar 134, when the use of the low D in the Alberti section is much more shapely than in the modern version, with F sharp in its place. And so on – bars 145 to 147 are much more logical, since they no longer go outside Mozart's normal compass for the clarinet, and 148 is revealed to be of the shape indicated here. Obviously the original bar 145 is unplayable on even a basset-clarinet – so Mozart crosses it out; but in the recapitulation, not shown here, it would be possible, by using the low C, to have the passage in the three octaves as shown. Could it be that Mozart had this already at the back of his mind when he wrote this in the exposition? The only remaining surprise comes in bar 189 *et seq.* to the end of the excerpt, which is shaped in the way it should obviously be from a musical angle, but may not have been suspected by many modern players.

There can be no doubt, then, that the correct form of the concerto is for basset-clarinet in A, and several players have constructed complete performing editions with almost identical conclusions. The work has also been performed with great success in this form, and will certainly be played more frequently in future on the instrument for which it was written. Not that the modern basset-clarinet is really any nearer to the original basset-clarinet of Stadler than is the modern Boehm clarinet to his five-key instrument (fig. **8**). It must be stressed that in spite of the extra keys which produced the lowest notes in the case of both the basset horn and the basset-clarinet, the instrument itself remained acoustically unaltered.

Both instruments were still essentially five-key clarinets at the end of the eighteenth century, because the extra keys provided no over-blown register and could be used in the chalumeau compass only. The same applies to the most modern basset-clarinet, which is in effect simply an extension of the Boehm system or Oehler system instrument, and so cannot be said to reproduce the sort of conditions Stadler had to face. What it can do is to carry out Mozart's intentions more faithfully than any other clarinet.

It seems strange that this instrument, which was capable of inspiring such great musicians, should have proved to be a dead end. No such instrument has been preserved, so that it would seem that perhaps it was found to give the player more trouble, technically, than the gain in compass warranted, and so died out of favour. It is thus the more important that at last the sounds Mozart hoped to hear, rather than those he heard, can be produced by the use of a more perfect instrument than Stadler was able to obtain. An interesting example of a successful attempt to produce an older type of basset-clarinet is showin in fig. **8**. This is a box-wood clarinet, the property of Alan Hacker, and although not the sort of instrument Stadler had when Mozart wrote for him, it gives a sound idea of the sort of problems involved, and overcomes them in a remarkable way.

There are some twentieth-century examples in works by Richard Strauss, among others, of the use of the basset horn in its modern form – as an extension of the most up-to-date types of clarinet, pitched in F. These are very much more common than the basset-clarinet, in B flat or A, for the obvious reason that there is more practical use for them in playing the music of the eighteenth century, in particular that of Mozart. The basset-clarinet, on the other hand, can only be used in its fullest capacity in specially reconstructed editions of a few works of Mozart. Apart from Strauss's use of the basset horn, the only well-known composer to use it freely seems to have been Mendelssohn in the delightful duo-concert pieces with clarinet which he wrote for Carl Bärmann – son of the great Heinrich, for whom Weber had written his concertos and the duo concertante with piano. The first performances of the clarinet and basset horn pieces must have been events of sheer delight, played as they were at Königsberg in 1833 by father Heinrich, son Carl, and Mendelssohn himself. They must also have been displays of incredible virtuosity, since both clarinet and basset horn at that time were essentially instruments, acoustically, of seven keys only.

Müller's refinements

It seems that at this stage the clarinet was waiting for a man of real genius as an inventor and designer to come along and revolutionise it. It is true that extra keys were still being added by players who felt that this could give them more purity of intonation rather than greater facility. There were reports of a six-key clarinet as early as 1791, and also one of eight-keys a year later; but the leaking of air from the felt pads, the weak springing and the generally clumsy key-disposition were a high price to pay for anything gained, and there is little historically to show for any advance at this time. True, the Frenchman Simiot of Lyons invented the A-B trill key, which is still our easiest way across the 'break' of the instrument, and by 1820 he is said to have displayed a clarinet of no less than nineteen keys; but it was the important visionary work of Ivan Müller which really pointed the way to the future.

Müller was a Parisian, born in Russia, and a man of great musical talent as well as incredible tenacity of purpose. He needed both these attributes, because there can hardly be a case of a great innovator suffering more resistance by authority. Oddly enough, although all clarinettists know his name, few are aware that he was a much-travelled virtuoso. It seems incredible that he should have had time in such a busy professional life to give so much detailed attention to the construction and modification of his instrument. True, he had at his disposal a number of excellent craftsmen to carry out his instructions – men like Gentellet and Simiot of Paris, as well as a great many who later took his clarinet as a pattern and made it the new instrument of the period.

Müller's experiments were a pre-occupation from quite an early age; before he was twenty and while he was still an Imperial Russian Chamber musician at St Petersburg he was experimenting with novel types of key-work. Later, in Dresden, Berlin and Leipzig, he specialised in basset horn solos, and won much praise. It was in 1809 that he gave a recital on a clarinet of new design made for him by the Viennese craftsman Merklein, and this seems to have been a sensational event. One of those present who was suitably impressed was the Viennese composer Philip Riotti, who promptly wrote a most showy concerto dedicated to Müller, who played it several times in the months which followed. It was this new clarinet, which does not seem to have been described in great detail, which was probably the basis of Müller's next important move – the establishment of his new clarinet as a pattern for large-scale production. It seems he was a remarkably forthcoming young man, liked by almost everybody, and certainly a most familiar figure in Vienna while he was there. Soon he moved to Paris, and in no time he had a wealthy patron, a M. Petit, ready to provide him with the money necessary for his project. Petit was himself a clarinettist, but his money came from another source – the stock market.

In 1812, Müller presented his newly designed clarinet to the Conservatoire in Paris for examination by the Commission there – an important body whose yea or nay could make all the difference to the prospects of the instrument. The new instrument was one of thirteen keys. This in itself was possibly not an earth-shaking event. What was of infinitely greater importance was the way in which these keys were constructed, disposed, vented and padded. It represented, most observers would now agree, the furthest advance since the work of Denner (see fig. **11**).

Müller claimed – with somewhat questionable justice, that his new key-disposition presented an instrument capable of playing in any key with comparative comfort. His methods were new. First he did away with that greatest of all bugbears, the flat felt pad covering an open hole. His holes were all countersunk, so that they presented a raised and bevelled ring to the pad. The pads themselves were of leather with a soft yielding filling of wool, and were held in a hollow cup which was soldered on to the end of the key in such a way that it left a sufficient opening or 'vent' for the tonal air to escape when the key was in the open position. The disposition of these keys was much more logical than any had been hitherto, and therefore gave an infinitely improved acoustic result.

It is true that Müller's was not the only many-keyed clarinet to be found at that time. Bärmann himself had a ten-key clarinet, the Finnish virtuoso Bernhard Crusell used one with eleven keys and the heavy demands of Spohr's concertos forced that composer's own favourite clarinettist, Hermstedt, to increase his keys from five to no less than thirteen. None of these experimental instruments was so successful that it stood the test of time, because the acoustic lay-out was less advanced than the technical ingenuity, leading to many notes of poor quality. In any case they were less technically advanced than Müller's new clarinet in the padding, venting, spring and disposition of key-work.

It must therefore have been a heart-breaking experience for Müller when his new *clarinette omnitonique* was turned down by the specialists of the Paris Conservatoire. The reason for this was rather a strange one, and almost certainly the result of bigotry. Because Müller claimed that the new clarinet could be played with ease in any key, it seemed that the only necessity for the future would be the B flat instrument, as being of a convenient size and a pleasant tone. The musicians of the Conservatoire, bred and born to the belief that each clarinet had its own special musical character and sound, according to its pitch, decided that these diverse characters were of significant musical value, and should be preserved. Yet composers had always used the clarinet which played most easily in the key of their work, whatever the character of their music – a fact which seemed to contradict this view. In spite of this, the panel recommended that Müller's new clarinet be rejected.

Müller was made of very stern stuff, but could not hold out against this reverse in a practical sense; he had to close down his works and stop the production of the new instrument. One can be reasonably sure that he knew that time was on his side – particularly as he had, in his own ability as a soloist, the means of demonstrating the superiority of his clarinet. By 1815 he had established it as the finest yet produced during his solo tours in England, Holland and Germany, when he played not only difficult works by Reicha and Ferdinand Ries, but several of his own compositions. It was upon these tours that his work in the development of the mouthpiece and reed of the instrument began to attract attention. First he abolished the clumsy and often insecure binding of the reed to the mouthpiece by a length of cord, replacing this with a metal ligature very similar to that in use today. Next, he very noticeably thinned and tapered the reed, making it responsive to the much more curved facing on the mouthpiece. This meant that he was able to produce a greater variety of articulation than was usual – his double-tongueing was described as 'unsurpassed' and he seems to have given a lot of pleasure to his audiences by his gradations of breath control – though on occasions the shrillness of his tone brought adverse comment.

All things considered, Müller can be said to have been the second great figure in the world of development of the clarinet; and as can be seen in Chapter 1, one important section of clarinet design at the present time, the German clarinet, is founded directly upon his work. He was a thorough reformer, and his work satisfied the demands of players for many years to come. It was seized upon and added to by later inventors in much the same way as was the Denner clarinet in the early days of the instrument – added to, but not vitally altered in the acoustic sense.

Klosé and the Boehm system

There remains one more great innovator in the history of the clarinet – the only man who altered its course to so vital an extent as Müller. This was Hyacinthe Klosé, the inventor of what has since become known as the 'Boehm system' clarinet.

Properly to understand why this should be so, it is necessary to know the work of the great Theobald Boehm, a Munich instrument maker and flautist, and the manner in which he had, only a few years before, revolutionized the design of the flute. Boehm was convinced first that the purity of tone he wanted could be obtained only from a flute with large holes, properly 'vented' so that no 'stuffiness' remained. He determined to design a flute which would have its tone-holes in the mathematically correct places, and went to much trouble to experiment and evolve the formulae necessary to create such an instrument. An off-shoot of this very painstaking activity was his invention of a series of ring-keys by which a finger can close a ring when covering a hole, and by so doing operate another key to cover a different hole at some distance. The result was that the fingers could cover holes well outside their normal reach, so that such holes did not have to be made smaller or moved closer to accommodate the structure of the hand.

This, and only this, was the basis of Klosé's work upon the Boehm principle – no acoustic subdivision of the clarinet was in his mind as it had been in Boehm's. The name 'Boehm system' clarinet is thus a misnomer; but it has been with us now for so long – since 1839 when it was first exhibited in Paris by Klosé – that it would be silly now to try to change this title.

Klosé was French by descent, and born in Corfu. Upon the return of his parents to Paris, he became a clarinettist in the Royal Guard, and before long was an Army bandmaster. Later he studied at the Paris Conservatoire with the great Frédéric Berr, and succeeded him upon his death in 1838 as professor there. This was his proud hour and he seems to have prepared well for it. A year or two before this, he had been in touch with Louis Buffet, the well-known instrument maker, and had explained to him his reasons for wishing to use the Boehm method of ring-keys. An instrument was designed adopting this principle on the lines suggested by Klosé, and in 1839 the Paris exhibition awarded it a medal – for Buffet. Neither Boehm nor Klosé were honoured, but there can be no doubt that Klosé was the mainspring of the idea which gave birth to this vital prototype of the clarinet now used by the majority of players the world over (see fig. **12**). The number of keys in Klose's instrument was the same as in most of those in use to this day. Seventeen keys and six rings help the fingers to control no less than twenty-four tone holes and it is proof that the earlier work of Müller and others in padding and venting had taken full effect that the instrument was so easily played and maintained in a leak-free condition.

There can be little doubt that there were many advantages in the new system of fingering not only from the point of view of technical facility, but of acoustic soundness of arrangement. One of its advantages is the avoidance, in the all-important right-hand area, of crucial 'fork-fingerings' which are not only clumsy in execution, but poor in sound. The left hand is a little less well catered for in this respect, since it simply changed a 'forked' F natural for an equally forked F sharp – but it must be remembered that the original F sharp of the Müller system remains to be used by those who are not too lazy to use the lower two so-called 'trill' keys. The fact that the notes

could be obtained with the little fingers of *either* the left or right hands, leaving the other free to move to the other notes which were obtainable only by sliding perilously on the Müller clarinet, meant that many passages and many trills and shakes were possible for the first time. It was therefore an instrument which could be reasonably termed *omnitonique* and this characteristic was seized upon by many composers with considerable advantage when they began to realize the possibilities of the instrument. This took some time, but since 1900 composers have indicated a willingness to treat the clarinet as an instrument far from fixed in any key-centre.

The Clarinet

The Buffet-Klosé clarinet was an improved instrument in more than mere musical, acoustic or technical terms. It had a much enhanced aesthetic appearance: it was graceful slim and elegant, owing to the disappearance of the ugly raised bosses upon which other clarinets pivoted their keys. The keys were pivoted at their ends, on long tubular barrels as now, and in addition the long joined lever keys of the Müller clarinet were replaced by neat side-operated, remotely articulated levers (see fig. 12).

There were of course several other makers who were at the time working hard at new developments for the clarinet. One of these was the Belgian Adolphe Sax, who was the inventor of the saxhorn (that foundation-stone of all the various instruments to be found in the Brass Bands of England today) and of course of the saxophone. In 1835 he is said to have produced a clarinet of twenty-four keys,which made very little impact upon the musical world; but in 1842 he produced the instrument which can be said to be a step on the way to the modern German clarinet. Sax retained Ivan Müller's system of fingering, but added a most important pair of rings to the lower joint which trued up the pitch and sound of the all-important B natural/F sharp twelfth, as well as other refinements of key-arrangement. From that time to the present day there have been a great number of inventors who have added to the Müller clarinet many of the advantages of the Klosé system, and at least one which is not available on the French instrument. This is the B natural to C sharp trill immediately above the break, and was solved by what is known as the 'patent C sharp' usually thought to have been the work of Mahillon of Brussels. This makes possible the smooth legato passage from B to C sharp by simply raising the right hand little finger – a feat which is the envy of Klosé (or Boehm) system players to this day (see fig. 15).

Later improvements

Space allows a detailed description of only a few of these

later improvements. They have been continuous to the present day on the German clarinet and can be appreciated by a comparison of the modern instrument described in Chapter 1 and the Müller clarinet mentioned above. The first important advance upon the work of Müller was made by the great virtuoso and teacher Carl Bärmann, who not only elaborated some of the keys, but based his fine Tutor upon the use of these extra facilities. As a result the developments he himself introduced soon became more or less standard; they consisted of extra extensions to keys so that they could be played by different fingers, or the duplication of keys so that the opposite hand could be used. There was also a considerable emphasis upon the correction of the intonation of several notes by the use of ring-keys, and it is significant that it was the sound of this clarinet as played by Richard Mühlfeld which inspired Brahms to write his glorious quintet, trio, and the two sonatas.

There were others besides Bärmann who helped the Müller system clarinet along the road to its present position in Germany. At the end of the nineteenth century Robert Stark experimented with improvements which combined some of the advantages of the Boehm system with Müller's arrangement. The Oehler clarinet of today is the result of many of these improvements and its present form is a monument to the work of Oskar Oehler himself, while reflecting the basic soundness of the Müller instrument upon which it is founded (see overleaf). The work upon this instrument took place over many years during which Oehler altered the position and shape of almost every key, adding an extra vent-hole here and bridging an awkward touch-piece gap there until the instrument was tailored to the hand of the player, and as acoustically perfect as it could be made. In many ways the mechanism is much more complex than that of the Klosé clarinet, but the mechanics are sound, the workmanship superb, and the whole concept most thoughtful. In one or two instances there are extensions to keys which provide smooth legato trills, but can be disconnected when not required. Oehler was also very much concerned with the problem of 'forked'

The Oehler system clarinet today.

notes, and his ingenuity has overcome this basic disadvantage of the Müller clarinet. A forked note is simply one in which the fingering forces the air column to emerge from two holes, with a finger forcing the lower of these into action when acoustics would demand otherwise. A 'fuzzy' tone is the most obvious result. To prevent this, Oehler provides an extra key governed by this guilty finger, which opens another hole at the side of the clarinet, so that the note is produced as perfectly acoustically as if the un-forked fingering were employed. This has later been applied to the Klosé clarinet by Geoffrey Acton of London with great success, since it has the effect of trueing up the harmonic series of the right-hand holes.

More modern systems

With the consideration of the Klosé, Müller and Oehler systems it can be said that the history of the clarinet is brought up to date, because the vast majority of players the world over use one or other of these. At the same time one must not overlook some systems which failed to attain popularity, and several which may well be a pointer to the future development of the instrument.

One feature of a clarinet once extremely popular in Britain, which has advantages enjoyed by no other, was due to the work of the French oboist Apollon Barret. This invention applied to the upper joint of the clarinet, using a ring-key spring-loaded against a single side lever which produces the notes E flat – B flat and F natural – C natural as a side-key fingering (see the Quilter clarinet in fig. **15**). As a result of this many progressions, trills and shakes are possible more easily than on any other clarinet, notably:

etc.

The adaptation cannot of course be made to apply to the Boehm system clarinet, and seems now to have died out without anything of equal advantage taking its place. This instrument is most often called the 'Clinton' model because it was introduced by a well-known professor of the early twentieth century, G. A. Clinton of London.

Later, Clinton had some success in combining the alternate levers of the lower joint (the main advantage of Klosé's system) with a Müller clarinet which also incorporated Barret's upper joint improvement. He called this the Clinton-Boehm clarinet, and it is an interesting hybrid of an instrument, capable of many good things. It was used by some important players in Britain but has now ceased to be produced. (See fig. **19**.)

From this time onwards almost every attempt at advancement of clarinet acoustics has been concerned with either the perfection of the 'throat' B flat or with the improvement or digital accessibility of the other 'throat' notes A flat and A natural. The weakness of the note B flat has always been known to be due to the dual function the speaker hole is asked to perform, since it has to produce perfect twelfths as well as its B flat. This is demonstrably impossible, since as a speaker-hole it should be much smaller, and much higher up the instrument, while as a B flat it should be much lower, and further down – in fact, exactly where the 'side' trill key of that pitch is now situated.

Makers for almost a hundred years have been conscious of this duality of purpose, and many of them have set about solving the problem. Among these were Ernst Schmidt, formerly of Mannheim, who in 1912 succeeded in producing an instrument with a separate key-opening for each purpose. Later Wilhelm Heckel of Biebrich, more famous for his reform of bassoon construction, refined this arrangement and added a special mouthpiece aimed at assisting the same equalisation. Still later, in 1934, the Leipzig musician Hans Berninger approached the problem from a different angle, opening the 'trill' keys to give resonance to the 'throat' B flat – an arrangement said to have considerably improved the note.

The work of William Stubbins of the USA in this respect is certainly worthy of very serious attention, since it is at present in production, and is as ingenious and worthy a solution as has been so far achieved. There is no need here to describe the finer details of Mr Stubbins's work – the so-called S.K. mechanism which he invented in collaboration with his friend Mr Kalmus; he has done so himself adequately in his own very interesting book, *The Art of Clarinetistry*. It is sufficient simply to outline the facts. The real problem lies in the upper register – the 'over-blown' notes of the top joint – which require a very small speaker aperture if they are to speak easily, and without the 'ghost' of other lower partials which are always present but must not be audible.

Clearly it is essential to have *two* holes to separate the two functions at present attempted by the one speaker-hole – a small one higher up the tube, and a much larger one, further down, in a position where it can produce a perfect and resonant B flat. These two holes must come into action automatically so that there is no alteration in the established fingering arrangements of the instrument.

Fig 12: *Left:* Early example of Klosé system clarinet by Buffet-Crampon, in cocus wood. 1870. *Below:* The all-important lever keys of the Klosé clarinet, acting in conjunction with keys on the other side of the clarinet to provide alternative fingerings. (Modern example.)

Fig 13: *Centre:* Modern Boehm system lower joint with Acton patent vent mechanism avoiding 'forked' notes.
Fig 14: Larger modern clarinets, Boehm system. *Left:* basset-horn in F. *Right:* bass clarinet in B flat.

Fig 15: Clarinet by Quilter of London. 14 keys, early 20th century, showing 'patent' C sharp (the two lowest holes on the left of the picture).

Fig 16: The 'S.K.' mechanism for the separation of the functions of the speaker-key and the note B flat.

Fig 17: Clarinets (*from left to right*) of the first half of the 19th century: (a) d'Almaine. London c. 1805. 6 keys. (b) Key, London. 11 silver keys. c. 1830. Ebony and ivory. (c) Camp, London. 12 keys. c. 1840. (d) Anon. 13 keys mounted and arranged very much in the Müller manner. c. 1845.

Fig 18: Clarinets (*from left to right*) of the mid 19th century: (a) F. Schutz. Mid 19th century German. Steel screws mounting beautifully shaped cup-keys. Large tone holes. No needle springs. Interesting extra keys, including left-hand A flat/E flat. A forward-looking instrument for its period. (b) Boosé, London. 13 silver engraved keys on pillars. Made for the 1851 Exhibition. Plays superbly. (c) Breton. Clarinet in C. 14 brass keys. c. 1850.

Fig 19: Clarinets (*from left to right*) of the late 19th century: (a) Henry Distin, London. Before 1857. 12 keys. A very early example of a clarinet made of brass by a famous maker of brass instruments. (b) Clinton, London. Before 1871. 13 keys. Modern cup-shapes. (c) Quilter, London. An odd instrument, with Boehm system lower joint and the Barret patent on the upper. c. 1890. (d) Clinton, London. Simple systems. An attempt to make an instrument to play in both A and B flat by turning a concentric silver tube with prepared holes. Work carried out by Albert of Brussels. c. 1899.

Fig 20: Interesting later clarinets: (a) Besson, London. Contrabass clarinet, c. 1910. Maple wood, simple system. Experimental lay-out with three speaker-keys. (b) Clinton Boehm. Boosey & Co., London. One piece body. An interesting combination of the work of Klosé, Müller and Barret. 1890 and after. (c) Boosey & Co. Full Boehm and extension to low E flat. Made for Manuel Gomez and including several extra keys of his own design. Early 20th century.

(a)   (b)   (c)

These conditions have been provided by Mr Stubbins and his partner in a most ingenious manner, certainly not for the first time, but equally surely with a success not surpassed by others. In their clarinet (see fig. **16**) the 'throat' B flat is obtained by the normal fingering; but the effect is very different, because the speaker-hole remains closed, and a large and resonant tone-hole opens for its benefit. As soon as the thumb-ring is operated to produce the clarinet register (i.e. across the 'break' to B natural or above) this large hole is closed and the extra small speaker-hole opens.

The twelfths produced by this arrangement are far superior to those normally achieved, and the B flat is much purer in sound and more definite in pitch than it could otherwise be, even with finger corrections such as are suggested later in this book.

As a result we have in the instrument fitted with S.K. mechanism a series with a great future – an example of vision upon which Mr Stubbins and his colleagues are to be congratulated.

Another prominent player and designer, Rosario Mazzeo, the highly gifted late bass-clarinettist of the Boston Symphony Orchestra, has given much study to the improvement of this area of the clarinet – the 'throat' notes – and has come up with a very different solution. In his clarinet (see overleaf) it is unnecessary to use the normal Denner-inspired keys for A natural and B flat, because these notes can be obtained by using the ring keys of either hand, either singly or in any number desired or convenient; one or all of them, in fact. This patent arrangement avoids the clumsiness of the normal fingerings for the throat notes, thus freeing the thumb and first finger of the left hand for much of the time. A natural is obtained by playing 'open G' and adding any ring, and B flat is achieved by playing the normal A natural and adding any ring from either hand.

The lay-out of this is stunningly simple, as well as mechanically sound in principle and practice. As a result, rapid passage-work normally involving the use of thumb and first finger is much more secure, once the transfer to this system of

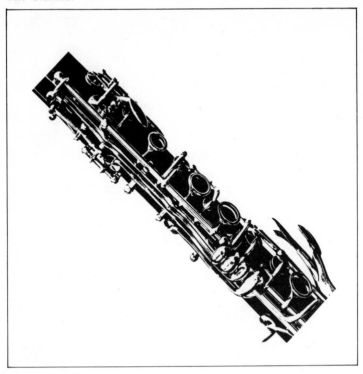

Lay-out of upper joint of Mazzeo system clarinet. Four deceptively simple looking arrangements with far-reaching effects

keywork has been mastered. In addition to the advantage of extreme dexterity, the notes B flat, A, G sharp and G – the throat notes – now using the bigger holes, are more open in sound and therefore more easily wedded to the registers above and below.

There can be no doubt that this arrangement carries a promise of great advantage for the future, and one can only regret that its adoption will probably take all too long. The fault lies in the players, not the system, and arises from the deeply ingrained habits of most of us. Over the years, every good clarinettist learns to resonate the throat notes (as detailed in Chapter 5) by adding several ring-keys to the normal fingerings. He also anticipates a leap across the 'break' by already having the necessary fingers on the second note while playing one of the 'throat' notes. These habits die hard, and if attempted on the Mazzeo system lead to complete chaos. The inventor of the system has foreseen the difficulty and arranged that the mechanism may be unlinked at will, so that the player may come to it gradually. This is a worthy idea, and, given courage on the part of the older player, should work. For the young there is no problem, since the finger-patterns are easier to acquire than those of other systems – provided, that is, there are teachers of sufficient honesty and courage to teach what they may or may not themselves do. This unlinking of the patent mechanism, however, can be said to be begging the question, as it is difficult to see how an instrument perfectly tuned for one system of fingering can respond with equal perfection to another when the unlinking takes place. Nor is there any point in having the extra mechanism involved unless it is to be used, even though this is by no means great in extent; any dead weight of metal is a hindrance to resonance.

The true value of this fine system will not be fully realised unless and until it is taken over completely by a number of really fine players. Mr Mazzeo, himself, used no other for a great many years, and this is certainly a fine testimonial to its possibilities. When his system is finally adopted – which may take a generation – there can be no question but that many passages, now almost impossible on the Boehm and Oehler clarinets, will be played with ease; so it is to be hoped that older players, while they may not themselves be prepared to adopt the Mazzeo system, will at any rate be prepared to teach it and so give their pupils the advantage of its facility.

In addition to the improvement of the 'throat' notes, the Mazzeo system has a key-articulation which makes for a true legato between the 'bell' B natural and the tone above – C sharp. The lack of this has always been a serious disadvantage of the traditional Boehm clarinet. In such a passage as this famous one from Ravel's 'Bolero', this can mean the difference between a 'lumpy' performance and the legato the composer had in mind.

Also, on the most advanced model, the note

can be obtained as a 'forked' note of considerable purity, facilitating many passages which are normally very difficult because of the necessity for perfect co-ordination with the side E flat key.

One disadvantage of the Mazzeo system which is independent of the previous experience (or lack of it) of the player, is in the approach to notes across the 'break' from open G; this requires the G to be played as a really 'open' note, with no fingers at all to support the instrument or to prepare for the big jump in acoustic difference between the registers. This is not only difficult to accomplish, even with practice, as can be verified on any clarinet, but quite 'lumpy' in effect when achieved. It is probably the only interval which is fundamentally made more difficult by the system. Certainly the same sort of progression from A or B flat is easier, since the fingers which play the lower note can be chosen to be those required for the upper.

An interesting system of fingering which has so far made no inroads into the general market for clarinets, and may in fact never do so, is the so-called Double Boehm, illustrated opposite. The area of experiment in this case has been the left-hand main tone-holes, instead of the throat notes. The underlying theory is that it is illogical to have a different sequence of fingerings to produce the same intervals in each hand. In the normal Boehm system the raising of each finger

MAIN CHARACTERISTICS OF THE " D-B " CLARINET

Similar "BŒHM" fingerings on both hands

Connexion suppressed

New easy and surprising resources

in the medium (left hand) and alto (right hand)

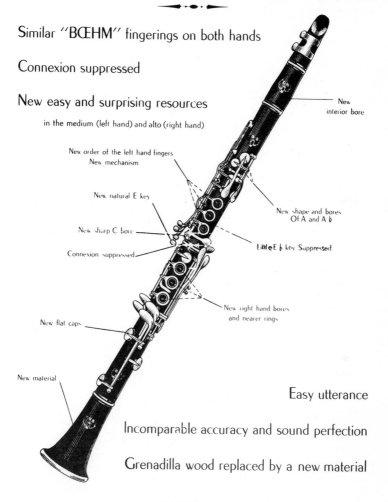

New interior bore

New order of the left hand fingers
New mechanism

New natural E key

New sharp C bore

Connexion suppressed

New shape and bores
Of A and A ♭

Little E ♭ key Suppressed

New right hand bores
and nearer rings

New flat caps

New material

Easy utterance

Incomparable accuracy and sound perfection

Grenadilla wood replaced by a new material

MODÉLE BREVETÉ S. G. D. G.

of the right hand, starting from the lowest, raises the pitch one tone, followed by a semi-tone, followed by one tone. The left hand sequence produces tone, tone, semi-tone. In the normal right-hand fingering the missing semi-tone between the third step and the tone above is produced simply if imperfectly by a 'fork' fingering. In the Double Boehm the same lay-out is adopted for the left hand, so that E natural is a forked note (second finger alone) and E flat is unforked (first finger). This of course greatly facilitates any passage involving, for instance, the C minor arpeggio; it also greatly complicates anything which requires C major or its relatives. In addition it adds one more 'forked' note to the acoustic mêlée of the clarinet, whereas most players and makers would much prefer one *less*. At the same time it must be said that this experimental system is worthy of investigation. An interesting side-issue which can be considered to be an advantage of the Double Boehm system is its abolition of the link between the upper and lower joints – the 'connexion' in the USA, the 'correspondence' in England. This is because the E flat – B flat twelfth is so much more accessible, and does not require the right hand in any way. There is certainly considerable logic in the lay-out. However, the E natural – B natural now requires the same key as was previously used for the E flat – B flat – the fourth 'trill' key at the bottom of the top joint. An obvious difference, also, is the much closer spacing of the left-hand tone-holes, possibly uncomfortably close for large hands, but certainly comfortable for the young player. This spacing makes necessary much longer keys for A natural and G sharp in the 'throat' register: this makes their operation lighter, but at the same time reduces the 'venting' to a marked extent. These holes can now also be bigger. Acoustically the makers claim for the system a considerable improvement in the second overblown register (fifth harmonics – i.e. from high E natural upwards) especially in *pianissimo*, due to the more logical left-hand lay-out, and a great increase in brightness in the throat B flat due to the increased size in the tone-holes of A and G sharp. Lastly, the removal of the 'link' between the joints means that the most misplaced key of all – the C sharp – G sharp little-finger key – can now be more correctly placed while retaining its normal shape and action.

There still remains room for the cross-fertilisation which may in future occur between these newer systems. It is a long time since Klosé developed the Boehm system clarinet. There would seem to be room for a truly modern clarinet with lighter key-work, more positive closure, improved acoustic response, and a better all-round artistic possibility. There are several reasons for the absence of such a clarinet from the scene today, most of them economic. There is also the distinct possibility that the removal of some of its defects altogether, rather than the rendering of them less intractable, might de-humanise the instrument and make it as impersonal as the clarinet stop of the computerised electronic organ. At the same time it must be said that the development of the clarinet is by no means at an end; its acoustic richness gives it an interest which is bound to result in the exploration of all sorts of possibilities.

Three
Acoustic Characteristics

To most clarinettists, a study of the acoustic characteristics of their instrument is a sad chore, taking them unwillingly back to the schoolroom, with references to such apparently unconnected phenomena as decibels, units, frequency, cycles per second, reversals of phase, nodes and anti-nodes, and end of tube corrections. Occasionally, even, the dreaded intrusion of a formula may be necessary to illustrate what happens in a given set of conditions when the clarinet is played.

It is usually at this point that the clarinettist retires from the scene, not so much defeated as discouraged, because it seems to him that this is effort in the wrong direction: he wants, in short, to know how to *play* the clarinet, not how to study the effect of what he is doing in scientific terms. His departure at this point is a pity, because a clear understanding of what he is doing is not merely important – it may well be essential if he is to take his playing far along the road which starts with elementary achievement and ends with serious art. He may be lucky, and be an instinctive player who can do without such knowledge; but it can do him no harm, and may do a power of good, because it is the point at which a real understanding of the clarinet may be said to start. There are things he should know.

First – what is sound? Sound is just an excitation of the ear-drums due to energy from air vibrations (or waves). Decibels are used to measure sound, from one DB (just audible) to the start of a pain in the ear from its intensity (in most people about 140 DB). As clarinettists, what we really need to know about decibels is that the clarinet produces a rather larger slice of this range of dynamics than the other wood-winds. It is quite capable of one DB, since in a 'diminuendo al niente' it can fade to complete silence. It can, in contrast, certainly outshine the flute and bassoon, and in almost every case the oboe, in loudness.

Next, leaving the question of loudness or softness, we should consider 'lowness' or 'highness' of notes. This is an un-scientific description, but the image is nonetheless a very vivid one, and immediately understood. This is where the 'hertz-unit' comes in, because it measures the number of vibrations or cycles which determine the pitch. This is perhaps best illustrated by a musical string in vibration, where one cycle is clearly the motion from a central point, at rest, to another central point:

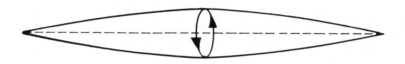

This is in fact the simplest sort of vibration, and is similar to that of a pendulum swinging from side to side. It takes no account, in pendulum form, of the passage of time. This can be represented by imagining a sheet of paper being pulled across the path of a pendulum while it is in motion. This gives the resultant course of vibration against time – or in fact impulses or vibrations, or cycles per second. This curve, known as a sine curve, is a picture of pure sound, with no disturbing overtones or harmonies, and looks like this:

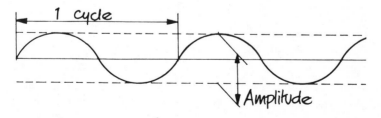

The Clarinet

The lowest sound audible by the human ear is that created by about 25 such impulses per second, and is described as 25 hertz. As the number of these impulses or cycles increase, the note is raised in pitch until it finally reaches the limit of human audible capacity at about 20,000 hertz. Dogs and bats, among other animals, can hear sounds above this limit, but are not usually naturally musical.

This is certainly not very complicated information to assimilate; and in addition to this, it is necessary only to remember the effect upon sound of two external conditions. The first of these is temperature. Air at a higher temperature vibrates faster, so that the note produced is higher in pitch. Would that the designers of most concert halls had heard of this! The second fact is that the density of the air affects pitch to a marked extent, and as the density is increased considerably by an increase in the water content, this affects the clarinet after breath condensation has begun to take effect – a quite short time after commencing to play. Moist air vibrates more quickly, producing a rise in the pitch of the notes produced.

The reed

What exactly is it, then, which produces this sound, when the clarinet is blown? (Here the word 'exactly' is probably better ignored, because in the strict scientific view there are several side-issues; these must for the present be disregarded because they cloud the main issue, so far as the player is concerned.)

The first point which must be clearly established is that it is not the clarinet itself which is vibrating, but the column of air it encloses. The shape and proportions as well as the length of this column dictate the sort of sound, as well as its pitch. The air column of a clarinet, for almost its whole length, is cylindrical. That of the oboe is conical (see fig. **21**). This determines the difference in character between the two instruments.

Whatever the shape of the tube, it is essential to have some external source of vibration to excite the air column. In both the conical oboe and the cylindrical clarinet, this is the reed.

The reed of a wind instrument is, in scientific terms, simply a valve – that is, something which opens and shuts, cutting off and re-starting the supply of air to the column inside the instrument (see below). The reason for its so doing is to be found in a study of air-dynamics – the reed is deflected by the passage of air over its surface; it snaps shut, cutting off the air supply, and since it is in fact a wooden spring, it then immediately returns to its open position, and so repeats the cycle. This action provides a rapid series of puffs of air to the column inside the instrument, and these contain the basic potentials for different harmonic patterns. They are found to vary in speed according to the shape and size of the tube to which the reed is attached. An interesting variation – a vital one – is the length of time during which the valve remains shut; if it flies open and shut very rapidly, it can admit air for only about one-twentieth of the series of its cycle of movement. If it does this, it has the potential of producing the full range of overtones or harmonics possible in the instrument concerned. It may, on the other hand, open and close so slowly that it admits air for a full one-eighth of a cycle, in which case the range of harmonics possible is much

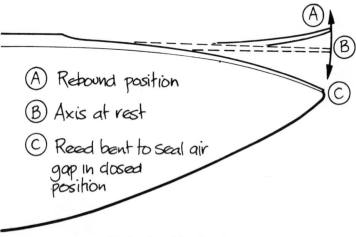

Blade of reed in vibration.

more limited. In practice, on the clarinet played in normal conditions, the reed opens and shuts more or less quickly within the framework of its cycle according to the desire of the player, who uses the damping effect of the soft lower lip, as well as the greater or lesser tension of the spring of the reed as controlled by this, to produce the sort of sound he requires. Generally speaking, bright sounds are produced by more tension and quicker opening of the cycle, more mellow sounds by a slowing of the opening and closing action. This is the most vital of all aspects of approach to playing a reed instrument, because it is what makes one player sound totally different from another – and it is simply a question of control of the vibration of the reed, and the limitless variations which are possible within the range of tension and speed of reed movement from its open to its closed position. It is not essential to know this fact, because from the earliest players it has always been a question of 'feel' rather than cogitation; but it is a fascinating aspect of our study of wood-wind tone production and can open one's mind to many new aspects of it.

There is of course an essential difference between the reeds of the oboe and the clarinet. The oboe reed is a self-contained generator of sound, while the clarinet reed, on its own, is silent – merely a potential producer of the essential vibrations. Any musician can recall the characteristic 'crowing' of an oboe reed – among the most maddening of all sounds in orchestral mêlée before the start of a rehearsal. To achieve a similar (even bigger) sound, the clarinettist must remove the complete mouthpiece with the reed attached to it – an indulgence he rarely, happily, takes unto himself. If he should do this, he has in his hand the exact equivalent of the oboe reed – the generator of vibrations of his instrument. This source of vibration is set in motion by the breath of the player – a statement which may at first seem simple, but is worth examining, because it is a fairly remarkable phenomenon. To set the 'valve' of the reed into its rapid opening and shutting cycle, the spring (which is the reed) has to be loaded. This is achieved by embouchure pressure; that is, the tightening of the lips around the mouthpiece at a point nearer the tip than the fulcrum or the end of the mouthpiece facing.

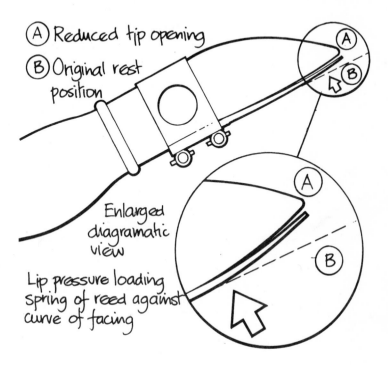

(A) Reduced tip opening
(B) Original rest position

Enlarged diagramatic view

Lip pressure loading spring of reed against curve of facing

Examining the pictures of the mouthpiece shown in this illustration, it should be noted that in its rest position there is no possiblity of closure between the reed and mouthpiece – a current of air will simply pass down this opening with a hissing sound unless pressure is applied as in the diagram of the reed in its loaded or playing position. The point at which the lip-pressure locks the reed against the facing of the mouthpiece is determined by the curvature of the facing, and is a vital factor not only to the comfort of the player, but to the range of sounds which are at his disposal; this is a subject better dealt with later, in our discussions of artistic approaches to playing the clarinet, but it is worth noting here as possibly the most powerful source of variety in clarinet tone-production. With this spring-loading, the generator is ready to do its job of setting the air in the column of the clarinet in vibration, and this simply requires a stream of air to be passed between the reed and the mouthpiece, when the valve action described above commences. As this happens, the reed is bent quite remarkably at every point beyond the locked position, as we saw on page 63.

Wave forms in a closed pipe

Having excited the air column inside the clarinet into vibration by the attachment to it of this quite powerful generator of impulses, the question now arises – what pitch of sound will result, and why?

In these circumstances it has been found that the lowest or fundamental sound produced depends not only upon the capacity of the tube, but its shape. The larger the cavity, the lower the sound; but cavities of different shapes give different shapes to their wave forms, and the clarinet is unique in that it presents a cylindrical cavity. This gives it the characteristics of a 'stopped pipe' – like that used in organ building; and the most obvious of these characteristics is that the pitch of its fundamental note is very much lower than one would expect from such a comparatively short tube. It is quite possible by some very complicated mathematics to calculate the optimum measurements for a clarinet in a given pitch. In practice this has been obviated by many years of trial and error, so that now we have clarinets which are more or less equal in length but of fairly divergent bore sizes, each having its own advantages and disadvantages from an acoustic and practical point of view. No doubt one day computerisation will present us with the perfectly proportioned clarinet from one aspect or another. It is hard to imagine that it would meet with universal approval, since people seem to require very divergent characteristics in their instruments – a fact by no means to be deplored, if we are to have clarinet performances of individual and recognisable character. At all events the clarinet will continue to respond as a 'stopped pipe' and to retain the acoustic idiosyncracies of that type of tube.

The pulses which form the basis of the vibrations in a tube are formed by the compression of the air molecules followed immediately by a rarefaction as the valve of the reed snaps shut. These pulses travel the length of the tube until they meet the open air at the end of it, and one after another they emerge there. At this point they rebound from the outer atmosphere, which reacts against them and sends back a resistance wave down the tube. The interesting factor in this resistance wave is that it is a direct reversal of the pressure-points of the outer wave – the compressions have become rarefactions and vice versa. Diagramatically it can be represented like this:

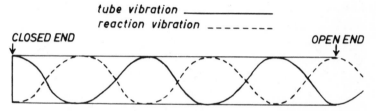

This is the wave form present in an open pipe, but, as can be seen, the reaction travels all the way back down the tube until it reaches the *closed* end – in the case of both oboe and clarinet, the reed-gap. The complexity of vibration does not end here, because obviously the vibration rebounds once more from the closed end as a reaction wave, again exchanging compression for rarefaction (a phenomenon known as change of phase) before retreating to the open end, changing once more, and returning again to the reed. This is a wave form of such complexity that it almost defies diagrammatic representation, but would seem to be something like this:

The Clarinet

Thus a simple open tube has two series of waves of opposite phase at any given time, one going and one coming, while a closed pipe has four sets, two of outgoing phase and two of incoming. As has been said, the clarinet is a 'closed' pipe – closed at one end by the reed; and it therefore responds by delivering the same sort of sound from a frequency point of view as the closed pipe of an organ. It is also true that the oboe is a closed pipe, and that in practice it responds as an open one – as if, in fact, the reed were not there. Much scientific elaboration and examination is required to explain why this is so. Most of this is not only incomprehensible to a non-scientist but completely unnecessary to a clarinettist. Whatever the detailed reasons, it seems certain that in practice the oboe acts as an open pipe because of its conical bore, while the clarinet, being cylindrical, responds like the closed pipe it is.

This four-wave form has only one major modification which must be noted. In theory, the ending of a pipe in the open air should be the reversal point of the impulse, and the change of direction and reversal of phase should happen neatly and tidily at that point. In fact this does not happen, because some energy escapes from the wave at that point and is not reflected. So the air beyond the end of the pipe is in vibration to some extent, and must be reckoned as part of the pipe for purposes of pitch. For this reason a pipe always produces a sound of slightly lower pitch than theoretically it should. This is a factor known as 'end-correction' and is an important aspect of clarinet construction. Incidentally, these stray end waves tend to be spherical in form and are the reason for the shape of the bell of the clarinet, which helps to radiate them smoothly and without undue back pressure. It is also important to remember that this 'end correction' phenomenon applies not only to the end of the tube, but to the air above every tone-hole of the instrument, coming into operation when this tone-hole is the lowest one in use. The air above the holes in these circumstances is in fact a part of the tube itself, so that closely fitted pads or fingers held close to the holes can have a damping effect. This is the reason for the care exercised by the best makers to obtain what is known as correct 'venting' – the correct distance from the hole of the pad, and the use of pads with a property of 'reflection'. It is also a point of study with the best players, who can obtain a great variety of effects tonally, and interesting corrections of intonation, by using the fingers at varying distances above the holes.

The harmonic spectrum

A study of the extremely complex wave form of the clarinet makes it obvious why it has such a wonderfully rich sound spectrum, as well as many characteristic acoustic advantages and disadvantages.

The first advantage is in the matter of the depth of the pitch which the clarinet can produce from a given length of tube. The clarinet can achieve middle C

(*on the B flat clarinet*)

from about one foot of tube. The oboe, in contrast, requires two feet of tube for the same sound. As a result of this a clarinet, which is only a little longer than an oboe, can descend six whole tones lower, and is a match for the viola in its lower compass, whereas the oboe cannot even compete with the violin, as it struggles with its bottom B flat against the G of the violin. In the upward extension, too, the clarinet seems to have the upper hand, because although exceptional players can now extend the oboe to a top C *in altissimo*, so can exceptional clarinettists (the written top D in this case) and certainly many modern composers are much more ready to accept the clarinet in the five tones below this than they are the oboe. This then is the first big advantage of the clarinet – it's stopped pipe' acoustics give it an extremely large compass.

The most obvious disadvantage of the clarinet's characteristics is that, since it produces such a low note from a relatively short tube, the scale upwards from this must consist of sub-divisions which are themselves small, and therefore critical in the calculation and construction of the holes which produce them. In other words, the error of $\pm$ .001in. is inevitably much more serious in a clarinet than it is in an oboe, and infinitely more telling than it could ever be in a bassoon. Nor is this the end of the matter, because when the lower or fundamental, register is left behind and the over-blowing of upper partials begins, these are at a much greater distance in the case of the clarinet than the others, and are therefore less controlled. But this is 'jumping the gun' somewhat. To understand it it is necessary briefly to examine the underlying harmonic lay-out of these overtones, or upper partials, of the clarinet.

No sound, or at any rate no decent instrumental sound, consists of one note only. Scientifically it is possible to pro-duce a sound which is a single note – it may even be necessary to do so. Musically it is a dull and unprofitable experience. The average tuning fork makes almost such a sound, but even this contains traces of others, which make it at least bearable to the musical ear. If one produces a deep, rich note on any musical instrument, and listens to it with care over a fairly long period, other higher notes soon begin to make themselves audible in the sound, and to emerge into the consciousness, most of them pleasantly related harmonically but a few of them slightly dissonant.

As a particularly vivid example, take the note of a large and deep-toned bell. This can be a most impressive sound; but at the top of its spectrum there is often a really tooth-shattering jangle of overtones which make it quite impossible, orchestrally, to accommodate it from the point of intonation. The fundamental may be perfectly in tune. The overtones are not. This is by no means applicable to the experience of listening to a low note on the clarinet. Certainly when one does this it is the effect of a whole *series* one is listening to – and it is a different series from that which is present in a low note of the flute or oboe; but it is not really a discordant series. It is quite simply a series of overtones which ensures that it does sound like a clarinet, and not a flute or oboe.

The complete spectrum of possible overtones for any given note has been found to contain the same series of intervals, and the pattern of these is shown by this series upon middle C:

All these notes are present when the fundamental is played, but they are in different proportions in different sounds, and in some instruments many of them are for practical purposes completely absent.

Obviously one can ignore numbers 10–13 in the case of the clarinet, except for freak effects such as are now (rather sadly) demanded. In any case they are hardly recognisable as the notes they are supposed to represent.

The clarinet's overtones

An examination of the clarinet spectrum playing this same middle C – in this case the written note, not the concert pitch – can be easily carried out, and underlines the remark made above concerning the unrecognisable upper partials. Simply fingering the fundamental note, even without raising the speaker key, and certainly without the aid of an open tone hole under the index finger, it is possible to obtain numbers 1, 3, 5 and 7 by lip pressure. It is quite impossible to obtain numbers 2, 4 or 6. This once more is very much in line with theory, because this is exactly the behaviour of a 'closed pipe'.

Two things emerge from this simple experiment. The first is that number 7 turns out to be not a top B flat as in theory it should be, but a usually well-tuned A. This is at first confusing; but in fact the note is really a very flat B flat. It is perhaps extremely fortunate that this flatness so accurately places the note as an A, because in fact it is the only one obtainable on most clarinets.

The other observation to be made from this series is that numbers 1, 3 and 5 together make a very strong major triad, and this shows very clearly why baroque and later composers found it essential to use the cadence known as the *tierce de Picardie* – the conclusion of any passage in the minor made by a final cadence to the major. Obviously with, for instance, a rank of stopped organ pipes all sounding their inherent major thirds above the fundamental tonic, the major chord is present already, and the minor third is a very strongly clashing dissonance. This effect is particularly strong in the case of massed clarinets, because of their spectrum.

The harmonics listed here are of course all assisted by the use of the speaker-key, and many of them by the raising of the first finger of the left hand. It must furthermore be remembered that this is merely a pattern of harmonics, and that in theory the same series of intervals can be obtained over every single semitone of the fundamental, or chalumeau, scale. The first jump is a twelfth, the second a sixth above that, because the clarinet includes all the odd numbered overtones (Nos. 1 to 7 or 9) and none of the even numbered ones in any strength. At this point theory and practice diverge. The twelfths are usually quite acceptable. Many of the sixths are not. Worse than this, they vary not only according to the length of tube in use, but from clarinet to clarinet; even two excellent clarinets may be found to differ greatly in this respect. This is particularly noticeable in clarinets of different bore-size, and present-day clarinets vary from as small as .575in. to as big as .600in. or more. This second over-blown series also varies in respect of the various tapers which many makers find necessary to introduce into the bore of their clarinets in order to correct the all-important relationship between the chalumeau and the twelfth above it. As a result, while most of the twelfths are fairly correct and certainly acceptable without any change of fingering (other than the addition of the speaker-key) there is little rhyme or reason in the third series, a sixth above. Luckily, many of these fifth harmonics are not used or necessary. The 'bell' B when over-blown gives a very gusty G natural which should be a G sharp

– a typical bugle-sound. The A natural harmonic of the C natural above is also usually poor and somewhat forthright. This also applies to the harmonic B above the D, which is in fact obtained rather well as the harmonic on C sharp, and can be used to advantage as a grace note in such passages as:

↑   *(fingered as)*

It is only with the harmonic on E – the usual top C sharp in use today – that we come to the overtones which have been properly tamed. This, on some clarinets, is very flat, and has to be raised by the addition of the E flat key (fourth finger right hand); the same applies to the top D, harmonic of F below, and the E over the G. This is a feature concerning which many makers seem to be unnecessarily complacent, even proud. It is obviously better not to require that extra finger – in a hurry it can mean the difference between success and disaster.

With the top F natural above A flat there is usually more stability, except that there is a wide divergence between the results of bores of different sizes. The partial tends to flatness in the case of the small bore clarinets, and to sharpness in the larger bore instruments. Sharpness is probably the lesser evil, because of the ease of control by the embouchure in the downward direction, and the impossibility of raising the pitch by lip-pressure alone. It is worth noting in passing that on most simple system clarinets a very good top F can be obtained as a harmonic of the A below – it should be an F, but this, again, is beside the point. One uses what one can of this particular slice of the clarinet overtone spectrum.

We come now to a consideration of the harmonic on the B♭ (third harmonic)

The Clarinet

This theoretically should be a top G, but is in most big bore instruments an excellent F sharp, and should be used much more often. It is particularly useful in Messiaen's 'Quatuor pour la Fin du Temps', when it enables the two completely unrelated notes bracketed to be played with the same fingering:

The harmonic on B natural in the clarinet register is once more a very flat fifth harmonic. It should be a G sharp in theory, but is a delightful G natural on many instruments, bright in tone and readily attacked. On small bore instruments, again, this is a disappointing flat note, and inaudible.

There are several important lessons to be learnt. The first of these is that even the first over-blown register may need a great deal of adjustment and humouring to make it viable as a musical compass; and above that there is no set pattern to which one should attempt to adhere. There must, in this third register, be a ready acceptance and forgiveness of weakness and waywardness in the character of the clarinet, together with a resourceful mind filled with the ingenuity necessary to invent ways of overcoming these traits. Here there is a limit, and that limit must not be exceeded by the makers of the instruments. Although the weaknesses in the harmonic structure of the clarinet are readily understandable and forgivable, they must be kept within the bounds of possible control. The clarinet in its most perfect form is a strange beast – if it is imperfect, it is also completely untameable.

In its most perfect form, most players now seem to agree that the most vital characteristic to look for is *flexibility*. If the clarinet answers back when a determined attempt is made to correct it, it is a very poor clarinet. A good clarinet is a complicated acoustic bag of tricks, but predictable.

The 'throat' register

All this discussion has so far left out of account the one register which most players agree is the part of the instrument which most requires attention – the 'throat' register, consisting of the notes

This is a part of the instrument which is not generally thought of as taking part in the normal acoustic scheme. It is not overblown in the normal way, though any advanced player finds himself using its harmonics with great satisfaction. The fundamental register of this part of the instrument is so important that it warrants a special discussion all to itself.

Here it is wise to pause and reflect just why the clarinet has failed to match up to its scientific possibilities in its development so far.

There can be no doubt that in some respects – size and position of tone-holes, venting and equalisation of resonance – the clarinet is still suffering the results of crude experiments made in its earliest days – tricks of the trade handed down generation after unthinking generation long after intelligent thinking should have eradicated them. Just one small example (and this is not at all appropriate to an acoustic discussion) is the characteristic sight of a player blowing the water out of his C sharp – G sharp key before playing a solo, or after spoiling a solo with its gurgling tootle. On the vast majority of clarinets this key has always been wrongly placed – underneath, where the water can run into at will. It usually still is, and is a *very* dangerous feature. There are many others. Some of these are acoustic failings which should have been eradicated decades ago. It seems certain that future developments will do this, with the removal of many of the present snags – though it is to be hoped that this may be accomplished without serious alteration of the character of the instrument.

The first of these snags is due to the use of the speaker-key hole, continued in almost every case to this day, as the tone-hole for the 'throat' B flat. This goes back to very early days indeed, and simply stayed like that when the clarinet developed its 'bell' B natural, at which time the two keys at the top of the instrument settled down as the A natural and B flat keys they are today. This was, at the time, the best that could be hoped for. Today such a set-out is quite a travesty, because modern technology should have swept it away long ago. Every clarinettist knows the most obvious results of this long-continued practice. This B flat is by far the worst note on the clarinet, largely because of the extremely small size of what is supposed to be a 'tone-hole' but in fact has to operate as a speaker-hole in addition. It is, even so, far too large to be an effective speaker-hole; to fulfil this function it should be very much smaller and much nearer to the mouthpiece. To produce the note B flat it should be not only larger, but much further away from the mouthpiece. This indicates that the two functions must separate – a special tone-hole for B flat must be provided, and a proper speaker-hole as well – both actuated by the left thumb as before. This has been attempted with much ingenuity by several clarinet designers, some of which work is described in Chapter 2, and the results they have achieved are very successful. But these results cannot yet be said to have come into general use. Possibly 98 per cent of clarinets are without such acoustic advantages, and here we must try to deal with things as they are usually found. This is in no way to minimise the work of such thoughtful inventors as William Stubbins, who among others has solved the problem not only of the properly placed B flat but of the correctly sized and located speaker-hole. These factors can be said to have pointed the way to the eradication of the faults detailed in this chapter. The same can be said of the work of Rosario Mazzeo, proceeding as can be seen in Chapter 2 from a slightly different angle, but with the same aim. Unfortunately such designs must still be said to belong to the future.

Meanwhile, there are several possible ways of dealing with the faults which are present in clarinets as they found in the vast majority of players' hands at the present moment, whether they play the so-called 'Boehm' system or one of the German-type clarinets. The problem of the feeble B flat is really not so serious; the fact that the speaker-hole which produces it is acoustically misplaced for its other duties is much more so, because it is the main factor in the displacement of the upper harmonics of the instrument, and gives rise to most of the fingering problems we must consider later.

So far as the B flat is concerned the solution lies in the statement of its weakness – it should be bigger and further from the mouthpiece. In fact, it should be where the present so-called B flat trill key is, and of that size. The solution is, therefore, simple enough – learn to use this trill key as a melodic note instead of an adjunct. In recent years, happily, most of the young players have adopted this fingering and use it with great skill and aplomb. Thirty years ago its use as anything but a trill key was rare, and usually mistrusted. A few adventurous players then began to include it as a melodic note, and evolved the method which should have been obvious from the start – of contacting the touchpiece of the key with the second knuckle-joint of the right first finger, a sort of rolling action which allows it to be included in the most legato phrases when care is used, because it is unnecessary to remove the fingers of the right hand from the holes and keys of the lower joint and they are ready for immediate use even in such passages as:

x *side B flats*

to say nothing of its more obvious use in passages which require a much more sustained B flat. This is a practice to be applauded, and incorporated into the regular technique of every advanced player. It is the perfect answer, when it can be used.

There remains still the odd occasion when it is impossible to get to the 'trill' key, and the old, traditional fingering has to be

The Clarinet

resorted to. Even then the battle is not lost, because then one simply resorts to resonance corrections by special cross fingerings which improve the character of the note out of all recognition. Think for a moment of the effect of striking a note of the xylophone. If there is no resonating tube, the sound is dull and lifeless. But if the instrument is given an additional resonator of the right length (a metal tube of the same diameter as the width of the bar, suspended below it but not in contact) the effect is immediate, satisfactory, and dramatic. It gives a rounded musical sound of definite pitch and even a measurable duration. It is this sort of resonator which is required to make our throat B flat into a decent-sounding note. How to resonate it? The tube of the resonator is certainly there ready-made – the tube of the clarinet itself. It simply fails to act as a resonator because it is full of holes. Fill these up by adding fingers, and it will work. Oddly enough it will not work if completely enclosed, because of the end-correction effect mentioned below. The B flat will be hopelessly stifled if the F natural or F sharp holes are covered, but from that point to the bell, the player has his choice of fingers to put on or keep off, and it is for him to discover what works in his particular set of circumstances. This may vary according to his instrument, the temperature, the type of reed and mouthpiece and possibly other even stronger factors. They may well vary from time to time. Certainly one such fingering which seems to work is:

But it must be remembered that this is no more than a guide, because the resonation of this most important note must be the personal pre-occupation and discovery of every player, and he has every right to disagree heartily with the findings of every other player. Now that he has a treasured and corrected B flat he will undoubtedly find himself dissatisfied with his A natural and A flat, and must experiment until he finds the best resonant fingerings for his purpose. Two fingerings which have been successful, but with which, naturally, many will disagree, are:

The player will then certainly find that he has left himself with a dull note which originally he may have thought quite bright – the so-called 'open' G natural. Two reasonable resonance fingerings are:

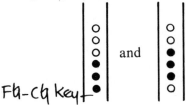

and there are several much more complex fingerings which one can use to vary the pitch of this very movable note. Having discovered all these optimum fingerings, he must then incorporate them into his technique until they become second nature to him. This may not be easy at first. Few players, having achieved their best A natural, can use it in this little solo from Beethoven's Sixth Symphony at first without quite awkward results.

The twelfths

We need now to consider the effect this misplacement of the speaker hole has upon the twelfths of the instrument. Clarinet makers have striven over the years to perfect these twelfths. They have been very much aware of the necessity for this, and have in fact reduced the seriousness of many of the defects, by reshaping the bore at various points by tapers of different lengths and intensities and by altering the 'flaring' of the bell, the weight of socket and bell, and the 'broaching' of the bore – that gentle swelling which starts usually just below the third finger-hole of the lower joint and terminates in the bell, which it must exactly match. They have constantly re-designed the interior of the mouthpiece and even experimented with the effect of different widths of reed. A further refinement is the under-cutting of the tone-holes – a feature which requires very careful examination to detect, because it can only be seen from the inside of the bore, and only detected by an eye used to the size of the original parallel holes. In fact a tone-hole may be anything from parallel

to extremely obtuse in its undercut shape:

This undercutting has the effect of making the note produced by the hotel much more flexible and movable in pitch. It can also make it more diffuse and even less resonant, and this undercutting requires a great deal of care and discrimination in its application.

With all these efforts, no maker has truly been able to root out all the 'original sin' of the clarinet. There still remain many weaknesses of intonation. The best place to start to discuss these is the midpoint of the clarinet – the area of:

There is no real excuse for this twelfth to be out of tune; it is so *natural* that there is virtually no sense of a big leap in the music when the interval is played. Herold knew this when he wrote his 'Zampa' overture, which contains the famous solo which begins with this twelfth:

It is a delightfully easy solo – to begin – for this reason. Having established that this twelfth is perfect, the facts to remember are (a) twelfths further down the instrument are usually narrower and (b) twelfths further up usually wider. This poses an interesting series of problems for the maker. If he takes a pride in the perfection of his chalumeau tuning, he is going to be left with a clarinet register very flat at the bottom and painfully sharp at the top. If he regards the clarinet register as more important from the intonation point of view (and there may well be something in this; for instance, a sharp C in the clarinet register is much more offensive to most people than a flat F in the chalumeau) he is going to produce a chalumeau register of such imperfection that even the beginner who starts with this register will think him a fool. This may very well have an interesting historical background. There are several instances of works containing both clarinets and chalumeaux. As has been said elsewhere, it is astonishing that although· there are excellent examples of clarinets in most museums, some of them from the time in question, there are no chalumeaux at all, anywhere. Could it be that in fact some of the clarinets in these museums were never used as clarinets, but tuned as chalumeaux – that is, without a proper overblown register? Certainly some of them seem to respond in this way when an attempt to play them is made, while others play quite pleasantly as clarinets, but miserably in the chalumeau register. This would be a short chapter in the history of the instrument, because quite soon works were being written which exploit the whole range of the clarinet; but it is a possibility which might explain several mysterious historical facts, the disappearance of the chalumeau in its simplest form among them. All this is of course of merely hypothetical interest. To the maker, as to the player, the fact of the imperfect twelfths is what counts.

The Clarinet

And as the maker is usually an intelligent person, he leaves us with a clarinet which is imperfect but predictably so. It is perhaps worthwhile at this point to summarise quickly the approximate state of affairs of the first two registers as they are usually found today, after the most skilled makers have tried their best to balance them:

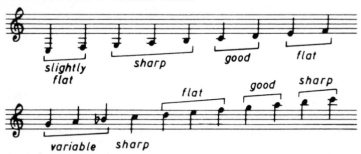

These faults are present in all clarinets, but in greater or lesser degree; the good clarinet is the one in which they are present, but both minimal and movable. The maker has done his job, within the framework of present practice. It is now the task of the player to do likewise, and the detailed method of doing so is indicated in our section dealing with artistic approach in Chapter 5.

The first and most obvious method of affecting the pitch of a note is embouchure control, tightening or slackening the lips around the mouthpiece and reed to sharpen or flatten the pitch. In effect, this allows a greater or lesser amount of the reed to vibrate, and obeys the normal laws of acoustics – that a small vibrating body has a higher vibration potential than a large one, and therefore produces a higher note. So a tight embouchure which stifles the reed to a point higher up the curve of the facing, i.e., nearer to its tip, raises the pitch of the note produced. The effect is in fact not very marked because most good players find that a fairly tight embouchure produces the sort of tone they appreciate, and there is little leeway in an upward direction. Slackening the embouchure has a much more marked effect; the note moves easily, and if the curvature of the mouthpiece allows, the pitch of the note can be pulled down almost a semi-tone – with, it must be added, a very great loss of beauty and clarity of the tone. A skilled player can do much to balance intonation from note to note in this way without this fact becoming obvious. he is grateful for notes which are slightly sharp, if they must have a fault, rather than flat.

Fingering corrections

Embouchure control should not be the only method of dealing with pitch faults. There remains one which is used surprisingly little by most clarinettists except in the upper register, where it is essential – fingering corrections. This involves the ignoring of the usual fingering chart which is assimilated when the instrument is first learnt, and the use of cross-fingerings, 'half-holings', and the *invention* of fingerings for any note where this may be necessary. A table of a few such fingerings is given on p. 84, and will repay careful study; but this is merely a start. The clarinettist must follow the tradition of the best recorder players in this respect; and it is certain that in doing so he will be following in the footsteps of the greatest clarinettists of the past. Even today many players use the fingerings ⃒ ⃒ for the note

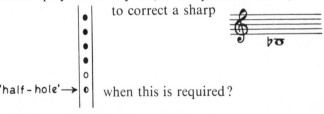

when an impossible slur demands it.

In doing this they are reverting to the only fingering available on the first clarinets ever made. Why then should a modern player so rarely use, with equal confidence, to correct a sharp

'half-hole' → when this is required?

The Clarinet

Any fingering is good enough for any note, provided it produces the note. Appended here is a list of such fingerings as experienced by one player. Others will certainly be able to invent a great number of additions to this list, for to be a clarinettist is to be an *inventor* of clarinet fingerings.

Auxiliary fingerings (*Boehm system*)
Some of these are for purposes of facility but most of them are improvements of pitch or tone. They should be taken as a guide only, since not only do different makes and bores of clarinets vary, but individual instruments as well. The key numbers mentioned refer to the picture of the instrument on page 97, at the end of the chapter.

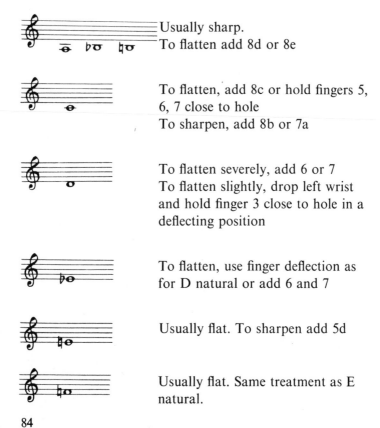

Usually sharp.
To flatten add 8d or 8e

To flatten, add 8c or hold fingers 5, 6, 7 close to hole
To sharpen, add 8b or 7a

To flatten severely, add 6 or 7
To flatten slightly, drop left wrist and hold finger 3 close to hole in a deflecting position

To flatten, use finger deflection as for D natural or add 6 and 7

Usually flat. To sharpen add 5d

Usually flat. Same treatment as E natural.

Should be in tune when taken with first finger alone, but is a forked note. See maker and change thumb bush if this is not so. Failing this, flatten by adding finger 3, sharpen by adding 5d

To resonate, add 5 6 7 according to pitch, or 3 5 6

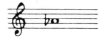

To resonate, add 5, 6 or 3, 5, 6

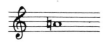

To resonate, add 2, *3*, 6, 7 and 8d (sometimes 5 as well, if pitch allows)

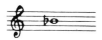

To resonate, add as A natural plus 4

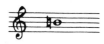

Normal fingering plus G sharp 'throat' key to give *ppp* attack. NB: do *not* attempt C natural like this

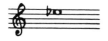

To flatten severely, add 4c

To sharpen, add 8b
To flatten, add 8a

Adjust as above for E natural. More responsive to treatment, because less risky

The Clarinet

To sharpen add 8b
To flatten add 8c

Flatter, but less resonant when
played {Th 1, 2, 3/5, 6
       {Sp

A multiplicity of fingerings usually
of varied pitches. Select for
context, rather than ease of
approach. Know which are flat, or
sharp

These can be played as harmonics
of

they are quite raucous

Have a different harmonic
spectrum when 5, 6, 7 are added –
and a softer sound

A useful *pp* attack is given by
{Th 1, 2 and 5c 5d
{Sp

Can be played melodically using its
'trill' fingering if 3 is added to
flatten
        {Th   5c 5d and 3
ie:{Sp

'Open' D (played as a harmonic of open G) is useful in a hurry. There are possible occasional uses for
Th 5b and: Th and A flat
Sp   Sp
Half-holing the first finger with the usual fingering flattens well
On some instruments the normal fingering includes 8b. This is a nuisance and should not be

Several very useful variations:
(a){Th – 2, 3   7, 8a
    {Sp
(b){Th A – a most useful fingering
    {Sp
    not nearly sufficiently known
(c){Th A flat 2, 3   5 – 8a to flatten
   {Sp
(d) Ditto with 6 instead of 5 to sharpen
One of the most variable notes on the clarinet

(a){Th A flat,1, 2, 3 to flatten
   {Sp
(b){Th A and A flat 1,2, 3, to sharpen
   {Sp
(c){Th A and 5b (an excellent trill
   {Sp
   with (b) of the E flat)
(d){Th 1, 2, 3, 4, 5, 7a – (a flat one)
   {Sp

The Clarinet

1.{ Th 1, 2, 3, 4, 5, 6, 7 the 'closed'
  { Sp
    F – flattish on most clarinets
    and stable
2.{ Th A 2, 3, 5b. A sharp
  { Sp
    fingering
3.{ Th A flat 2, 3, 4 8b. Slightly
  { Sp
    sharp on most clarinets

Avoid normal fingering, i.e.:
{ Th 2 whenever possible
{ Sp
better are:
(a){ Th 1, 2   5 6 7 8a (masked in
   { Sp
     sound)
(b){ Th 1, 2 5d (bright in sound)
   { Sp

Many fingerings possible. Among
the most useful are:
1.{ Th 1 (an 'open' sound but
  { Sp
    brittle)
2.{ Th 1, 3, 5, 7, 8b (useful for
  { Sp
    legato approach)
3.{ Th 1   5, 6, 7, 8b (flattish)
  { Sp

Avoid usual fingering{ Th 2, 3, 6
                     { Sp
when possible.
Better are:

1. ⎰ Th 2, 3, 5, 6, 7, 8a (sharper
   ⎱ Sp

   without 6)
2. ⎰ Th 1, 5c, 5d (can be brittle)
   ⎱ Sp
3. ⎰ Th 2, 3, 5, 7a 8b (sharp)
   ⎱ Sp
4. ⎰ Th 2, 3, 5, 8a (sharp)
   ⎱ Sp
5. ⎰ Th 3, 5, 8b (good smooth)
   ⎱ Sp

Add to normal fingering:
5d to sharpen
8 a, b, c or d to flatten

1. ⎰ Th 1, 2, 3, 4/5, 6, 8, 8d (the best
   ⎱ Sp

   for general use)
2. ⎰ Th A flat, 2, 3, 4,   8B   (flat)
   ⎱ Sp
3.   Sp 1, 2, 3, 5, 6, 7, 8d only (easy
     attack)

⎰ Th 3, 7, 8a
⎱ Sp

⎰ Th – 2, 3, 5, 6, 7, 8c. A firm and
⎱ Sp

usable note

⎰ Th – 2 – 5
⎱ Sp

Almost impossible to attack, but
approachable from the D natural

So much for the intonation aspect of clarinet acoustics. There remains a side of its characteristics which is less obvious at first, but has as great an effect upon its performance. This is a marked imbalance of 'pressures' between the various registers and the different parts of the bore, and is what has given rise to the fallacy that the clarinet must sound different in various parts of its scale. This chameleon-like quality is by no means essential. The clarinet can be made to sound like one instrument from bottom to top, but only if its inequalities of pressure are taken into account, and dealt with. Overcoming these is the key to success in the sound of the clarinet.

These inequalities arise from the proportions of the bore of the instrument, and are best illustrated by once again examining the defects of the 'throat' notes. Having corrected the B flat, as suggested above, by resonance fingerings, it is found necessary to do a similar correction upon the A natural, A flat, and open G. The reason for this necessity is not the same as for the B flat. In these other notes the tone-holes are of the correct size, and in the right place. In fact, they are probably the only holes for which a maker has complete liberty of placement, because they fulfil only one function, not normally being overblown. The reason for the poor quality of sound they normally produce is the extremely low pressure which exists in that part of the clarinet, owing to the proportions of the bore at that point.

It must be remembered that, unlike the oboe and bassoon, the ratio of the width to length of the bore varies greatly in the clarinet from top to bottom. Owing to its conical construction, this ratio in the oboe is almost a constant – possibly about 21:1. That is to say, if you open a tone-hole at the top of an oboe about 5in. from the reed, the bore at that point may be about $\frac{1}{4}$in. If you play a much lower note, with a tube length of about 20in., the bore is about 1in. (It must be said here that as this book is not about the oboe, the measurements given are just for illustration – no attempt at accuracy is necessary.) The ratio length/width is, therefore, of the order of 20:1, for the whole bore of the instrument.

With the clarinet the cylindrical bore changes all this. Play the A natural 'throat' note, and you are employing a tube some 5in. long and ½in. in diameter. The bore/stroke ratio, as a motor mechanic would put it, is 10:1. Now move to the note D natural in the overblown part of the instrument: you are using about 20in. of tube and still the bore is only just over ½in. The ratio is now 40:1. This difference in ratio is the real reason for what has always been known as the 'break'. in the compass of the clarinet, which is not really due to the change from the fundamental to the overblown part of the clarinet and the consequent introduction of a whole new set of harmonics. If these had the same sort of resistance as the notes below them, there would be no problem – but this is not so. Nor is there any real digital difficulty in crossing this 'break', because the player quickly learns that he must have fingers already on the holes and keys necessary for the B natural while he is playing the A. He could learn to switch from one to the other both rapidly and smoothly but for one serious difficulty. At first, the B natural eludes him. It takes far too long to speak, and the music will not wait for him.

It is the difference in the *pressure* of the two notes which he has failed to take into account, and the *legato* between the A and the B is entirely dependent upon his realization of this phenomenon. The A natural, because it uses a fat, short, tube, has a very low atmosphere pressure. To make it into a firm note, it requires not only the finger corrections suggested above, but the feeding of a considerable volume of air through the tube, to raise this low pressure. This is not a process of blowing, but of speedy and controlled exhalation, so that the resistance to this pressure is *just* felt, and exactly over-ridden. The next note, the B natural, on the other hand, with its 48:1 ratio of length to bore, is a very firm note which has a natural high pressure. When it is played, there is a feeling that the aim is not to pass air through the tube, but that the note requires the air to be retained in the instrument, to fill it and to sustain this high pressure which is natural to it. There is an immediate tiny 'kick' to the diaphragm if this interval is properly bridged. If this is not so, the note will not only speak too slowly but it will 'bulge' badly when it does speak, and will contradict the sound of the A natural which precedes it by its sheer physical unwieldy weight. Once this interval has been properly felt, the difference in air pressure necessary to control and bridge it will become completely instinctive. The player will be able to 'cross the break' for the rest of his playing life.

One aspect of this solution to the density-relationship between notes is at first disturbing. The notes at the lower end of the instrument sound very smooth, while those at the upper end, having a more quickly-moving air supply, tend to be overlaid with a hiss. This need not disturb the player, as he certainly hears it much more than anyone; it is quite inaudible at more than about three feet in any reasonable acoustic surroundings, and is rarely picked up by even the most sensitive of modern microphones. Certainly it is less carrying than the pronounced reed-buzz which results from the other method of equalizing the uneven notes – that of using a very thin reed. This merely masks the inequalities by overlaying them with reed-sound, producing an invariable and monotonous tone. It is a method of playing the clarinet which can be said to beg the question: it ignores the problem by covering it up, and so does not permit all the expressive possibilities which can follow its solution. The most notable of the pressure differences has been examined above – the crossing of the 'break' from A to B; but this is only one example. Because the clarinet does not overblow in octaves, the pressure areas are spread over its compass in a remarkably haphazard way. They are in fact quite logical in sequence in the 'feel' of the instrument – 'rare' notes at the top of the tube, dense notes at the bottom – but when examined in rotation, they have a most complex appearance

These pressure areas must be studied and carefully corrected

in the way already described for the crossing of the 'break'. The only way in which they can be moulded into a matched musical progression is to know what to expect from each note approached, and to balance it in relation to the one it follows by careful diaphragm support. This may seem to be a complex operation. Add to it the resonance finger-corrections we have discussed and it becomes more complex still. Luckily it becomes an instinctive operation fairly soon, and the main obstacle is to make oneself think in this rather new way. It is certainly the very stuff of which real clarinet playing, as opposed to elementary note-spinning, is made.

Clarinets are transposing instruments

While discussing clarinet acoustics it may be worthwhile to try to deal with that question, deceptively simple at first sight: 'What *is* a B flat clarinet, and why is it different from an A, and E flat, or any other pitch of clarinet?'

The simple answer is that a B flat clarinet is one which, when it plays its own C major scale (its simplest one), is really playing the B flat scale of the piano. An A natural clarinet is one which plays the A major piano scale in the same circumstances. And so on through all the other keys in which clarinets are made.

The use of at any rate three different clarinets arose quite early in the instrument's history for a very good reason – the impossibility of playing in any remote key because of the appalling intonation of the clarinet in its many sharps and flats. Diatonically the clarinet could play reasonably well in two or three sharps or flats. Chromatically it was fairly disastrous, even with the greatest skill in half-holing, cross-fingering and embouchure control. As a result, the first use of the clarinet usually found an instrument employed which was pitched in the key in which the composer had written. In C major he would use a C clarinet, and so on. What did this mean, exactly? It simply meant that in each case the player did not see a single sharp or flat. He simply played in C major all the time; and the B flat clarint played the scale of B flat, the A clarinet the scale of A and so on. A simple enough scheme, so far.

Since, however, music is written in all sorts of other keys and it is quite impossible to imagine a whole rack of clarinets ready to accommodate each one of them, we come to the somewhat complex use of several clarinets playing the keys which lead to the least complications. Of course they soon departed from simply playing in C major, but they went the shortest possible distance from this which was capable of producing the composer's requirements. Take, for instance, a piece of music written in E flat. If no E flat clarinet is available the choice may have to be between a B flat and an A. Remember the B flat, when playing its C major, is really playing the composer's B flat. So his music must be written one tone higher than required to sound. The A clarinet, similarly requires music three semi-tones higher than it sounds. So in the composer's score of E flat, the B flat clarinet plays in F and the A clarinet in G flat. Clearly the B flat clarinet is the one used for this piece in E flat. Similarly, if a composer writes in the key of E major, the B flat clarinet has the key signature of F sharp major to cope with while, the A clarinet gets away with a simple G major. Obviously the A clarinet is the choice for this piece.

This is an explanation which seems entirely logical to clarinettists – and the facts behind it are such as may well gladden the heart, because they may make life a great deal simpler in a practical sense. To non-clarinettists such explanations are most unreasonable and quite incomprehensible. What all this means in strictly practical terms as seen by composers who wish to write well for the clarinet, is this: If one wishes to keep the written key signatures within reason – say up to four sharps or four flats, a judicious use of just B flat or A natural clarinet can cover all the keys generally used. It is still worth considering this, in spite of the populra fallacy that the modern clarinet takes no serious account of key signature problems. Certainly the problems are much greater than is the case for the flute and oboe. Anyone who doubts this should examine carefully the reaction of an excellent clarinettist who later becomes a saxophonist. Always within a few months he is playing in extreme keys on the saxophone (on which the upper register, like that of the other wood-winds but not of the clarinet, is an octave, and not a twelfth, above the lower) with an ease which he will never, to the very end of his career, achieve on the clarinet. Modern composers, who daily make the most extravagant demands upon the technique of every wood-wind player, often find that slight editing may be necessary if they are to get the same effect from all the wood-winds. Their editing in the case of the clarinet is usually the avoidance of quickly played repeated awkward intervals which simply will not speak in time, and is due to the inability of the instrument to cope with extremes of accidental intervals. Less forward-looking composers, still using key-centres as part of their musical outlook, can content themselves with the following facts: The B flat clarinet plays with ease the keys of C, F, B flat, E flat, A flat and D flat as well as G and D: and of course their relative minors. A is obviously best left to the A clarinet (playing C major); so is E major (playing G major), B major (D major) and even F major (A flat major). This, obviously, covers the whole range of keys, and never uses more than four sharps or flats. It may seem to be the lazy man's way out, and there is a fairly strong school of thought which suggests that it is an archaic hang-over and that the composer should simply write the score in concert pitch and leave it to the copyist to sort the matter out. This may well work perfectly if the copyist in question is really skilled and knowledgeable; it may even be successful if the composer is not too particular as to the sort of legato he is going to get. But the fact remains that even today the difficulties which gave rise to the use of transposing clarinets have not entirely disappeared. This becomes obvious with shrewd observation of some of the finest players today, who may be seen from time to time swiftly changing from one clarinet to another, even when no instruction has been given to do this by the composer. They know well enough how to obtain the effect he intended to get, whereas he may not. It is, after all, very special knowledge, and if the player is a serious and experienced artist, he will have given this a lot of thought. He should also make sure that the instrument is changed when acute difficulties lie ahead, and that there is time not only to change, but to play a few notes, before the vital passage is at hand. Elgar was a master at this kind of thing. Rarely, in his works, does one have to make a solo bass clarinet entry completely cold; usually he manages to find a few notes to play, probably inaudibly, but in preparation for the important solo so that one has at least a sporting chance of entering at the right pitch.

Having established that the B flat and A clarinets are both necessary, and the obvious advantages of one over the other at a given time, we now come upon yet another thorny question, this time one without an answer. This is, simply: 'Do you think there is really any fundamental difference between the sound of the B flat clarinet, and that of the A?' To this question there will always be a variety of answers, because no two players can agree. Certainly anyone who plays both can instantly recall the difference in 'feel' between them: there is a subtle mellowness about the tone production of the A which contrasts with the apparent slightly greater brilliance of the B flat. This, however, could be simply subjective. Logically the reason for this difference, if in fact it exists at all, is by no means obvious.

To begin with, it is not cogent to identify this comparison with that which can be made between the B flat and E flat or even the C clarinet. In both these cases there is a different bore, a different mouthpiece, and a narrower reed, all of which contribute to the very great difference in feeling, as well as effect. With the B flat and A clarinets the same mouthpiece is used and usually the same socket. The bore is identical, and it is simply a question of the differences of layout of the tone-holes, in that for any given note the same length of tube is in use – though the size of hole which terminates this may in fact vary it to some extent. Nor does the overall length of the instrument determine the difference some people are certain exists, because if the B flat clarinet is furnished with a low E flat key and the A is not, as is usual, the two instruments still seem to retain their own characteristics, in spite of their now identical lengths. Here the word 'seem' is probably the operative one, because anyone who has listened with care to his own recording knowing that he has for some reason changed clarinets *en route* will testify that it is extremely difficult for him – even him – to know where this happened; and if he continues to listen while thinking of the fingerings of the other instrument, he may be unaware that he has in fact made the change at all.

A careful analysis of the way in which composers have used the various clarinets only increases the confusion. Many seem to use the instrument which simplifies the key-signature, but some – like Schumann in his Op. 73 Fantasy Pieces – use the A clarinet obviously for the sort of sound they think it provides.

So, although one can prove scientifically that the sounds of the B flat and A clarinets are identical, players and listeners alike tend to believe in the B flat for brilliance, and the A for romance. They could possibly be right. In either case it is essential for the player to be acutely aware of the acoustic make up of each of them, if he is to do justice to himself and to the works he is to interpret.

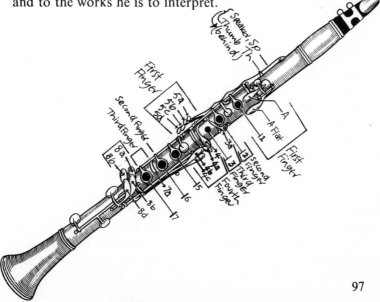

Four

The Practical Clarinettist

There can be no doubt that the act of playing a wind instrument is a physical one, whatever its intellectual overtones; and the control of such a complicated piece of mechanism cannot but be aided by a knowledge of what is involved, from a purely mechanical point of view. It seems little less than a miracle that any concert involving wood-wind instruments should be anything but a dismal series of disasters, when one considers the multitude of tiny moving parts – the delicate reeds and springs, the finely adjusted pads, and the water-logging of the whole process by breath condensation. That it usually does get off the ground is certainly a feather in the cap of the instrument maker or repairer – but it may also very well be to the credit of the performer himself, who has possibly avoided such catastrophe by the timely insertion of a piece of cork or the skilful application of a rubber band only a few minutes before the scheduled starting-time. He should be trained to do this, and should encourage himself to rely upon his own knowledge of the working tools of his trade, however artistic he may feel himself to be. Here are a few of the things he should know.

Keywork and bore dimension

One must assume that the player has decided upon the sort of bore he wishes to make his own – the small French bore with its tight sound, the medium American-French with its versatile characteristics, the large German with its wide sound, small mouthpiece and hand-made reed, or the large English bore with its French mouthpiece, its great flexibility and its characteristic ability to take on the personality of the player.

Whichever of these bores he uses, the player has to have keywork which suits his needs, and here the choice is wide; not so wide as it used to be, for keywork today is usually of the drop-forged type, and basically of nickel silver, often called German silver. (See fig. **22**). This is not silver at all, but a mixture of nickel and brass, with more nickel in the better quality than the poorer. Drop forging is simply dropping a huge weight from a great height upon a thin bar of the metal, stamping it into a 'die' upon which it has been placed. This both shapes it and hardens it; but it is not so hard as it used to be in the days of hand-forging, a couple of generations ago, and not so rigid as it used to be when 'sand-cast' – melted and poured into a hollow mould in smooth sand. As a result of this softness, it may wear fairly quickly if the quality is not of the very highest; but the plating with which it is often finished gives it added strength and, of course, beauty.

Such plating is normally of two types – nickel, which may be very thin or quite generous, and silver, which is often specified for the best quality instruments. Chromium plating is sometimes applied, but has the disadvantage that it can peel off if the key is bent, as it probably will be at some time during its life. It is, however, wonderfully hard-wearing on the bearing surfaces, and comfortable to use if one does not object to the very smooth, almost slippery effect. Silver, on the contrary, tends to 'drag' on the fingers, especially if it is of the heavy-gauge type applied to the best clarinets. It also tarnishes black if left for a week or two, and can be rendered quite thin by persistent cleaning. So, by and large, good nickel-plated keys seem to promise best. They do not tarnish, do not drag or slip, and are capable of a most handsome finish.

Given an instrument with drop-forged keywork which is flexible, a great many adjustments are possible, and the player can do many of these for himself if he goes to the trouble to make sure of his material. Keys can be bent cold, with care, using small pliers with the jaws covered with a duster, to protect the key-surface. Thus the 'venting' of the tone-holes can be modified, by making sure the pad is not too close to the hole, causing a 'stuffy' and vague sound. The keywork should in reality be made to fit the hand of its owner, and this can often be achieved by the second factor:

Corking

It is not always necessary to bend keywork to achieve the correct clearance. At the end of its action, whether the key be an open or closed one so far as its rest position is concerned, it has a cork buffer to prevent it from producing the percussive effect it obviously would do otherwise (see fig. **24**). The thickness of this cork is crucial, and by thinning it or adding to it it is possible to alter the 'venting' of any key one wishes. A word of warning is essential here, because so many keys are dependent upon one another that altering one may put another out of action, or may alter its venting in an undesirable direction; but knowledge of what this cork does – and it has an important role – is essential to an understanding of the instrument. It is not simply for silence; it is an integral part of the balance of the shape of the key-pattern, and must be of the finest quality as well as of perfect proportions. Champagne corks are an obvious source of supply for the player repairer, using a sharp single-edged razor blade for the necessary thin slicing; and modern 'contact' adhesives make it possible to apply this to the plated surfaces of keys with reasonable security. It must, however, be stressed that this is a job certainly better suited to the skills of the professional repair-man, if one of these rare individuals can be found. He should be entrusted with the whole range of maintenance jobs mentioned in this chapter, and at least every two years should be given time to strip the instrument completely and refurbish it with all its appurtenances, if it can be spared for a sufficient length of time. At such a time the player should if possible spend an hour or two with him for the final checking of this vital matter of cork-thickness, because it is of very great acoustical importance.

Fig 21: A comparison (*above*) between the bores of the clarinet (cylinder) and oboe (cone). Note the very large bore at the top of the clarinet and the tiny tube at a similar point in the bore of the oboe.

Fig 22: Modern keys (*below*) of drop-forged German silver units, silver-soldered and nickel-plated. A typical leaf spring is attached to one of them. The rest require needle springs.

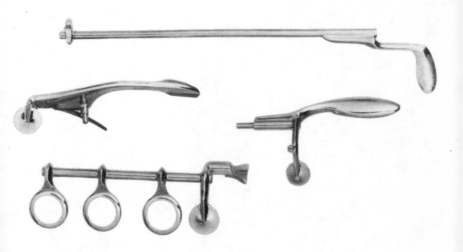

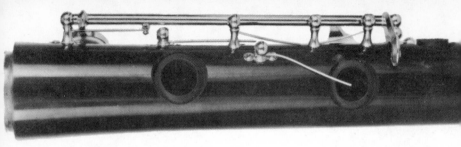

Fig 23: Needle springs (*above*), loose and in position in the key notch.

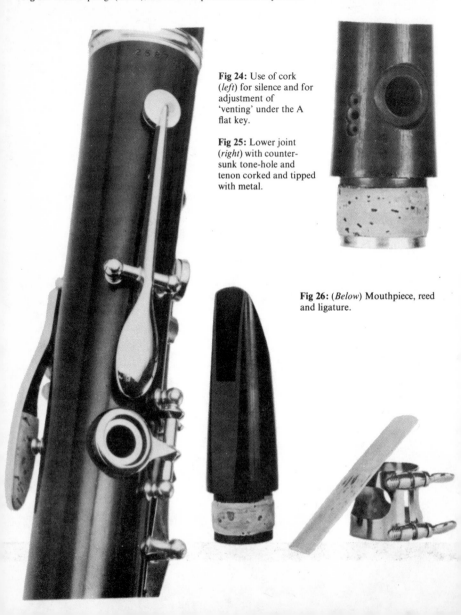

Fig 24: Use of cork (*left*) for silence and for adjustment of 'venting' under the A flat key.

Fig 25: Lower joint (*right*) with counter-sunk tone-hole and tenon corked and tipped with metal.

Fig 26: (*Below*) Mouthpiece, reed and ligature.

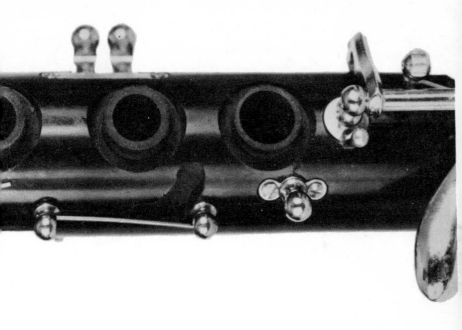

Fig 27: (*Above*) Anchored pillars (*right and top*) and an un-anchored, with needle spring attached.

Fig 28: (*Below*) Types of ligature: *left:* Heavy plastic with screws on top; *middle:* Popular rigid metal band, with screws below; *right:* Light and flexible plastic.

Fig 29: (*Above*) Types of clarinet barrel: *left and middle:* of boxwood with ivory tips, 18th and 19th century; *right:* of grenadilla, with metal band (current practice).

Fig 30: (*Below*) Types of clarinet bell: *left:* 19th century; *middle:* 18th century; *right:* 20th century.

Fig 31: The clarinet from log to finished tube: (a) Billet of grenadilla (lower joint); (b) Bored tube (undersize); (c) Bored to size inside and out; (d) Holes bored, countersunk and prepared for keys and pillars. Tenon corked, and ring fitted to top at upper counterbore.

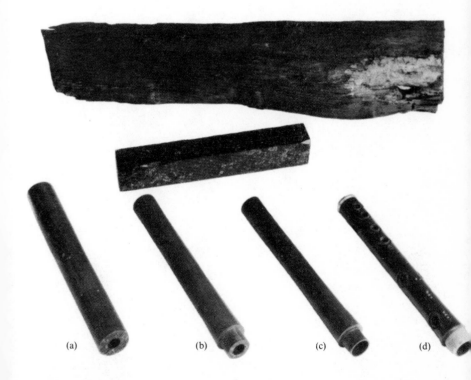

(a)   (b)   (c)   (d)

Fig 32: (*Right*) Popular type of reed-cutter. The shape of the tip-curve is crucial, and varies in individual examples. A good one is a collector's item.

Fig 33: (*Below*) Thumb rests: *left:* popular type; *right:* adjustable type.

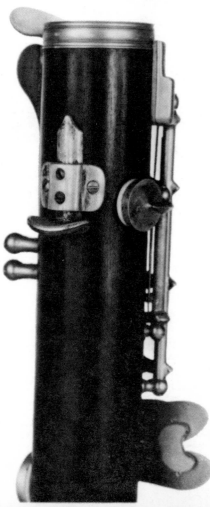

Fig 34: Relaxed fingering position.

Fig 35: The embouchure showing the 'flat chin' which prevents the damping of the reed by the soft tissue of the lips.

Springing

Also vital to the performance, 'feel' and balance of the clarinet is the springing of the keys. These must be so adjusted that the resistance presented to the finger by the touch-piece of the key is equal in every case: and this in spite of the fact that the weight, direction of movement and even the function of the keys is very varied. Springs used are of two essentially different types, as well as of several different materials. The first type is the needle-spring, which is simply a strong steel needle flattened at one end so that it can be held rigid by a hole through the pillar in which it is inserted (see fig. **23**). This needle is tempered and usually blue in colour, and is formed in a bent shape which gives it a rest position at an angle to the axis of the 'barrel' on which the key pivots. It is used on 'lever' keys – those which have a lever at one end of the barrel and an arm at the other to transfer the motion to the cup of the key which covers the hole. These lever-keys are of many different sizes, and of two types, open and closed. It is necessary, in other words, to hold some holes open to produce the note, and to close others. The holes which are in the closed rest-position govern the greatest possible lightness of the springing, since if they are not firmly held they can actually be blown open by a determined player. Having discovered by trial and error what this minimum safe holding pressure involves, the springing of the open holes can be carefully adjusted to it.

The second type of springing in the clarinet is used in the more simple type of key, the earliest historically, which is simply a see-saw over a central pivot, one end of which is the touch piece and the other the key-cup. This type of spring is a curved and tapered leaf-spring, one end of which is attached to the under-side of the key by a screw at the key-cup end, while the other extends under the pivot towards the finger and rides in a groove, usually metal-lined (see fig. **22**). These see-saw keys, seven in number on the normal Boehm clarinet, are all used to control 'closed' keys and happen to be all on the upper joint. Adjustment of them is both simpler and safer than is the case with the needle spring, since they are more robust. Obviously they give stronger springing when bent away from the base of the key, and this is easily possible without the embarrassment of fracture, which so often attends the amateur in his similar efforts with needle springs. This risk is somewhat less in the case of some needle springs now being fitted by more enterprising makers, since they are of a softer and more ductile material, such as beryllium, and can be more safely bent to pattern; but it must be left very much to the choice of the player as to whether he prefers these springs or not, since some people detect a difference of speed in the response, or imagine they do so, which is probably just as important. The vast majority of clarinets are still produced with blued-steel springs, and most of the best performers seem to prefer them. When properly adjusted, these needle and leaf springs can present a remarkably even resistance to the fingers, and a truly skilled mechanic can make them extremely light while at the same time not losing the 'positive' feel or the safety of a closed pad against air-pressure.

Padding

The third factor in the mechanical make-up of the modern clarinet is the pad, that extension of the finger-tip which exactly reproduces the function of it at a great distance from the source of pressure. To seal the tone-hole completely requires several carefully regulated factors. First, the tone-hole itself is more easily sealed if it has a counter-sunk bed-place with a bevelled rim (see fig. **25**). Next, the pad must be completely parallel to the surface of this bed-place at the point of contact, in spite of the fact that its movement is radial in the case of the lever keys and simply angular in the case of the see-saw examples. Finally it must be firm but soft, containing an impression of the bevelled rim as a permanent feature of its shape; it must not distort, or if it does so must return instantly to its original shape. It must also be impervious to moisture so that it does not simply become a balloon of water. If punctured, it must absorb moisture without serious distortion, and should dry out without hardening or cracking.

This is a fairly tall order and it is astonishing that in fact it should be achieved with reasonable success by several types of pads.

Of fairly recent development, the plastic moulded pad must be considered as a possibility for ubiquitous future use. It is waterproof, stable, and can be made of material of any degree of elasticity required and in any shape which presents a perfect sealing surface. It is still not in general use by the best makers on their top-quality instruments, nor is it in general demand by the finest players. This could be because of prejudice – the very word 'plastic' carries with it a sinister undertone of things cheap and mass-produced. There is certainly no reason why a very special type of plastic should not, in future, supply us with the perfect pad. There is also, as hinted in Chapter 5, no reason why the pad may not be dispensed with altogether, with possible revolutionary changes in the clarinet as a result. Meanwhile, traditional padding seems to maintain its hold, and has existed virtually unchanged for a hundred years. The traditional pad consists of three parts – a light paper or thin cardboard backing, a felt disc of appropriate thickness, soft but firm enough to take an impression of the hole-rim and a flexible covering which may be of fine leather, of animal bladder-skin or of thin plastic. The virtues of all three of these covering materials are varied. Skin is the best 'reflective' medium, approximating to the bright surface of the clarinet bore, and giving the best resonance. It needs careful fitting and has two disadvantages: (a) it punctures easily, and when this happens it can soak up water and put the clarinet out of action – a most frightening experience for the player, and (b) it can stretch away from its backing and become loose enough to act as a diaphragm, buzzing loudly in sympathy with certain vibrations of the instrument – not always those associated with the hole in use, making detection difficult. The thin plastic covering does not have this 'buzzing' trouble to the same extent, but lacks sufficient stiffness to 'stay put' against its backing. As a result it has a less positive feel than the skin pad, and even though it may fundamentally have an equal reso-

103

nance response, this is marred by the lack of crispness in its sealing action and its slight tendency to 'cling' when leaving its hole-rim. The leather covered pad does not suffer from either of these troubles, but has a defect of its own; it has a less perfect reflective surface and therefore a slightly less resonant response. It is, however, extremely hard-wearing and stable, and used with success by a great number of players. It also takes a perfect impression and in many ways is easier to fit, making it a good pad to carry around in the case for emergency use. This is not so true of the pad which is probably the most recent fashion, particularly in the USA – the cork pad. Of very high quality cork, this pad has the virtues of all the above types – waterproof, stable, reasonably resonant, silent and long-lasting. It does, however, require perfect fitting, and must be a perfect specimen of its type, since it cannot, by finger-pressure or other methods, be made to fit itself to the hole as can others – a disadvantage it shares with the moulded plastic pad. Certainly the perfection of padding can make all the difference to the possibilities of any clarinet, since it governs a large share of its resonance. There is room for future improvement of this aspect of the clarinet.

Pillars

An important adjunct to every key is the pillar upon which it pivots. (See fig. 27.) The alignment of this, and the smoothness with which the key can work while held by it, are factors vital to success. Nor is the design and application of the pillars a simple affair. To start with, the attachment to the instrument must be firm, and must remain so even if the wood of the tube expands or contracts with temperature or moisture. Next, although the pillars may be screwed into the wood, it must be remembered that the tube of the instrument is quite a thin shell; some say the thinner the better for resonance response, provided the wood is of fine quality. Certainly in most clarinets it is of less than $\frac{1}{4}$in. thickness, so that a pillar of more than $\frac{1}{8}$in. penetration is dangerously close to a break through. One excellent method of avoiding this risk is the 'anchored' pillar (see fig. 27), in which only a short parallel rod is inserted into a hole in the tube's surface, and this is prevented from turning around its central axis by a small plate anchored to the surface of the tube by either one or two small screws. This is a somewhat complicated solution, and expensive, but very much to be applauded. It has, however, to be well designed if it is to be strong.

The task of pivoting the keys upon these pillars can be solved in three ways. The first of these, that of the screwed rod passing inside the barrel of the key from pillar to pillar, is used in every clarinet with the leaf-sprung keys, where its length is usually less than $\frac{1}{2}$in. In the longer keys, such as the lever keys of the lower joint and the ring-bearing arrangement of both joints, other methods are often used; but where this is not done, and long rods are utilised, often over 5in. in length, the bearing surface is so great that the key may be expected to work smoothly for forty years or more. The objection is often made to this practice that in the event of an accidental blow, the rod will be bent inside the barrel of the key, causing it to bind upon rotation and making it difficult to withdraw. In fact this rarely occurs, and in the life-time of most players the sort of accident which would cause it is almost unknown and would probably seriously damage the instrument anyway. Certainly the normal everyday knocks seem to take no toll of this mechanism and from the point of view of normal wear and tear this arrangement can be expected to outlast three replacements of any other type.

The second method of suspension used for the longer keys is by point screws through the pillars (below left). This method relies upon a remarkably small bearing-surface, and as German silver is in contact with hard steel, it obviously soon begins to wear. This can be prevented by insets of harder metal in the ends of the key-barrel. When even this wears, adjustment is simple. Longer point-screws can be fitted to take up the play in the ends of the key-barrels, or the existing screws recessed further into their pillars, producing the same result. This method of suspension is the cheapest and probably the most practical for general use.

Mountings on pillars.

The third and most modern method is the use of a combination of the two already mentioned – pivot screws which are parallel instead of tapered and thus present a bearing surface similar to the screwed rods, but of only about $\frac{3}{16}$ in. in length (above right). Because of this parallel bearing surface, working against a similarly untapered inside surface in the key-barrel, wear is very much reduced, and as a result the intervals between maintenance are greatly increased. The disadvantages of this compromise solution is that when wear does take place, the fitting of oversize pivots is the only solution – no amount of end adjustment can be employed.

Further than these three methods, suspension of the key and silence of action can be aided by the fitting of nylon bushes into the ends of the barrels. This is a rather rare practice at present, and one which must await the test of time. For the player, the most important aspect of his pillars must be lack of play and avoidance of tightness which can cause slowing of his technique. The obvious aid in these two factors is a fine grade of oil, sparingly applied to all bearing surfaces. The dangerous expedient is the packing of the loose joints with paper or cellophane, which can clog the mechanism and cause a complete stoppage.

Bore conditions

Of all the variations in clarinet design, those involving the bore are the most crucial in effect. Discussion of these variations is better dealt with in an acoustic sense, since it is not merely the effect upon instrumental efficiency which is involved but the very being of the clarinet itself. Whatever the bore of the instrument may be so far as shape is concerned, there are certain factors it must have, and must be encouraged to retain. It must have as near a smooth mirror-surface as possible; no grain must be allowed to rise, no dirt allowed to settle upon it, no material deliberately placed there which will mar this superb reflecting surface, which should almost dazzle when seen end-on against average sky-light. Secondly, it must be waterproof, so that moisture will collect on its surface in globules and then run away bell-wards, with a reasonable chance that these miniature torrents will not enter a tone hole en route and cause fluttering gurgles against the pad when this is opened. If it settles in a damp pool, this is proof that it is in fact sinking into the wood; and this, causing expansion, is extremely bad for both the acoustic proportions and the mechanical safety of the clarinet. The globules of condensation are obviously best removed before they become too big or numerous, and a mop of exactly the right size should be used for this. Design of these mops is an aspect of clarinet maintenance which is seriously neglected by makers, and is most often left to the ingenuity of the player. The hard and hairy wire-mounted mop which is pushed through each joint in turn is a menace, since it is a very efficient method of enlarging the bore. It merely distributes the water more widely over its surface by breaking up the globules and can leave behind short fibres which get into tone holes. It is supplied by most commercial instrument-makers, possibly with sinister intentions for the long-term future. The best mop for a clarinet is the pull-through, a triangular piece of cotton material about half-a-handkerchief in size attached at its apex (by stitching rather than a knot) to a length of tape about a foot long, which terminates in a small weight – possibly an inch section of flattened lead rod – inset into the tape. This weight passes smoothly down the bore, and the moisture can then be removed in one smooth sweep – obviously better taken from the mouthpiece to bell, since the main condensation appears first in the top joint. At least one maker supplies such a mop, covered with advertisement; but in the instrument cases of most players there are to be found many variations of home-made design, only vaguely similar to this model. Keys and nails are dangled down the bore on the end of spirally sprung pieces of garden twine. Old handkerchiefs are knotted largely to this twine, often of a size so large that there is a great danger of their being jammed in the bore, especially should the knot become untied. Occasionally a beautiful silk or rayon handkerchief is sacrificed to this end by a devoted owner – a misguided generosity, since the hardness of the fibres makes such a mop a really first-class abrasive tool to wear away the bore, and in any case there is very little absorption of moisture. One such home-made variation, however, is good – the small mop of chamois leather, very much smaller than the cotton mop, but similar in shape. This must be changed fairly often, since it does not work so well after it has been washed, having lost its natural oil. The secret of its success is in this very fact, since in its use it leaves behind a very slight deposit of this oil, and this is extremely beneficial. It is possible, indeed, that this is the best way of giving the bore all the oil it requires; certainly the majority of players tend to over-oil the bore of their instruments to the detriment of the reflective surface of the bore.

Oiling the bore

The whole question of oiling a clarinet is debatable. The methods of manufacture of many large firms of instrument makers are shrouded in secrecy; some of them undoubtedly employ oil in treating the wood they use – almost invariably these days grenadilla, a dense African ebony – with oil or other substances. This treatment may be under considerable pressure or under none, and may be done at any stage of manufacture from the rough wooden billet, split or sawn from the log, to the finished instrument. The intention of them all is to produce a clarinet which will be impervious to moisture and so remain dimensionally stable and less liable to split or crack.

A side issue here is the method of cutting these billets;

there would seem to be logic in the theory that a billet split from the log by an axe, following the grain, would provide a more naturally straight-grained tube, without out-croppings of grain, than the sawn product. This should prevent cracking due to stress even when swelling or shrinkage takes place. It does not seem always to do so.

The same applies to oiling, whether at an early stage of manufacture or late – or even during the long playing life of an instrument. Cracking is of course a complete disaster, and can completely ruin the finest clarinet. It can be 'pinned' to prevent spreading provided the crack is a 'surface' one; but if it has penetrated to the bore, and especially if it passes through one or more tone-holes, there is no treatment other than replacement of the joint concerned.

Nor does there seem to be logic in the incidence of cracking. Careful owners who oil their clarinets lose them in this way, even though they religiously take them apart after each playing to dry out each joint and tenon, keeping them in moisture controlled cases and avoiding violence of any sort. Others who appear to neglect their instruments thoroughly seem to have no trouble of this sort, though it has been known for it to suddenly happen to one of their number after thirty-five years of such behaviour, and to keep on happening steadily over the years which followed. It is certainly the duty of any maker to provide an instrument which is as safe from cracking as may be, and if oiling seems to produce this, it will obviously be used by them. They also usually suggest further oiling by the player from time to time. What must be avoided most carefully is the piling up of this oil in the bore of the instrument as a sort of 'toffee' which not only kills the resonance, but even alters the internal dimensions. Even on the external surface this is undesirable and unattractive to the touch, while the smell of the raw linseed oil which is usually used in this way is by no means artistically stimulating. So the rule of oiling should be 'as little as possible, as often as available'. The wood of a clarinet should feel like that of a fine piece of furniture, with a natural patina which comes from handling. The grenadilla wood is itself quite beautiful,

The Clarinet

and an instrument made from it without any attempt at staining or unnatural oiling is most attractive. It is also worth noting that in the experience of many players, the heavier the wood, the better the resonance. That is not to say that a heavy clarinet is the best, because the weight may be the result of heavy key-work or a serious over-dose of oil. It is just a fact that in identical instruments it is the one made from the most dense wood which is usually best at producing the naturally 'dark' sound which characterises a fine clarinet.

The mouthpiece

It is quite impossible to over-stress the importance of the choice, design and maintenance of the clarinet mouthpiece. Discussion of its effect upon the artistic approach to the instrument is left to Chapter 5. Here a few of the details of its construction are sufficient (see below). Of whatever material it is made, the mouthpiece has certain features which must be understood and checked regularly. These features are also illustrated in fig. **26**.

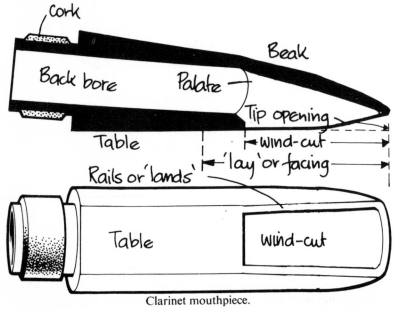

Clarinet mouthpiece.

(a) The table must be perfectly flat, since it is the anchorage of the reed: no air must be able to escape between the reed and the table, nor should any moisture penetrate, causing swelling of the blade of the reed. Some makers insist that a slight depression in the middle of the table is desirable, since it springs the reed away from the facing of the mouthpiece and appears to give it added life. This is difficult to prove, and obviously results in a reed which is working under stress. Certainly the favourite mouthpieces of most players, when examined, are found to have a flat table.

(b) The rails or 'lands'. These must be exactly equal on both sides, giving a perfectly controllable curve for the embouchure. The shape of this curve is probably the most individual part of any clarinettist's equipment. This is the 'lay' of the mouthpiece, and the possible variations are almost without limit. At the tip it may vary in the gap it makes with the reed from .005in. to .050in., and the length of the opening from top to point of contact while at rest – the length of the 'lay', in fact – may be anything from $\frac{3}{8}$in. to as much as 1in. Between these two points the curve may have almost any shape, though usually it is more steep towards the tip than at its lower end; this curvature is governed by the skill of the maker, and is almost always a hand-crafted factor, which results in an almost religio-fanatic attitude in the minds of many players when they are looking for the perfect specimen. The rails are thus the most variable aspect of the mouthpiece, because they present the facing upon which the reed beats; and with them one must include the continuation around the tip. Generally speaking, thin rails are more popular than thick ones, though there should always be sufficient thickness to ensure perfect sealing and a reasonable wearing-life. More is said about the choice of 'lay' in Chapter 5.

(c) The 'palate' or roof of the interior. This must be smooth, and can be of several shapes, according to the sort of sound it is intended to produce. A convex palate tends to brilliance of sound, a concave one to darkness.

(d) The walls or 'chops'. Narrow walls give intensity, wide ones flexibility and a more 'spread' sound. Some designers believe that a narrowing of the walls from entry to the bottom of the mouthpiece focuses the sound more perfectly.

(e) The wind-cut. This is a little appreciated part of the construction of the mouthpiece. Obviously if the current of air passing over the flat under-surface of the reed is suddenly confronted with a bulky obstacle at the end of the wind-cut (see caption) this will cause an added and unproductive resistance; so the wind-cut should be sharp at the junction with the table, flat and making a fairly acute angle with it, and should enter the bore of the mouthpiece at the lower end without unevenness or any trace of ragged edge or 'burr'.

It can be appreciated that with all the variations possible within the scope of these several mouthpiece characteristics, the permutations of variety are endless, and that in fact every single mouthpiece is an individual phenomenon; much more than is a clarinet, because the effect of the slightest possible change of dimension is so much greater in the case of the mouthpiece than it is in the instrument. There is no hard and fast rule as to what sort of mouthpiece must suit a player. It may take time, but he will finally decide on the type of mouthpiece which is comfortable for him; provided this comfort also allows him to play with control and expression, this is the one he must use, however odd his choice may seem. At the same time it is as well that his choice be made from as complete a range as possible. He should consider all the materials available – ebonite (hard rubber), glass or crystal, metal and plastic. All these materials have their good and less good characteristics, and there is a case for having more than one sort in one's armoury, especially today when demands upon the player are as varied as they are.

There are already players who prepare themselves for this by having mouthpieces in several different materials. The vast majority of the best players use mouthpieces of ebonite; next on the list seems to be crystal (glass), plastic (a cheaper grade of mouthpiece), and finally metal or metal-faced mouthpieces, which are very rare. The use of ebonite as a favourite material is justified because it has a warm sound, is easily moulded, carved or ground, and the reed can easily be seen in relation to the rails, because of the colour-contrast. Glass also gives a surprisingly warm and satisfactory sound, and some excellent players use it with great success. It has two slight disadvantages: (a) it tends to collect condensation, causing 'frying' in the sound, and (b) the lay is difficult to see, since the rails disappear owing to their transparent nature, and consequently the reed is difficult to attach and adjust.

The metal facing or mouthpiece is something of a surprise, because its effect is so much warmer and softer than the feel of the metal would suggest. Silver is the favourite material, and this is often used as an insert in the ebonite to the depth of about $\frac{1}{8}$in., after which a facing can be carefully filed upon it. The sound produced by such a mouthpiece is dependent, as it is in all others, upon the exact nature of the curve of the facing; but it does tend to produce a sound which is pleasing to hear and comfortable to produce, with warmth and easy control. It has only one disadvantage, that of weight, which can be disconcerting when the mouthpiece is in the act of entering the mouth – even dangerous if carelessly handled, as it may strike the lower lip. This is a small matter, and it seems certain that this is one special sort of mouthpiece with a great future. The all-metal mouthpiece is another matter, because the solid silver and even gold mouthpieces, though theoretically a good idea, are extremely expensive in addition to being so heavy that they are difficult to apply to the clarinet, however well they might succeed with the saxophone. The same applies to the brass mouthpiece, which is usually gold or silver plated. The best possible compromise is the carefully produced model in which the main tube of the mouthpiece is hollow, with an inner plug leaving a considerable gap between itself and the inner walls, while the rest is solid silver. There are some fine examples of this by a famous maker of hand-made mouthpieces, and it seems certain that they are a pointer to the future.

These contrasted materials tend to give slight differences of tone, which can be intriguing and interesting, and such a collection gives a wide range of flexibility and dynamic contrast. Probably two grades of ebonite, one of crystal and one of hollow silver or ebonite/silver would be an ideal collection for a player of the future.

The ligature. The function of the ligature would at first sight seem to be obvious – that of binding the reed at its thickest point, the heel, to the table of the mouthpiece, so that the blade can vibrate freely against the facing and then return to its rest position. William Stubbins is quite emphatic on this point, stating: 'It is a fallacy to suggest that the whole length of the reed vibrates and that consequently it should be held loosely on the mouthpiece in order to achieve this total vibration . . . A ligature is designed to hold the reed firmly on the mouthpiece lay without distortion.'

Others are not quite so certain, even though they may agree that far too much fuss is made by the third group, who insist that the material of the ligature is of great importance, as are the number of contact-points it makes with the reed, their relative pressures at such points and the fact that it may bruise the uncut surface bark of the heel of the reed. It is true that a reed which has pressure marks deep in the bark at this point may play perfectly, and that another which has had no such rough treatment may spontaneously twist or warp; but there is often a necessity to change the position of the reed slightly on the table, and such grooves may make this quite impossible. Again, whether it is psychological or not, the actual material surrounding the mouthpiece and reed do seem to many players to affect the quality of sound produced. The Germans have no doubt on this point. For them the simple cord wrapping which is their birthright and has been used since Denner's day (see drawing on page 23) is the solution. Using this with great skill, they fix their hand-made reeds to mouthpieces which have been made with grooves around their exterior surfaces for just such a purpose. It is a scheme which works perfectly. All other players are faced with a choice – how must they use a metal ligature to the best advantage, and which type is best suited to their smooth mouthpieces? There is no answer to this question in an absolute sense, because many types seem to work well. There are single screw ligatures with a centre plate which compresses the reed with out grooving it, the normal two-screw type which does groove it, special thin metal ligatures with raised spots aimed to contact at only two points on either side of the reed, plastic bands which are similarly constructed but claim to be more gentle and leather and felt bandages, tightened by boot lace thongs, which are supposed to be the gentlest of all.

Provided that any of these (a) hold the reed firmly but without distortion and (b) prevent air or water from escaping down the 'table', they provide a usable ligature. If one or the other seems to make a better sound, that is the one to use. There may be a good reason for it, or none at all. The ligatures in fig. **28** are of two types: (a) screws on the blade of the reed and (b) screws on the top of the mouthpiece,

The clarinet reed

There is undoubtedly scope for the writing of several large books on the subject of the reed. Elsewhere, details may be found of methods of hand-making of both the German and French types of reed. Here, it is proposed simply to examine the simplest aspect of this tortured subject – which is that of the mass-produced article used by the vast majority of clarinettists other than those of the German schools. The important facts of this aspect are:

(a) The reed is made of a piece of bamboo called *arundo donax*, or sativa, which grows in many parts of the world but probably as well in the South of France as anywhere. It is a tall plant, many feet in height and of varying diameter. Obviously the size of this diameter is the guide to the sort of reed which will be the final product. It may be big enough for a bass saxophone or contra-bass clarinet or small enough for the E flat clarinet. After being cut into lengths one and a half times as long as the finished reed, it is usually split longitudinally into four strips, and then flattened on the back or inside to a thickness appropriate to the purpose – possibly $\frac{1}{32}$ in. for clarinets but more for larger reeds. Whatever its final size, before this is done it should have been matured in the sun for three years after cutting. This may or may not have been done, because by kiln-drying a fair imitation of this process is made available to makers who have a large output to maintain. The result of this seasoning is usually a change in colour, so that often a good quality of cane may be detected by its rich golden hue; green reeds are immature, brownish ones over-ripe – a simple analogy with many a familiar fruit.

(b) Having obtained this 'blank', the task of the reed maker is to produce, in the material at his disposal, the very complex shape which is the clarinet reed. This, as shown here, is no simple taper in any direction, but requires a

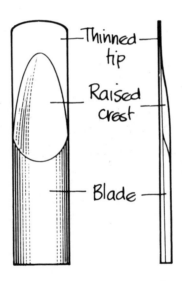

The shape of the reed. The taper is constant from blade to tip and from centre to sides. There is no flat surface.

raised crest in the middle and a tip of fan-like structure of sufficient but not excessive thinness, together with sides of sufficient flexibility to allow embouchure control to take effect. The method of cutting this shape is usually secret, and may involve rotary diamond cutters moving either from tip to heel (or vice versa) or a longitudinal planing action by blades guided remotely by a model forming-pattern. This need not concern us here. What is important is that reeds so produced may not be by any means as perfectly graded for strength as the maker would like. A box of medium reeds may contain 30 per cent hard and 30 per cent soft in spite of the efforts of the maker to test them by spring-loaded gauges and the like. Indeed, one maker has stated that the finished strength of his reeds depends not upon the dimensions at which he aims, but upon the resistance offered by the cane to his cutter. Cane is a substance of varying density and this may well vary within a single reed-sized portion. So this maker actually tests his reeds on the mouthpiece and so is able to grade them accurately – surely the only possible method for success. This does, however, give us a pointer to the best type of reed to try to obtain. Hard cane resists too much, and is therefore brittle in sound, even when thinned. Soft cane is 'mushy' even when thick. Medium cane resists more evenly and therefore it is in the medium range that most players find their best results.

(c) Given this fact, the player must find some way in which to tailor the reed to his exact needs. To do this, he will be wise if he discards any reed which cannot be made to respond because of impossible dimensions. These occur when the raised crest has been in some way impaired, causing the reed to be 'spineless' or when the wings are so uneven that they cannot be made to match. If one of these is too thin there is no way of replacing the lost material. Given a reasonably proportioned reed, the response can be greatly improved by attention to a few simple rules.

The first of these is never to touch the raised crest of the reed unless the overall strength is hopelessly too great, in which case the reed will probably never respond to treatment. Next it is necessary to determine whether the reed is too 'hard' or too 'soft' for comfort and beauty of sound. If too soft, the tip must be progressively shortened by the use of a special reed-clipper (see fig. 32) until it is either perfectly correct (an unlikely event) or too hard, when the following methods of treatment should be applied. Reeds which are too hard are incorrect in one of two ways: either they are too hard to blow, or they are too hard for the embouchure to close them against the facing into the operating position. These faults must be eradicated little by little, by scraping the surface of the reed with either a sharp blade, a folded piece of abrasive paper, or a piece of 'Dutch rush' – the dried stem of a species of wild grass believed by many players to have special qualities as a reed-shaping agent. It leaves a smooth surface and seems not to tear the cane-fibres. Whatever the scraper used, it is essential to remove a very small amount of cane at a time, testing the effect frequently and working at the part of the reed which produces the required effect. The areas shown below are

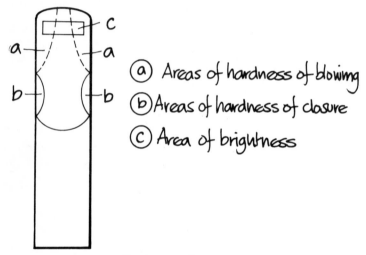

(a) Areas of hardness of blowing
(b) Areas of hardness of closure
(c) Area of brightness

Reed proportion areas.

worth bearing in mind. Scraping the areas marked a, it is essential to keep the two sides in balance; the effect of thinning these 'wings' is to make the reed easier to blow. A very slight excess of thinning causes complete collapse. Removal of material from areas marked b eradicates difficulty of closure by the embouchure; here it is less essential to be modest in the amount removed. Finally, adjust 'brightness' by gently scraping area c.

Having arrived at a reed of the correct strength, its true sound can now be heard. This may well be very disappointing because the hard reed it was originally had a spurious brightness which was attractive if useless. The reed may now have to be rejected. It has not really been ruined; it simply never was a good one. But there is just one more adjustment to be tried before this rejection. The area c is the area of 'brightness'; so if the sound is 'stuffy' a few tiny shavings must be removed from this area alone. There is nothing to lose at this stage, and this final adjustment can work wonders. It is one which must be carried out within fine limits. The vexed question of the flat back of the reed and its correct treatment is one which must be left to the discretion of the individual. Often this surface, although flat, is rough in texture and covered with a tenacious layer of bamboo-dust which is the perfect type of surface to collect dirt and soak up moisture. This is better removed with great care by stroking with a wettened handkerchief while the reed is securely supported from the other side against a hard flat surface. Further polishing, especially with fine abrasives, gives a highly glossy surface. This is undesirable since it retains moisture in globules and produces an extremely embarrassing 'frying' sound. Some players can soften a reed by sliding it across a perfectly flat plate (a mirror or piece of plate-glass, for instance) upon which has been placed a sheet of fine abrasive. Usually two or three careful and skilful passes are enough, because the thin tip of the reed is affected even more than the blade, and may well collapse.

One further factor remains – the 'seasoning' of the reed while it is in use. There is no doubt that a good reed is usually not at its best in the first couple of hours of its life. At this time it seems to resent its new-found moisture-content, and may even sound 'soggy' after a short time. The test comes later, after it has dried out. If it is a fine piece of cane, it will have retained just sufficient moisture to become pliable and sonorous, and if carefully nurtured it should have many hours of useful life before it develops a pale and stony look which indicates that it is becoming brittle, and a cutting sound which goes with this. Some reeds do not enter the sonorous stage at all, and must be discarded as poor material. Opinions vary as to the best method of maintaining the reed when not in use. Some players remove them and keep them in special reed cases which ensure flatness. Others dry them and put them back on the mouthpiece with great care in exactly their original position. Still others leave them *in situ* without any drying, and seem to have success in this way. Whatever the method, one thing seems certain – the moisture content is important, especially in its quantity. A reed which dries out completely usually 'crinkles' and often does not recover fully from this, so it is advisable, whether the reed is to be left on the 'lay' or not, to moisten it slightly before shutting it away for the night.

Attempts have been made over the years to use a variety of materials other than cane, including bone and metal, to make reeds. None has been really successful, though the prayers of many a player have been directed to this end. During the Second World War, when a wealth of acrylic plastic was first available for such experiments, the plastic reed was marketed with a loud fanfare. Many players, having already made experimental reeds of their own, knew what to expect. The trouble with the plastic reed is that it absorbs no moisture, and though it is invariable, it is an invariability which is relentless and soon tires the average embouchure. The 'feel' is altogether different, so that although some players can produce a reasonable sound from the plastic reed, very few can enjoy the experience. Most of them feel that the difference is that of a flat smooth surface contrasted with that of a tight bundle of hollow threads, which is what a piece of bamboo resembles. A cynic might say that if a reed were required to trigger the H bomb, a perfect plastic product would be produced overnight by the millions of pounds or dollars lavished upon it. A still greater cynic would say that if this happened it would be such a perfect replica that among its other characteristics would be the cane reed's lack of durability. Meanwhile the plastic reed remains one of fairly low potential for serious performance.

The barrel or socket

This part of the instrument is really an extension of the

mouthpiece. Older clarinets did not possess one, some having a longer mouthpiece and others a simple extension of the top joint. The intended function of the barrel (otherwise called the socket) is as a tuning-device, since by pulling it out at its tenon-joint with the clarinet a lengthening of the tube is achieved. It is a crude method of flattening the instrument, since its effect upon notes at the bottom of the tube is negligible while that upon the 'throat' notes is disastrously great. The theory of having sockets of varying lengths to play the instrument at different pitches is a fanciful one: a clarinet can play only at the pitch for which it has been constructed. The inclusion of a barrel in the design of a clarinet does, however, permit the individual to re-tune the instrument to his own needs permanently. A player who wishes to flatten his clarinet can adopt a long barrel, and then sharpen the 'throat' notes he has ruined by enlargement of the tone holes. Sharpening the instrument overall is achieved in the opposite manner – by filling in the tone-holes of the affected throat notes while employing a short socket.

The issue is somewhat complicated by the efforts of some makers, who taper the bore of the barrel, reducing it as it descends, as a control measure to lower the upper twelfths in the left hand. Whatever length of socket is used, the bore at its base must leave no 'step' as it merges with that of the top joint of the instrument.

Variations in both density of material and in thickness of the barrel do seem to produce differences of tone-quality. The light socket, particularly of ebonite (hard rubber), gives ease and clarity of sound, with light articulation and a short warm-up period from cold. The heavier socket, of dense wood and considerable thickness, gives a 'darker' sound, full-bodied and 'woody' with a heavier but more impressive staccato. It takes longer to warm up but retains its temperature and is in many ways a more stable piece of equipment. It is worth some trouble to decide the type most suited to one's needs. Possibly two sockets of different characteristics can be used. Whether or not this is decided upon, it is wise to use only one socket for a pair of instruments, ensuring that the tenons have been made so that this can be done. This means both that a larger part of the clarinet is at playing temperature when the change is made and that there is a large handful when changing in a hurry, avoiding the embarrassment of pulling off ligature and reed at a crucial moment.

The bell

The shape of the clarinet bell, its weight, and its density all have important roles. There is little point in discussing this here, because all makers have worked at the perfection of the design of this component and supply the bell they consider to be most suitable. The ring around the bottom of the bell has no effect upon tone, but obviously strengthens the bell. It adds weight to the bell and a further burden upon the tortured right thumb. When it works loose, as it often does with shrinkage of the wood, it can cause vibrations in the sound. It is however an excellent protection for the bell-rim. A dense bell, even a fairly thick one, gives stability to the tone produced, particularly to those notes produced by the middle part of the tube. It is painful to support but is worth the effort acoustically. The inner proportions are of vital significance and difficult to check. The whole purpose of the bell is the smoothing of the sound and the adding of resonance by its weighty presence. There is reason to believe that weight of socket and bell – the ends of the tube – steadies the vibrations of the instrument. There is probably room for experiment in the perfection of them both. Figs. **29** and **30** illustrate some early, and some modern, designs.

The embouchure

It is necessary in any chapter dealing with the practical side of clarinet playing to include a discussion of something which is part of the equipment of the player and not of the instrument. The 'embouchure' is a term used to describe the method of blowing the instrument, deriving obviously from the French *la bouche* – the mouth. This is an aspect which is most frequently forgotten by players and teachers alike, since stress is almost always laid upon the function of the lips alone – a function which one may call 'labiture' or what you will, assuming that it is a function which needs to be dignified by a special title of its own.

Certainly the lips have an important part to play, as have the teeth which support them in their role. It seems possible that the muscular tone they enjoy, in particular that of the lower lip (since it is in contact with the reed and acts as a cushion to its vibrations), has a direct bearing upon the type of sound produced by the player. It may be that the incredible personal variations of sound which can be distinguished between players of otherwise equal ability may have their roots in this very factor (see fig. **35**).

None the less, the embouchure is a much more complex problem than the mere combination of lips and teeth. The size of the mouth, the resonant cavities it presents, the slackness or tension of its walls, the position and function of the tongue – all these have vital parts to play in the production of clarinet tone. There is no space here to deal with the scientific aspects of the embouchure from either the medical or dental point of view. The orthodontics have been very skilfully dealt with by Maurice Porter in his book *The Embouchure*. Mr Porter is a very skilled dentist as well as a most enthusiastic clarinet-tist, and his work on this subject can be regarded as fully authoritative and expert.

The lay point of view is simpler and shorter. Generally speaking, clarinet embouchures are described as being of two types, single or double. In the single embouchure, the reed is placed against the lower lip, which covers the lower teeth, and the mouth is then closed so that the upper teeth press upon the top of the mouthpiece. The jaw muscles then compress the reed by the action of the lower teeth pressing the lower lip against it, bringing it close to the facing of the mouthpiece so that it can be set in vibration more easily. The double embouchure works in exactly the same way, except that the upper lip is also tucked in between the upper teeth and the top of the mouthpiece. Advocates of this type of embouchure claim that it gives a more sensitive 'feel', in that an all-round live-tissue contact is maintained; certainly *feeling* comes into the picture here, because it is a much more painful process. Equally certainly, the sound produced often seems to the player to be smoother, because the vibrations of the mouthpiece itself, otherwise conducted to the head by bone-conduction, are damped by the upper lip. They do not cease to exist, however, just because they are not felt. One further factor remains – the thickness of the upper lip does undoubtedly make for a more open mouth and a greater resonance cavity – very desirable for the type of clarinet tone most desired by many players. This can, however, be obtained in other ways – by a fatter mouthpiece, for instance, or by a conscious resonation on a mouth-opening vowel, as suggested in Chapter 5.

This is not to suggest that the double embouchure is in any way fundamentally wrong. There have been, and are, many fine players employing it. Nor is there anything demonstrably superior in its technique to that of the single embouchure, whose advocates probably include an even greater number of first-class performers. If the similarity of effect produced by the two methods proves anything at all, it is that the lips themselves are not at all the factors of vital importance they are often claimed to be. Players should be encouraged to take their choice of method by assessing the comfort and ease with which they can employ the one or the other. There are in any case many players with upper lips too short to stretch over the teeth. Nor should a player who has started one method be afraid of changing to the other if he feels it is better for him to do so. There are many examples of important players making this change, some of them after as much as fifteen years of experience: and in no case did those around them detect any change in the sound produced. The use of the lips is a matter for comfort and endurance, and the function of the lips is very simple indeed: it is no more than that of a movable and infinitely adjustable elastic band surrounding reed and mouthpiece.

The purpose of this band is twofold. It must apply the

pressure to the reed as described above, and must seal the mouth so that the air it contains under pressure can be directed into the instrument and not allowed to escape. It must be capable of movement up and down the lay of the mouthpiece, to lengthen or shorten the vibrating portion of the reed, and also of exerting greater or less pressure upon it. This done, the rest of the complex business of resonation – the real 'embouchure' in fact – must be left to other factors which affect tone production whether one uses a 'single' or a 'double lip' embouchure.

In addition to labial placement and activity, there are three important factors to consider in embouchure control. These are:

(a) the muscles of the cheeks, which are responsible for both the size of the cavity of the mouth and its reflecting characteristics, since they form the all-important walls at the side of it;

(b) the jaw muscles, which govern not only the pressure exerted on the reed, but the size of the resonating cavity in a vertical direction, increasing or decreasing it at will by the movement of the base of the tongue;

(c) the position and muscular tension of the tongue.

There can be little controversy about (a), because obviously the cheek muscles must be firm to give any possibility of labial control. Even though there is an enlargement of the oral cavity when the cheeks are puffed out, this is offset by the flabbiness of the walls surrounding it; and the relaxation of tension seriously affects lip-support. The cheeks should therefore be held firmly, but not rigidly. There should be little evidence that they are containing an air column under pressure. Concerning (b): the function of the jaw muscles is so complex that it is better to deal with it in Chapter 5, when it combines with other oral functions in the resonance of vowel sounds. It is possibly the most variable of all the aspects of embouchure from note to note, and is responsible for much of the balance which is the essence of correct tone-production on the clarinet.

In (c) it is essential to remember that the tongue is a muscle, and has the same properties of tension and relaxation as all other voluntary muscles. Its most obvious use in playing the clarinet is its attack upon the reed and consequent production of staccato of many sorts. This is also an aspect dealt with in Chapter 5. The purely static position of the tongue as part of the established embouchure is quite simple: it is simply drawn back in the mouth as far out of the way of the movement of the reed as is reasonably possible in view of its requirement for attack in a split second, when needed. The very withdrawal in this direction has the effect of tensing the tongue; so that, with the firm walls provided by the cheeks, the hard palate above, the teeth in front and the firm underside of the tongue below, the vibrating reed is enclosed in a large and resonant cavity. It must be the aim of every player who wishes to enjoy the finest sound his instruments can produce to ensure that his embouchure fulfils these requirements. The lips are important – the remainder is vital.

The thumb-rest

Too little attention is usually paid by both makers and players to the design and positioning of this fixture. Historically it is of fairly recent origin; the original clarinets of the 18th century did not employ it at all, for the obvious reason that the box-wood clarinet, with its few keys, was light, and could balance easily enough on the thumb without further help. Besides, as time went on, the right thumb was employed otherwise; originally the E natural–B natural key (the one which in fact gave the clarinet its present shape) was thumb-operated. Basset horns and clarinets also used the thumb for the series of keys which extended the compass downward to low C – a most clumsy and hazardous function, it is true, but one which apparently worked. It was with the appearance of Müller and his contemporaries upon the scene that the thumb became unemployed except as a supporting agent. Thereafter it was not only an advantage to have a thumb-rest; the weight of the instrument made it absolutely essential, as can be verified by anyone who removes the thumb-rest from a modern clarinet and tries to play it. This essential adjunct is thus worthy of careful attention in design, since in many clarinets the word 'rest' is a serious misnomer – the shape of it seems to have been evolved with the express intention of providing a sharp edge at its inward side, digging into the thumb with such ferocious intensity that a very undesirable dropped wrist position is the only way of avoiding pain. The under-surface of the thumb-rest should be curved and corked in such a way that this cannot happen. A design which successfully avoids this is shown in fig. **33**. Should a clarinet be provided with a less satisfactory thumb-rest, there is no sense in continuing to use it unaltered. To do so will result in bad fingering habits and in uncomfortable corns upon the upper surface of the thumb. Alteration can be simply achieved by removing it from the clarinet and bending with pliers (a vice helps!) to the correct shape, afterwards padding the under surface with thin cork or soft felt. If there is sufficient room (i.e. if it is too far up the clarinet anyway) the whole operation can be carried out by affixing a shaped piece of cork of any thickness and the most comfortable shape, which can easily be discovered by experiment.

This brings us to the other aspect of the thumb-rest which is worthy of attention – its position. There seems to be little doubt about this in a radial sense – it should be absolutely at the back of the clarinet, in line with the reed and the thumb-hole and ring. Vertically it is a matter of taste, and seems to respond little to reason. Simply holding out the right hand in its relaxed playing position would seem to suggest that the obvious position is underneath the first-finger hole. Lining it up in this position usually makes it too high for the player, since it prevents easy movement of the first finger up the clarinet to operate the trill-keys of the top joint. This movement is usually possible when the rest is placed opposite to the centre of the first-finger hole, making the thumb about $\frac{3}{16}$ in. lower than that finger in its holding position. This should be regarded as the highest possible fixing. The lowest position is probably $\frac{3}{4}$ in. further down the instrument, and only the player can decide at which point between these two his own comfort demands its placement. Unfortunately there is no way of testing an infinite number of positions; after about two false starts it is inadvisable to continue to experiment, though filling the unused holes with the most popular of modern epoxy-resin fixatives can be said to make the joint as good as new. The careful drilling necessary for this task is almost certainly best left to a professional repairman, who will be reasonably certain to do no permanent damage.

It is astonishing that so little has ever been done by makers to present an adjustable thumb-rest, though there have been many examples in the past century to provide pivotal examples for comfort. A simple solution to the vertical placement problem was evolved some ten years ago, but never produced (see fig. **33**). This was simply a pair of rails upon which the thumb-rest travelled, being arrested by a grub-screw out of the reach of the thumb. Players could experiment for a long time in each position before deciding finally what they really needed. Unfortunately the device tends to lead to restlessness and a lack of ability to settle firmly for a single position. Used properly, it could be a most important advance.

The tenons

In normal construction the clarinet has four tenons, fitted into four sockets, in its assembly. There are several reasons for this. The first is a question of convenient-sized portions of instruments – (a) the mouthpiece, (b) the barrel, (c) the top joint, (d) the bottom joint and (e) the bell, none of which is longer than about 10in. As a result, the instrument can be accommodated in quite a small case – even a pair of clarinets can be carried in an attaché-case. There is also the question of the depth of the log from which the joints are cut. If it is intended, say, to make an A clarinet with a one-piece body, the log must be of such a depth that to manhandle it requires super-human strength, and this discourages makers. A third factor is that, if a joint is to crack, it may as well be a short one, so that replacement is cheaper and simpler. Finally, both cleaning and mechanical maintenance are simpler in short sections than in long ones.

This being said, there is no doubt that acoustically the tenons are extremely undesirable. It is here that possible leaks, and mis-alignment of the key work occur. The instrument may even be out of truth because the joints do not present a perfect straight line, and careless assembly may be the cause of damage not only to the key-work, but of cracking of the wood. Also, in any change of atmosphere, humidity, or extremes of temperature, tenons may become too slack, or (much worse) too tight. They are therefore at best a necessary evil, and their maintenance is a vital aspect of clarinet care.

The first aspect to be studied is the material of the facing of the tenon, as well as that of the counter-bore into which it fits. Normally this is greased cork in the case of the tenon, and wood for the bore. These two materials can be extremely satisfactory, providing a perfect seal and a smooth assembly, but probably not for long. Usually the joint becomes slack when the cork dries out and shrinks, and further greasing helps only to a limited extent to seal the air-leak which results. Various types of cork grease produce different effects. Petroleum grease alone is poor in its most refined form, and the heavier water-pump greases are better, if rather more messy to apply. Certainly grease and tallow, mixed thoroughly, provide the most satisfactory lubricant, and the mixture has only one disadvantage – that of a most unpleasant smell, which must be borne by the owner and forgiven by his family and friends if he is to be safe from his loose-tenon perils.

Even with this super-grease, however, cork finally becomes slack, hard and useless, and must then be replaced. This is certainly not a job for the average player to tackle. It can be done by a skilled repairer quite quickly and with surprising advantage to the safety of tone-production. Before this luxury can be enjoyed there is an emergency method which can be used to tide over the owner who cannot get to a repairer.

Cork expands with steam. It is inadvisable to hold the tenon in a jet of steam from a kettle, because of inevitable expansion and possible cracking of the wood. The best method of swelling the cork is to wet it thoroughly, and then, rotating it rapidly, hold it in a flame from a spirit lamp or even a lighted match. This may blacken it a little, but it swells quite surprisingly, and with a gentle application of grease it is usually a much improved tenon.

Another method, and one used by a great number of busy professionals, is lapping the tenon on top of the shrunken cork with cotton thread soaked in grease. This should be fine sewing-cotton. The use of dental floss for this purpose is to be discouraged, as it is so thick that it simply sets up a series of ridges upon which the tenon rides, and around which the air can escape. Thin cotton can be lapped around the tenon so that it presents a continuous bearing surface, and if properly greased it is compacted by the pressure of the joint, making it into exactly the shape and size required to make a perfect seal. It can also be removed in part, or added to gradually, until exactly the correct amount is present for this result; and of course, if the wood of the joints it is connecting expands or contracts, adjustment is very simply achieved in this way. A cork joint which has deteriorated may thus be kept in use for years with very satisfactory results. It is, however, essential that the lapping material be of soft cotton, and be thoroughly soaked in grease – the tallow-grease mixture mentioned above is best, and the whole hank must be immersed in a melted pot of this noxious substance for several minutes – preferably out of doors or in the garden hut. It can then be removed, its surface wiped, and the whole wrapped up in cloth until required for use. It will last for years, and will in fact become much less offensive quite soon.

However carefully this tenon-maintenance is carried out, sooner or later wear of both the tenon and the counter-bore will take place, causing the joint to have too great a clearance and giving rise to 'rock' at the junction. This is usually due to a 'rounding off' of the tip of the tenon and an enlargement of the counter-bore, and in both cases the remedy is a thin metal facing – German silver is a satisfactory material, but Sterling silver is best (see fig. **25**). This is an expert's work, and advice should be taken as to when it is necessary. This advice will almost always be to have the operation carried out later rather than sooner, because it can cause trouble with a joint which is still swelling with moisture-absorption. A metal tip holding a tenon, while the joint to which it is attached swells, is a sure way of producing a crack; and a circlet of metal in a counter-bore which is shrinking is an equally certain invitation to disaster. So joints should start out with cork on wood, and end up years later with cotton on metal. Both can be satisfactory, carefully used. In any case, tenons are essential to the clarinet. It may be possible to dispense with the middle tenon, but the bell and mouthpiece will always remain separate, and of course the barrel must have its tenon for tuning purposes. A passing thought here is that in fact clarinets over the years have been made with special screw-adjustments on the barrel for this purpose, and some of these seem to have worked. It thus seems possible that normal tenons will disappear in the years to come – possible, but by no means certain.

Pitch and tuning

Of all the problems which face instrument makers, none can be said to be so completely impossible of solution as those of general pitch and individual tuning. Apart from national variations of pitch (which still exist in spite of attempts at international standardization at A = 440 c.p.s., and are mentioned elsewhere in this book) there is the puzzling fact that individual players do in fact produce sounds of different pitches from the same clarinet, reed and mouthpiece. This is understandable where the quality of sound is widely different, and especially when one player uses a hard reed with a wide mouthpiece opening and the other a soft one and a close facing; in this case one can be certain that the harder reed player will play much sharper than the other, for reasons touched upon in Chapter 3. What is much harder to explain is the case of at least one world class orchestra which employs two clarinettists whose sound blends perfectly, who normally play well in tune, who use the same model clarinet, the same grade of mouthpiece and reed, and who can in fact play each other's instrument in comfort and with pleasure – yet who, when they do so, find that the pitch of one is almost a quarter-tone above that of the other. (There must be a good medical reason for this.) The phenomenon is especially noticeable in the 'throat' register of the instrument; and here the cunning of the maker has been called into action over the years to such excellent purpose that the instruments these players use are in fact 'tailor-made' to their requirements. One player uses a fairly short barrel with opened holes for G, A and A flat, while the other requires a longer barrel with smaller holes for these notes. The moral of this is that it is always best, when ordering a clarinet, to be in touch with the man who makes it, or at least to be in contact with a firm of manufacturers who are willing to admit that their clarinets, however perfect they may be, must be liable to alteration to individual requirements. There is no such thing as a perfect clarinet, except in abstract terms. The instrument can, however, be brought nearer to that ultimate goal if care is taken in this way. Alterations must be gradual and informed, but they must none the less be undertaken in a spirit of comradeship by the maker, who is wise if he respects the individual 'quirks' of the finished performer. To alter a clarinet radically for a beginner is of course stupid and wasteful, but it is no reflection upon the maker when a mature player requires something out of the normal line of acoustic set-up to make the clarinet fit his needs.

Five
The Artistic Approach

Skill is just a beginning

Once the purely mechanical business of simply producing the notes of a scale or a tune on a clarinet has been mastered, the most important aspect of playing the instrument can begin to be considered – the channelling of this acquired skill into reasonable artistic achievement. Certainly the simple act of producing the correct series of harmonic overtones, using the right fingering to divide the tube into its correct relative length and reinforcing the partials as necessary by embouchure pressure, has almost nothing at all to do with music. No more, really, than has the same series of sounds produced by a series of tuning-forks or steam-whistles. Such sounds are simply the raw materials of the music it is intended to perform, and the player must now ask himself how he can transform these unrelated notes into what the composer meant them to be. How can he turn them into a *tune*? Unfortunately, in the case of the clarinet, there are certain difficulties to be overcome before the general rules of phrasing can be made to apply. First must come a careful study of the techniques which one can use to add to the expressive range of the clarinet; and these, it must be said, add immeasurably to the difficulty of playing the instrument.

Take as an example the adjustments and modifications essential to play the opening phrase of one of the great sonatas of all time – Brahms's F minor, Op. 120 No. 1. The achievement of the notes themselves is not really very

The Clarinet

difficult, for Brahms certainly had the clarinet very much in mind as he wrote, and uses the typical wide leaps of which it is so capable:

The balance of the first four notes is a classic example of acoustic problems and the way in which they have to be overcome if an artistic result is to be achieved. The reasons for this are set out in Chapter 3, and a study of the characteristics of each note gives one a clue as to the necessary approach.

(a) The D is probably slightly flat, and may be dull in sound. It is also in the dense part of the spectrum of the clarinet.

(b) The B flat is the 'windiest' and least resonant note on the clarinet, and a most unnatural neighbour of the D because it is in the least dense area of the instrument. It may be sharp or flat, according to the setting of the socket to tune, or attempt to tune, the pitch of the clarinet.

(c) The G is a similar note, but more resonant and its pitch more or less follows the sharpness or flatness of the B flat, but to a lesser degree. Being the 'open' note of the instrument, it has no character of its own at all.

(d) The top B flat is bright in sound – extremely so, almost uncontrollable. It can be played with less brightness as a 'long' B flat (first fingers of both hands only) – but not in this context, followed by a G. It is usually sharp when played as a 'side' B flat, and may have to remain so to match the sharp C natural which is its neighbour; but it must be played in tune all the same. Without going further, one can see that these four notes can give a very poor start to this great work. They must not be allowed to do so.

The method of approach must be thorough, gradual, and thoughtful. It will take time to get just these four notes in perfect balance, even before the musical meaning they are meant to convey is considered. An analysis of the experienced player's thoughts on the problem probably goes something like this:

(a) The D being flat and dense must be attacked firmly from the diaphragm and with a secure embouchure pressure. It must be 'held' in the instrument as much as possible, with a minimum waste of air from the bell.

(b) The B flat can probably not be played as a 'side' B flat unless the player has the sort of hand which permits this, when a slight rolling and a contact with the second knuckle is all that is required. If it can be played like this, the resulting note will be similar in sound to the D, but will require a slightly greater volume of air passing down the instrument to equalise it. If the normal 'throat' B flat is used, resonant finger corrections, as discussed earlier, must be instantly applied, and in addition the extremely low atmosphere pressure in the tube must be boosted by letting a large quantity of air pass through it. This should be increased until it is felt that the balance with the D has been made, without worrying about the hiss from the speaker-hole.

(c) The 'open' G also needs the same sort of support from the diaphragm, but slightly less in degree. While playing it – possibly also with finger corrections to amend its intonation – the mental preparation for the huge jump to the top B flat must begin. Before actually playing the next note it is best to feel where it 'lives' in the embouchure – and often to imagine that it is hovering over the top of the head and must be reached for, to get it without a 'scoop' or a squawk.

(d) The B flat, when reached, will be both bright in sound and sharp, especially played as a 'side' B flat as it must be in this context. Both sharpness and excessive brightness are avoided by feeling the note slightly further back in the mouth than the previous notes. This both increases the volume of resonance in the mouth, and slackens the embouchure pressure, producing a slightly flatter and duller sound.

Having balanced these four notes, all that remains is to ensure that the *legato* is perfect and that the *poco forte* indication has been observed, and the rest of the phrase can be given the same sort of attention. At this point it may be well to ponder just whether all those slurs should be honoured quite literally; but at present, assuming that they must, the following essential points must be borne in mind.

(a) Bar 4 is the most crucial. It requires a left hand C and usually a slight flattening as well as a slight under-playing of this quite brilliant note, followed by a top E flat which cannot be approached with a slur in its usual 'middle-key' fingering and so must employ one of the auxiliary fingerings shown in the chart on page 87.

(b) Bar 5 is complicated by the fact that the F sharp can sometimes be played with the same fingerings as the E flat which precedes it, adding the first finger of the left hand. Sometimes it cannot, because instruments vary greatly in this respect. Whichever way it is, we must not use a flat fingering, because the A which follows it will certainly be sharp, and the necessary embouchure adjustment will be noticeable. The F sharp must also be obtained with an almost *legato* attack, so there is little time for a dramatic change of fingering between bars 4 and 5.

(c) Bar 6 is the perfect phrase to use the side B flat, and failure to do this is extremely foolish. Oddly enough, most people do so fail for a long time.

(d) The short *crescendo* at the end should not be too dramatic, but more a sort of rounding off of the phrase, accompanied by a feeling of *tenuto*.

All this takes almost exactly ten seconds in performance, which suggests that clarinet playing is a fairly complex affair when approached in this very advanced way. This approach is quite essential, however, if the composer's intentions are to be realised; and it has its reward, because there is really no other instrument which can play this phrase so perfectly as can the clarinet, when it is well done. The wide spaced notes can, and must, be made to sound as if they are near neighbours, while still surprising the hearer at the wide span of the melodic invention.

These adjustments may seem to be so complex that nobody could ever manage them in the few seconds available. Luckily, we are helped in this by a most fortunate human characteristic. Repetition makes the most complicated muscular adjustment almost unconscious. Human behaviour patterns are easily and quickly acquired, and the most complex operations seem trivial in a very short time. A child of five can often tie a shoe-lace in the dark after a month or so of familiarity, though the operations involved in this task at first are found to be very complicated. It may be wrong to say that such acts are subconsciously performed, but certainly they can be at the very back of the conscious mind. The same can be made to apply to all the adjustments mentioned above. If all the various characteristics of each note are studied and balanced over the years with time to spare as they are played, very slowly, the whole series involved in this or any other comparable tune will naturally and easily fall into place. The effect is then unbelievably different from the bumpy and unattractive affair which is the best that can otherwise be managed. This slow process has then simply to be made sub-conscious, or nearly so, by familiarisation, speeded up, and the job of really *playing* the clarinet has begun.

This analysis of the opening of the Brahms sonata is just one example, giving a clue as to the correct attitude of mind. It may be taken as a model, but the real point is that this type of thought must be fostered and practised. It can make clarinet playing much more exciting, because there is literally no end to the adjustments possible. The permutations of finger arrangements, pressure control and support, and embouchure variation are almost limitless.

For beginners only

Playing in this manner is, at first, obviously living the hard way. There is an easy way, but it fails to produce the results, and is a dead end. This simple solution is to employ a feeble reed on a close faced mouthpiece, producing a characterless and invariable sound. There are no really bad notes with this set-up and no good ones either. It is obviously an attractive proposition, because it frees the fingers to produce showers of notes at will, unhampered by any pressure or embouchure adjustments. For the beginner this sort of mouthpiece and reed has its advantages, but it must be left behind as soon as serious musicianship can be allowed to take over. With a firmer reed, the production of a tune can be likened to the 'tasting' of each note in turn, because each exists as a recognisable physical sensation, and this sensation or 'taste' can be recalled and re-established at will.

A variety of sounds

Leaving for a moment the idea of a tune as a sort of vocalisation of the clarinet, the player must bear in mind that he has at his command quite a wide spectrum of different sounds, all of which he must learn to use with discrimination.

In some ways the sheer variety of sound-possibilities is one of the least explored aspects of the clarinet; perhaps not surprisingly so, since to achieve a single unified sound over the three and a half octaves of the compass of the clarinet is in itself a fine achievement. But when this has been managed, the advanced player must learn to produce several sorts of sounds, and unify them in turn so that he can produce them at will in any register of the instrument. The old idea that a clarinet had three or four registers – chalumeau, throat, clarinet and altissimo – has mercifully now left us. These are now just sub-sections of the compass, and the aim must be to produce them all with either one sound or with another.

It is undeniably true that different nationalities or 'schools' of clarinet-playing tend to produce their own very different sounds, and in many ways a study of these is advantageous because it gives a clue as to the possibilities of difference. It is also true that in some ways there are physical differences in the instruments used, which seem at first to account for the various sounds produced – different sizes and lengths of bore and different disposition of tone-holes, as well as widely different details of mouthpiece design. The question of mouthpiece material is also important in this respect; but in this vexed question of natural differences of sound, the main reason still remains the *desire* of a player to produce the sort of sound he achieves. The French player *wishes* to sound French, the German equally wants to sound German, and both would probably sound very much the same as they now do if they changed to an instrument of the type used by the other.

What is important is something which is still much more rare than it should be – the desire of each player, whether his fundamental sound be French, German, English, American or Italian, not always to produce the same sound, but to try to use the sound most appropriate to the music he is playing. The sound which most musicians would consider to be most appropriate to our Brahms solo is in no way typical of the ideal sound required to play, say, the familiar important fragment from Strauss's 'Ein Heldenleben' shown on page 140.

How to treat this solo?

To begin with, the required volume of sound is essentially much greater – about three times as great as in the Brahms sonata. Also, this is manifestly much sterner stuff, requiring a more compact, severe and masculine sound. In the first place, the approach to this problem must be a mental one. Focus upon the required sound, make a mental image of it, and half the battle is over. But this is not all. To achieve the metamorphoses from the intimate Brahms to the masterly Strauss, a much more firm diaphragm support is required, a greater lip-pressure to stiffen the sound, and the oral cavity generally must have a much firmer muscular tone. Also, on the bottom A flat, a breath accent, unknown in such gentle music as the Brahms, is essential to emphasise the tremendous drop in pitch from the top C and add drama to its sound. It is altogether a more forthright sound.

Mouthpiece characteristics

It is not really necessary to use a different mouthpiece or reed to obtain these contrasted effects; the best players can go straight from our first tune to our second without too much difficulty, and as time goes on players are becoming used to having to cope with an increasing variety of extreme requirements at a moment's notice. This is not to say that these extremes *must* be coped with on one mouthpiece alone; merely to marvel that it seems that they *can* be. With the increase in the variety of extreme effects which are being demanded from the clarinet nowadays, it is undeniable that it can be an advantage to have more than one mouthpiece at one's disposal. This facility can increase both the dynamic range and the flexibility of the instrument from the point of view of intonation, as well as reducing the fatigue which inevitably follows an attempt to push a favourite and familiar mouthpiece beyond its capacity in either direction. A great variety of sounds can be obtained from a single mouthpiece. An even greater variety can be obtained from two or more if they have been carefully chosen for the roles they have to play. This choice must be taken very seriously – the mouthpieces, although intended to produce different sounds and varied dynamic ranges, simply must have one thing in common – the sound they give must be the one the *player* dictates, not one which is built into them and cannot be in any way modified. By all means get a mouthpiece for orchestral use which will produce a *ff* twice as big as your chamber music mouthpiece without a sense of strain and without overloading; try to find one which will give a small direct sound for special use, or one which can develop a cutting edge that Duke Ellington would have welcomed. But avoid like the plague one which will produce only a buzzy and edgy, or a husky 'jumbo-sized' tone. Mouthpieces which have a shallow palate – that is, those in which the reed has only a small clearance from the inside of the top of the mouthpiece, or where the 'roof' of the tone-chamber has been made deliberately convex so that it bulges towards the reed –

invariably have a loud, brilliant, sometimes a 'gritty' sound. This was common knowledge with the old jazz clarinettists and saxophonists of New Orleans, who modified their ancient ex-army instruments by inserting a wedge of chewing-gum in the tone-chamber of the mouthpiece, and hence made themselves not only heard, but heeded and even feared! The mouthpiece which has an extra deep palate where this raised 'baffle' is absent, giving a deep, concave ceiling instead, always has a dark, sometimes hollow sound, lacking edge and definition. Like the shallow mouthpiece, it is often possible to use such mouthpieces for special effects, but such extreme cases are probably best left to the player who finds himself in conditions he cannot otherwise cope with. To use them for normal orchestral or chamber music activity is not only unwise – it may even be impossible. Also, where such extreme sounds are produced, it is often because the player concerned has a preference for them, one or the other, and produces them as a matter of routine. A safer method is to have a mouthpiece which *tends* in this direction or that, so that it can be pushed there if possible, or used in a more normal manner if it is so wished. It is a mistake to try to smooth out the sound of an over-bright mouthpiece, for instance to play the Brahms tune above, or to brighten up a cavernous one to attempt the Strauss; but two different mouthpieces, one tending to brightness and the other to darkness, will give great comfort and satisfaction, if you cannot manage both effects on a single mouthpiece. The 'middle of the road' mouthpiece, with slight variations upon it in the two directions of brightness and darkness, should be the aim. These slight variations include the depth of palate already discussed, and also two much more obvious factors: the facing or 'lay', as described in Chapter 4, and the materials used in the manufacture of the mouthpiece.

The 'lay' and the reed

The most important factor governing the type of facing chosen for artistic satisfaction must in the end be the comfort of the player. There is no point in straining the muscles of the embouchure (and this means those of the face, the jaw, the throat and the lips) unless what happens when this is done makes some difference to the quality of sound produced.

To respond to attempts at variety of expression it is essential that the facing be sufficiently 'open' to respond to variety of lip-pressure – it must have a 'squashiness' under the lip which means that when compressed the sort of compact, firm sound required by the Strauss extract above can be produced, *ff*, without any sense of back-pressure in the thorax. In other words, the instrument must be able to take everything a strong man can give it without overloading. This of course also means that the reed must have sufficient material in it to vibrate at a great amplitude while being held firmly by the lip in its 'damped' position. This 'squashiness' is something which can be felt, and once felt it is not easily forgotten; but it must not be excessive because a tiring factor of this sort leads to headaches, fatigue, sore lips and general depression which are at any rate as serious in their artistic effects as the buzziness of the close facing, and much more distressing to the player himself. Given this more 'open' quality, however, the world of expressive playing is revealed to the budding clarinettist. Now, should he wish to play the Brahms melody on the same mouthpiece as he uses for the Strauss, he will find that a more vocal, more relaxed and generally more satisfactory sound is achieved by a less generous lip-pressure, a firm but not forceful diaphragm-support for the air column and an enlargement of the oral cavity until the resonance of the sound reaches its optimum – this last something fairly rare in clarinet playing until recent years, but now happily more in vogue. All these circumstances require a facing which is not only more 'open' than the easy-going beginners' mouthpiece, but slightly longer too. Obviously the effort required to close a stiff, short and open 'lay' is too great to be sustained for long – and there is no point in making life difficult without any artistic reward to follow. So let the facing be such that it is possible to control it, rather than be controlled by it. Here a good teacher must help.

Those who have experience in such matters are still startled to hear the incredible effect when a student whose normal sound may be poor and undeveloped is allowed, with due attention to hygienic safety, to play the instrument, reed and mouthpiece of his professor. Almost always he produces the sound of the teacher, and feels so inspired that he cannot rest until the conditions of the clarinet he plays are approximated to what he has just felt. It is like the revelation of the 'groovy' feeling of a good golf-swing – suddenly things click into place, and what has been impossible before is now glimpsed and must be seized upon in passing and made safe for the future. At this moment of revelation it is the duty of the teacher firmly to ensure that the instrument mouthpiece and reed of his student are such that he (the teacher) could himself use them to produce artistic results which he would find satisfactory. One is aware that physical differences between the teacher and the pupil may make this more difficult; in practice this is not such a barrier as one might expect, because the physical energy expended in supporting the tone is not so great that it is beyond the capacity of the average person, at any rate after he has passed the beginner's stage – and the extremely weak physical specimen has so little chance of ever matching up to the demands of any wind instrument that he would be better advised to apply his talents elsewhere.

The student must go away not only with his teacher's sound ringing in his ears, the feel of his teacher's instrument in his body, but with an instrument of his own which can recapture at will, before the vision slowly fades and he once more settles back to his own sound and his own methods of tone-production, as of course he will do. This is the way of life of a clarinettist, and a cynic might say that even the best teacher can be of influence only when within ear-shot; but gradually, given a long series of such sessions of correction, one or two changes should emerge. Either the student finally crystallizes his production into a reasonable copy of his teacher's, or (even better) he may develop a style and character of his own which has something unique to offer. He will then be able to go out and add to the pleasure of his hearers as well as getting the personal satisfaction which comes from an inner knowledge of one's possibilities. It is not that he has rejected the teaching he has been privileged to enjoy; he has in fact absorbed it. By adding to it he may well cause some head-shaking among his elders; but he is right in that the clarinet must be more than a 'rubber-stamp' instrument, simply endorsing what has been common knowledge for generations. Production of sound can be so varied, so flexible and so expressive given the right set-up, that no two clarinettists need sound exactly alike, nor should they.

The super-mouthpiece

To many clarinettists, and in particular many mature and experienced players, the whole discussion of varieties of mouthpieces, different types of facings, materials, interior shapes, brings a sharp rise in temperature and the sharp response: 'Rubbish.' This is simply because they think they know very well the heart and truth of the matter. There is, and always has been, they are assured, only one perfect mouthpiece: all others are weak copies of it, and their owners are to be pitied but encouraged to get out of their choice as decent a sound as they possibly can. The mouthpiece in question is of course the one they have themselves used for 25 years. The idea of setting it aside to flirt with a lot of new-fangled modern mass-produced travesties is sheer heresy; and the very idea of using a series of different mouthpieces in the course of a few days' work is such extreme folly that nobody could take it as a serious suggestion. There is something so wondrously comforting about a mouthpiece one has come to know well. Fit it with a good reed, let it settle for a couple of days, and you have a friend; a friend whose very presence seems to ensure that difficult passages can be charmed into submission, no matter how difficult the surrounding acoustics. As has often been said of a favourite mouthpiece or instrument in the band room: 'This one knows all the operas!'

One must admit considerable sympathy for this point of view, because a really fine mouthpiece has an almost in-credibly wide range of dynamics as well as a great variety of tone colour. Also, either the reed 'plays-in' perfectly to the mouthpiece, or the player adapts himself to the reed, fairly quickly. It may be a little of both processes but it does result in a wonderful sense of completeness, the sort of rapport which can make the clarinet an instinctive tool, can make it disappear from the mental foreground and allow a concentration upon the sheer music itself, its shape, its progress and its interpretation. Blessed is he who has achieved this state of bliss. Long may he have it – or reasonably long, for it cannot, in the nature of things, last for ever. No mouthpiece of whatever material, shape or finish can exist for very long without marked physical changes which inevitably affect its performance. These changes are of several sorts. In the case of ebonite it is invariably a structural change in the make up of the material. This is a de-vulcanisation of the ebonite until it tends to turn more nearly to its original rubber state, a de-vitrification which changes its colour from glossy black to dusty green and its texture from steel-hard to mushy-soft. The shape usually remains surprisingly uniform, but in any case it too is subject to the next series of change factors. In use, a mouthpiece is being constantly beaten, hammered, set in vibration, wiped, cleaned and affected by saliva, which can be acid in the extreme. It collects deposits which have to be removed, taking with them some of the material. Pulling it through with a swab raises the palate and expands the sidewalls, as well as enlarging the bore and tone chamber. But it is the facing which inevitably takes the greatest punishment, for here the reed is in constant hammering attention, compressing part of the 'lay' more than the rest because of various thicknesses of reed in motion at any time, so causing a distortion which in time necessitates re-facing. This is the final deciding factor in the termination of the life of a mouthpiece. The skilled repair-man who replaces this facing starts first by flattening the 'table' of the mouthpiece – taking off a mere two-thousandths of an inch but making it essential to follow this right up the facing to the tip, where it has to be coped with. The top 'rail' is now found to be too thick, and is carefully reduced to match the side rails. The mouthpiece is now shorter: it is also shallower and so brighter in tone, because of the proximity of the palate to the reed. Its capacity is thus less, so that it plays at a higher pitch. It *does* play, and may give the impression of an entirely new life to its doting owner; but he had better beware, because if this is done three or four times, he is in reality playing on an entirely different mouthpiece. He is, with all the skill and experience he can bring to bear, compensating in every note he plays for the ever-increasing defects of his mouthpiece. He is developing habits which become so much a part of his method of playing that he regards them as an essential part of his stock-in-trade, even as one of the fundamental reasons for his celebrity. The danger of the whole business of the Super-Mouthpiece is that he may try hard to hand on this tradition of approach and control to his pupils; he may supply them with the sort of mouthpiece he thinks they need (a copy of the Master) and so he may spread what can at best be described only as an addiction. Most pathetic is his condition when his addiction is far advanced, because then only one of two things can possibly happen. Either his mouthpiece becomes so worn as to be useless even to him, or it is lost, stolen or damaged beyond repair. It is then he enters an underworld of torment, peopled by a multitude of new, glossy mouthpieces, good, bad and indifferent – but all utterly useless to him. The best one can then hope is that he has taken the precaution some time before to have a careful copy made of his late departed mouthpiece. This is most unlikely to be an exact copy, since almost any mouthpiece maker will flinch from the final distortions which would be necessary for this; but if it is reasonably close, there is a hope that he may be able to recognise in it something he can bend to his will – if ever he can forget his lost love. Failing this, he is a Paolo looking for his Francesca in the wilds of Hades – lost forever. This is tragic – but from the point of view of the clarinet world, much less serious than what could happen if he could breed a whole new generation of false mouthpieces, spreading the dread disease from which he does not know he is suffering.

His correct course, obviously, is to select with care a new

mouthpiece from the great variety available, after which the real business of how to make an interesting variety of sounds can begin. Here the natural musical ear is the prime factor, the same ear which has, in fact, been at work since the age of about six months, sorting out sounds, their meanings, and their translations into action.

Speech and music

The music of speech is the first music a child learns, and from this music he derives the meaning of life. Later he can apply it to the art of music as we know it, and there is no doubt that there is a close analogy between the two, a connection between the spoken word and music; between accent, dialect and the cadence of speech and the much more subtle and understated expression of musical utterance. To his language the average person brings such musical talent as he possesses, usually without conscious effort or realisation. As a clarinettist he is wise if he can learn to apply the same sort of attention, indeed the very same sort of sound-production, to his instrument. Much of the apparatus used is identical, many of the methods of resonation, articulation and projection very closely related. It is true that in speech the generator is the vocal chords, in the larynx, while in the clarinet it is the reed and mouthpiece in the mouth; but the resonation of the sound, once produced, is dependant in both cases upon the cavities of the head and mouth, and the articulation requires the same sort of tongue motion in each case. At this point it must be emphasised that there are many points of contact within the mouth which are useful in speech, but which the tongue should be discouraged from exploring in the articulation of the clarinet. There have been some good players who have achieved a satisfactory staccato and semi-staccato by attacking the roof of the mouth with the tongue. Some, but not many. The sound is usually an ugly 'quack'.

The connection between speech and clarinet tone production is emphasised perhaps more clearly in a comparison of the flute tones of various countries. Certainly the French tone can now be said to dominate the world scene; but this was not always so. A generation ago, for instance, England had a flute sound very much of its own. It seems certain that the reason for this lay in the different vowel sounds of English and French speech. The best illustration of this is in the pronunciation of the name of the instrument itself. Say '*la flute*' and you can hear the sort of narrow, tense and concentrated sound of the French school of flute playing. Follow this by saying 'the flute' in English and you have uttered a much more relaxed, open-mouthed and generally looser sound, so typical of the best players in the older English style. This is not merely a fanciful concept of a link-up between instrumental sound and language. It can be amplified greatly, because it is a fundamental factor, and can form the basis of a very wide study leading to a most desirable variety of tone-colour in the instrument concerned.

How can this link-up of language and instrumental sound find general application? It is something for the future, a new concept of wood-wind playing, for certainly no generation of players has so far given it a chance, if it has even been vouchsafed a passing thought. To a great extent its application is a question of playing and obtaining a resonance on the various vowel sounds not only of the player's own language, but of an international selection. The effect of this is immediate and dramatic. Form the vowel sound 'oo' in the mouth and it is projected in the sound of the clarinet as a typically 'white', pure and to some ears rather an old-time sound. 'Eee', 'oh', 'aw' and the French 'ou' all have their own flavour in the sound pattern and their characteristic equivalant clarinet sound. Inevitably the player will have his favourite among these, which is to a great extent the reason for the divergence of sounds into national groups. At present the 'aw' is typically English except in the military schools, where 'eee' is probably more common; 'ooh' seems to belong to the German method of production, 'ah' to the American. All these have been ingrained and made more permanent by the mouthpieces, reeds and instruments used in each case. It is up to the modern player to unearth them, to learn to produce tham *all*, even those with which he is not in sympathy, as a matter of duty. It is our job to provide any sound, good or less good, required by the music. Very few players enjoy the sound of a 'growl', a long glissando, or a series of flutter-tongued notes on the clarinet. Yet all these must be in our armoury. So must the variety of sound obtained by vowel-reinforcement of the embouchure, and in future this must be part of the training of every player. Incidentally articulation can also be affected by consciousness of vowel resonance. The German guttural 'ach' when combined with the French 'rr' (neither of course strictly vowels, but compound sounds) forms the basis of a controlled 'flutter' for use in such works as Alban Berg's '*Vier Stücke*' for clarinet and piano – an effect so very similar to the controlled violin tremolo that it opens up a new world of possible use. There is a great deal of progress yet to be made in this field.

These are just a few pointers on the way to be followed – and the way is obvious. The player of the future has the whole world as his stage, and will be unwise to regard himself as having a musical nationality. There is already a sign that younger players are rising to this challenge, breaking down the hard-and-fast barriers of nation and race, and approximating in their views; but there is a danger in this, the danger of a dull uniformity when one sound predominates and much that is good is lost in the process. They must now go further still, having at their disposal the sounds now typical of the French, the German, the English, the American schools of playing – a whole palette of tone-colours from which to choose. They must then go on and find newer sounds as yet unheard and unthought of. The number of sounds obtainable from a modern clarinet is incredible. It will be greater still in the future.

National schools

Meanwhile, a survey of the present wide differences between national schools of playing is illuminating, giving us as it does the whole palette of clarinet tone from which to choose.

The French School. This, not surprisingly, employs the Klosé or Boehm system clarinet, and usually of French manufacture of a small bore about .578in. to .583in. diameter. This, in combination with a mouthpiece of shallow capacity to give immediacy and brightness, of a fairly close facing and shortish 'lay', requires only the addition of a thin reed to produce an instrument of hair-trigger sensitivity and incredibly facile response. Such a set-up is responsible for the fact that, compared with any other institution, the Conservatoire in Paris has inspired or commissioned many more works of a florid, brilliant nature than any other. Some of these are of little musical value. Others, like Debussy's '*Rhapsodie*', are important additions to the repertoire and bring to the listener a new aspect of instrumental timbre which is at once light and superbly expressive. This is the strength of the French school, the virtue to be selected and retained by the player of the future. There is certainly no other school of playing which can claim to have a facility greater than the vast bulk of French players, nor a system of training more perfectly adapted to the attainment of this ideal. If this school has a weakness, it is the invariability of the sound produced; until fairly recently there were very few exceptions to the regular régime which produced players all of the same pattern. Happily there is now a more forward-looking attitude.

The German School. At present, the mode of playing in Germany is at the opposite extreme from that in France. The two schools are much farther apart than the contrast in the two most frequently used instruments (detailed in Chapter 1) would explain. None the less, instrumental difference unquestionably plays its part in this divergence. The differences of fingering can be discounted, since there is relatively little advantage in either, especially since the most modern forms of both the Klosé and the Müller patterns adopt additional keys to correct the 'forked' notes, which used to be the weakness of both systems. The question of bore is another matter and a more important difference; it is bigger, usually, in German instruments – in extreme cases, as much as fifteen thousandths of an inch bigger. The parallel part of it is also considerably longer. This results in an instrument of very much greater resistance than the typical French clarinet. The latter starts to increase in diameter fairly sharply from just below the third finger hole in the lower joint, a process known as 'broaching', so that by the time it reaches the bell of the instrument it may be more than 50 per cent broader than it was at the top. The German clarinet retains its slightly larger diameter until after it has entered the bell, when the sound is vented by an uncovered tone-hole some $\frac{1}{3}$in. in diameter (before the bell starts to flare for the remainder of its length).

Possibly the greatest factor in the difference between German and French clarinet playing is due to the great resistance set up by the type of reed and mouthpiece used. German reeds are hand-made and tailored to the mouthpiece, so that each player's set-up is in its way unique. Invariably the reed is heavy and the facing not only close but very long; this accommodates a reed which is so stiff that it would produce no sound at all if used in conjunction with a typical French mouthpiece. Even on the mouthpiece for which it has been specially made it usually has a formidable resistance, but one can never fail to admire the way in which this is overcome by the best German players, any more than one can cease to marvel at the way in which they dispense with the metal ligature and tie the reed on with a simple wrapping of cord – an operation which is as much a part of their very thorough training as is the making by hand of their reeds.

The effect of this extremely resistant set-up is to produce a clarinet tone of very considerable purity; a compact sound which can sustain a very beautiful *legato*. To players used to overcoming much less resistance it is astonishing how the best German players can support long phrases and achieve such a wide range of dynamics – from a robust *ff* they can *diminuendo* to a *pp* which is the inspiration of the echo-tone many of their composers are so fond of using. It is a gentle, edgeless sound which only at very close quarters has anything of a wind-hiss audible in it.

Articulation of the heavy reed is both more difficult and less satisfactory because its motion is obviously more difficult to arrest and re-start, and in fact takes fractionally more time than the thinner French reed. Nor can it easily provide the fascinating 'plop' which is caused by the sudden closure of a thinner reed causing an area of negative pressure – a partial vacuum in fact – in the tube. This explosive staccato is one of the finest effects obtainable on the clarinet and its loss is quite a serious one. At the same time it must be said that German players are very rarely guilty of 'quackiness' in their attack – the best of them certainly never so. The sheer stability of the sound generator means that it can be attacked powerfully without answering back. The hair-trigger, tightrope-walking act which is a feature of some French instruments is never a necessity with the Germans, making for playing of a broader, more sweeping style; and light staccato is certainly perfectly obtainable. The whole background is one of great expressiveness and vocal style in the case of their finest players. Only among the less accomplished is there a tendency to produce a slightly hollow 'cuckoo' sound, owing to the thick reed damping out the upper partials; certainly the tone has a less interesting harmonic spectrum than the French, simply taken as an isolated sound. It is what is *done* with the tone which gives it its interest. It can, as one critic has said, be 'the clarinet-cuckoo of the *Wiener Wald* – a pleasant bucolic sound, but scarcely richer in colour than that of the ocarina'. It can also be the gloriously rich tone, as produced by a Mühlfeld, which inspired Brahms to write some of his very great masterpieces – The Quintet, The Trio with cello and piano, and the Sonatas.

Certainly the finest German players are not only highly technically accomplished, but superbly and traditionally trained to become highly artistic performers. One basic difficulty they have to overcome in this training is the business of intonation-correction. With a moderate reed it is possible – easy, in fact – to modify the pitch of a note at the very moment it is played, by embouchure control. With the heavy German reed this is almost impossible, and it is really remarkable that so many of this school of players can play well in tune. This is often achieved by finger-corrections, cross-fingering and half-holing. In addition, the modern German clarinet is fitted with a mass of gadgets aimed at correcting the acoustic lay-out – little vent-holes, extra keys covering alternative finger-holes and the like. It still leaves something to be desired, so that even the best German players may be caught out by adverse conditions of pitch.

Other Schools. Many authorities suggest that in fact the French and German schools of clarinet-playing are the only ones, and that all others are simply off-shoots. William Stubbins is quite emphatic on this point, and is at pains to point out that there is no such thing as an 'English' school of clarinet playing. One must agree – the English, American, Italian and Russian styles of playing are all different, but they can be said to stem from one or other of the two main sub-divisions or 'schools', French or German. They are the 'middle of the road' styles. In this mid-position, however, there are now several examples of original style and artistic approach which can make some claim to independence. Perhaps the most interesting feature of all of them is that, even though they take great account of German methods and obviously have great respect for them, without exception they have now given up the Müller-type clarinet in favour of the Klosé. This is true now even in the USSR, which was an isolated example of the reverse until the late 1960s. It is also true in England, in spite of the fact that some of the best young players are now interested in the German sound and are playing instruments from that country. One has yet to see one of them playing anything but what the German makers call the 'Reform Boehm' clarinet – an interesting hybrid which includes all Klosé's finger-patterns with some of the acoustic features of the German system, though usually with a mouthpiece which owes a lot to French design. This is a valid departure from the tradition of either side, and is in fact an instrument capable of the sort of catholicity of approach which players of the future, must, logically, have as their aim. It is probably true that this model of instrument, certainly as much or more than any other, is capable of producing the several different varieties of tone which will be demanded of the next generation of accomplished clarinettists.

The Italian school of playing, quite naturally founded upon an operatic tradition, is an interesting mixture of the French and German approach. As might be expected, it has a marked 'vocal' quality, an open and smooth, if often fairly small, sound, and has been responsible through the years for the inspiration of some truly fine clarinet solos. A feature of Italian clarinet playing is the widespread use of crystal mouthpieces on Boehm system clarinets. The facings on these are fairly close, but by no means as close as the French, and this produces an even sound without much 'edge' which is perfect for the sort of conditions one usually meets in an opera-pit. It has certain limitations of carrying-power in the larger world of the concert-hall, but the best Italian players in the symphonic field are masterly in style and very fully equipped technically.

Leaving Europe, the next important school of clarinet-playing is in the USA, where there now seems to be a definite crystallisation of a style, following half a century of divergences owing to the importations from French, German, and Italian sources of their most important players. For a long time there were pockets of players of each nationality sticking fairly rigidly to the styles of this or that important professor. Now, on each successive visit, one is conscious of a levelling out of the differences of style, and in fact of a uniformity of approach which is nothing short of startling in a nation so numerous and so very wide-spread in a geographical sense. Any teacher who has a succession of pupils from different parts of the USA can testify to this uniformity. Somehow, the miracle of modern communications has brought them all together in a remarkable way. They all seem to make the same very pleasant and forthright sound by the same method. They play the same type and make of clarinet and mouthpiece – always French. The angle of attack of the embouchure, and of the arms and wrists in holding the clarinet, is always the same, and in fact the general result is without doubt extremely thoughtful and competent.

If the English school of clarinet playing has a feature, it is that in fact it has no recognisable set pattern to which all are expected to conform. There may not be as many styles as there are players – that is an exaggeration – but certainly there are several very strongly constrasted styles of playing, all excellent in their way, from the most delicate French sound to the most robust German, as well as at least two types of sound which can now be said to be indigenous to only Britain itself. Both of these contain an element of vibrato. The first is a firm round sound with a gently vocalised vibrato – very effective indeed when not overdone, and smooth and even when no vibrato is employed. The second is a hollow 'edgy' and 'spread' sound, usually with an unvocalised lip-vibrato; a copy of the first type which has usually gone wrong because the mouthpiece employed is of the wrong type. A sad sound, and one which it is to be hoped will soon pass. It is, in fact, produced by a fairly small proportion of players. The others play not only with style and beauty of sound, but with a technical elegance which would have been unthinkable in any but the greatest artists of a bygone age.

Fundamentals of tone production

Undeniably, a knowledge of the facts given in Chapter 3 concerning the acoustic phenomena of the clarinet helps tremendously in obtaining an excellent sound from the instrument. Just as certainly it is obvious that this knowledge is not *essential* – for there have always been players of unique natural gifts who have never needed to give a thought to the scientific aspect of playing. These happy people can and do produce a fine tone from the clarinet – usually any clarinet – because they have the 'feel' of it in their mouths, a sort of natural 'tasting' of the sound as it is produced, a bringing together of the factors necessary for success in this most important branch of clarinet technique. For the rest of us, however, it is necessary to analyse what in fact is going on as we play.

The first factor, surely, is a correct mental image of the exact sound it is wished to produce. Given this it is possible to experiment in all sorts of ways, constantly rejecting the results as they fall short of this image, constantly keeping that shining sound in mind and refusing to settle for anything less perfect. The ideal will of course never be achieved, but each step taken in this way will be one in the right direction.

Next, the mental image of the moving air-column employed must be constantly borne in mind. Too often the clarinet is regarded as an instrument to blow down, instead of a tube which contains a moving air-column which requires constantly varied and adjusted support from the diaphragm. The correct image is of one continuous air-column starting at the diaphragm, passing through the thoracic cavities, and resonated in the chamber of the mouth as it sets the reed in motion, after which it *continues* inside the clarinet and ends slightly beyond the bell-end or above the lowest tone-hole in operation. The whole column moves, volumetrically, at the same rate, and the constant piston-action of the diaphragm is what sets it in motion and supports this motion once it has been started. There is only one point of resistance in this system of movement – the aperture between the reed and mouthpiece, varied by the pressure of the embouchure. The rest of it must remain smooth and continuous. Many players describe the phenomenon of an 'open throat' to explain this – an odd description, since there is in fact no muscular action which can bring about this opening; but the feeling of this should be present, because any constriction at the back of the tongue causes uneven support of the column and can result in the ugly sound of a pressure-vibrato – the 'nanny-goat' sound of which some players of the past, and even a few of the present, have been guilty.

The next factor in tone-production which is worthy of attention is what happens in the mouth. There is no doubt that the texture as well as the size of the chamber surrounding the generator (i.e. the moving reed and mouthpiece 'beak') has an important bearing upon the sort of sound produced. If a clear, round sound is desired, the muscular texture of the whole mouth should be firm. Any puffing out of the cheeks when playing is obviously undesirable and the tongue should be drawn back and kept slightly 'clenched'. This seems to have the effect of bouncing the air between the tongue and the hard palate of the mouth above it, in just the way it will vibrate between the reed and the palate of the mouthpiece a split-second later – and there is something between the inter-relationship of these two events which puts them together under the control of the player.

Next, the size of the cavity is to some extent also under the player's control; only to a certain extent, because inevitably it is governed by the natural size of his mouth, particularly from cheek to cheek. So far as 'opening' is concerned there is great possibility of adjustment. It will be found that the resonation on different vowel sounds in fact opens or shuts the mouth involuntarily. 'Ee' is the closest, and to be avoided except for the special effect of shrillness it engenders. 'Oh', 'Ah' and 'Aw' are the remaining degrees of openess, and should be experimented with until the best sound is obtained. 'Aw' is usually found to offer less resistance to the moving air-column, as well as giving maximum resonance. But a lot depends upon the size of the mouth, and it is for each player to find his own answer to this problem.

The mechanics of tone production have already been dealt with in Chapter 3, in the section on analysis of the acoustics of the clarinet. What matters to the player is that he can hear, can feel, and can control the production of clarinet tone he is producing. A simple increase in pressure by the additional thrust of the diaphragm (not by simply blowing harder) and the volume of tone increases. This is an instant for careful listening, because the sound can easily be allowed to alter in character as it increases in volume from *p* to *mf*, and from *f* to *ff*. There are several sorts of clarinet tone available and easy to obtain if thought and care are applied; but mere increase in the dynamic level of sound must not be allowed to be the reason for one of these suddenly becoming another. A *crescendo* should begin and end with the same voice singing it, not start with an ocarina and end with what sounds like a trombone.

Here there are at any rate two factors to consider. First, it must be remembered that the density of the reed has an important bearing upon the range of dynamics it will take without distortion. A reed that is too thin will be only slightly 'buzzy' in *pp*, more so in *p*, rather harsh in *mf*, and unbearable in *ff*. A very thick, dense reed will have only a hoarse whisper in *pp*, be good in *f*, and can be magnificent in *ff* if the player has the lung power and lip strength to support it. Somewhere between these extremes there is a reed upon which the player may rely to get only a slightly hairy *pp*, a good *p*, and equally fine *f* and *ff* response. This must be the one chosen.

The next factor to consider is the effect of lip pressure upon control of sound-alteration with increased dynamic level. Given a fairly firm reed, increase from *mf* to *ff* will not produce a flattening of the pitch as it does with a thin reed. It will, however, tend to harshness in *ff* if embouchure pressure is maintained at the same level as that used in *mf*. It is too tight, and is causing the trapped reed to protest that it is being held too close to the 'lay' of the mouthpiece for its comfort at that high dynamic level. So the pressure must be gently relaxed, allowing a greater volume of air to pass into the instrument without overloading the reed. Care is needed of course to make sure that the bounds of intonation control are not crossed when this is done; the amount of muscular relaxation in question is quite a small one, and must never be big enough to lower the pitch of the note. A possible third factor in sound-sustaining and pitch-retaining is the amount of the mouthpiece taken into the mouth. Generally speaking it is best to take the maximum 'bite' possible without loss of control and consequent squeaks. This has the effect of opening the mouth, so that the 'aw' vowel is the one which would result in speech. Given a balance between these factors, tone-production on the clarinet needs the addition of only one thing – careful listening on the part of the player, and the ability also to hear 'at a distance'. It is of no use to produce a beautiful sound which is heard only a few feet away. The player must try to imagine what a distant audience will hear – certainly a smoother sound than he himself is hearing, and one in which the hiss of the reed has been filtered out, with the slightly hoarse sound of the 'throat' notes gently masked by distance so that they blend with the better notes below and above. Incidentally, the player must learn to modify to rooms of varied acoustic quality so that he makes the best of what is often a very bad job. The clarinet, more than almost any instrument, suffers from a lack of sonority in its acoustic surrounding atmosphere. Certainly the floor one plays over should be bare. Thick carpets are anathema to the instrument. But given bad acoustics, the only thing to do is to use the smoothest reed which can be found – firm but not hard – and above all, resist all temptation to *force* the sound.

There are many people who are prepared to insist that the angle of the arms and wrists in playing the clarinet, combined with the angle of the head, should be such that the instrument is as close to the vertical as possible. The reason for this is by no means clear, because there are certainly many fine players who hold the clarinet at almost 45 degrees to the vertical plane. The real truth is that the instrument responds best when the player is comfortable, so that in fact the angle may well be anything at all, and varied very much from one individual to another. It is worth experimenting with various angles, when usually it will be found that the one adopted naturally already will be the final choice, as it is the obviously comfortable one. One interesting thing to note here is that most people find that if they hold the head back and pull the wrists down, bringing the clarinet nearer to the vertical, the pitch can be kept down more easily in moments of sharpness or if playing with a flat piano – this is particularly noticeable in quiet chalumeau passages.

Transposition

Next it is worth considering the vexed question of *transposition*; not the reasons for the clarinet being a transposing instrument, which we looked at in Chapter 3, but the question of transposition involved in playing parts for clarinet in C on the B flat clarinet, as well as on the A; and parts for clarinet in A on the B flat clarinet. These are the most common and useful forms of transposition and can be learnt very quickly. As a rough guide, the following facts should be learnt:

(a) B flat clarinet to play C clarinet part. Add two sharps to the key signature, or drop two flats. Play the note next above that written. Exceptions: B natural becomes C sharp, E becomes F sharp, B flat becomes C natural and E flat becomes F.

(b) A clarinet to play C clarinet part. Add three flats to the key signature, or drop three sharps. Play as for bass clef, but two octaves higher, so that

Incidentally, the use of the A clarinet to play C clarinet parts is by no means common enough. Beethoven's Fourth Piano Concerto and his Violin Concerto (slow movement) are fine examples of advantage to be gained in this way. The effect is infinitely more pleasant, smooth and expressive.

(c) B flat clarinet to play A part. Simply play the part with a drop of a semi-tone in mind. Add flats to all notes except sharps, which become naturals. Remember that F becomes E natural, and C becomes B natural. This transposition is complicated at first, but becomes easy very quickly.

There are many works in which the wise player chooses to play on the instrument not chosen by the composer. There can be no doubt that what the composer wants is a facile and smooth performance, yet often he is without the necessary technical know-how to make sure of this by writing it for the appropriate clarinet. This is by no means an easy facet of musical knowledge to acquire, because it is not merely a question of key-signatures; it is essential to know the actual fingering involved, as well as the effect upon the articulation of the 'breaks' of the clarinet. So there should be no doubt in a player's mind as to his freedom to choose how he obtains the notes required by the composer; he should certainly use the one he finds easiest. In this case the easy way is undoubtedly the right way, because it does produce the right result.

Phrase markings

There is also the vexed question of how to interpret the phrase-markings a composer uses. Practical experience of playing works under the composer's directions tends to lead one to suspect that what they want may not be very similar to what one can see in the part. Nor are composers to blame for this altogether, because in fact much of their work may be edited after it leaves them, or it may in any case be phrased subconsciously in the manner of a string-melody, to accommodate bowing and other aspects of string technique. Leaving aside the works of such composers as Mozart, who left the phrase-markings very much to the player in his major solo works, so that what one now sees may be anyone's idea of phrasing, let us take a look at another famous Brahms phrase, the start of his E flat Sonata:

That is how the early editions of the work phrase it, so it is presumably as Brahms wrote it. It is also as it is played, nine times out of ten. But – did he really mean it to be cut up into little bits like this? A few passes with a phanton bow-arm will convince even a non-violinist that probably bowing comfort was in Brahms's mind as he wrote this phrase, even though the sound he had in mind was that of Mühlfeld's clarinet. If you ask a good violinist to play it, although he will *bow* it as phrased, he will do his very best *not* to make it sound fragmented. He will in fact just naturally try to make the whole series of phrases as *legato* as possible, with tiny touches of pressure as the bow changes occur. The same should be our aim as clarinettists. The opening of this sonata should in fact be re-phrased something like this

with just a gentle brush of the tongue at each of the points marked, or no sort of tongue-action at all, if it is felt that this is more natural.

Given this tiny example as a case in point, it is worth re-examining much of our solo activity with this sort of critical eye. In many cases the black and white phrases of the copy are good enough, and need not be altered. In others there will be great benefit in looking a little further, in trying to see behind the notes to the mind of the composer – not to be sensational in one's alteration of his intentions, but rather to be more true to his feelings. There is nothing more sickening than to hear a whole orchestra playing one single long note in a series of sequences which should obviously all be short – there are examples in both Beethoven's Violin Concerto and his Seventh Symphony – just because some editor hadn't the courage to print a note with a tail which Beethoven had obviously missed off. To anyone who has seen a Beethoven manuscript, this is a travesty, because the tortured scrawl of that impulsive genius obviously needed sensitive and understanding interpretation by those who had to get it into shape. Happily, for the most part, it got that. It is, of course, far from easy to know where to draw the line in this business of taking liberties with a composer's work. Living composers are usually most approachable in this matter, and are rarely dogmatic if there is a good reason for suggesting a change of phrasing.

The Clarinet
Tongueing

All phrasing is a question of use of the tongue. As a clarinettist one has to realise that the tongue is by no means a simple physical organ whose function is to start and stop the sound of the instrument. The real trouble is that the moment one really analyses what the tongue is doing, it seems to be doing something else altogether. Take the case of the first instruction in almost every clarinet-tutor or instruction book. 'Place the tongue against the reed, and as you blow, remove it so that the tone can start. Then replace it and stop the sound, by touching the reed as it vibrates.' One can hardly quibble at this, which is scientifically exactly what happens – until one tries to do it. Then, the removal of the tongue simply produces a loose 'tha' sound – precisely what one is trying to avoid as a clarinet attack. Psychologically, however scientifically inaccurate it may be, there is no doubt, that the sensation of a clarinet attack is an *impact* of the tongue upon the reed. In saying the word 'too' the tongue *starts* on the roof of the mouth. Similarly, it starts on the reed when trying to produce these six notes:

But in fact the feeling is that each of these notes has been started by *striking* the reed with the tongue, and then holding it back, away from the reed, and resonating the note produced within the mouth as one would do in speech or singing a vowel sound 'oo', 'ah', 'aw' or whatever is the sound of one's choice. So – the best advice is to *strike* the reed with the tongue.

Next, one may well ask – what part of the tongue, on what part of the reed? This is a question which is rarely dealt with in any sort of detail, probably because there would seem to be a fair number of methods in use, many of which appear to produce a reasonable *staccato* attack, and some of which in addition can vary the strength of impact, and so provide a more flexible and musically useful note-starting mechanical function. This is inevitable, since the angle at which the clarinet is held, and consequently the angle of approach of the tongue, varies greatly from player to player. Obviously, if the clarinet is held in a near vertical attitude, and the head is maintained at its normal position – to read music, say, while retaining peripheral vision of a distant conductor above the part – the only possible angle of attack is at an angle of almost 90 degrees to the blade of the reed. In other words, the tongue is pushing the reed towards the facing of the mouthpiece, and when it has pushed hard enough, the reed will come to rest against this, and the sound will stop until the tongue is removed. This obviously takes time. The amount of time will vary according to the distance from the tip of the reed of the point of impact of the tongue, but in any case, at this angle, one is at the mercy of this time-delay factor, which must make this method of tongueing more sluggish than it need be. A further factor to be considered in this respect is the thickness of the blade of the reed. A thin reed will respond more quickly to such an impact than will a thick one – in fact a really dense reed will simply not respond at all. So this angle of attack must confine its usefulness to the soft-reed school of playing, and this brings further problems in its wake; one of these is that if a soft and thin reed is attacked with a firm tongue it tends to 'quack' because it bends as it travels to the mouthpiece facing, and arrives there in various stages as a result. In the *altissimo* register this sort of attack is little short of disastrous.

Where the angle of the instrument is less vertical, the conditions in the mouth are very different, and it is possible to approach the reed at a much more acute angle. From a purely mechanical point of view, this is obviously less efficient – a force applied at right-angles is certainly more effective so far as simple closure is concerned, and will obviously take a shorter time to silence the instrument, as a result. But here another factor is introduced, when the angle is reduced from 90 degrees to about 45 degrees – the tongue, being of muscular tissue, is resilient and flexible, with the result that while part of it is engaged in pushing the reed towards the mouthpiece facing, another part, slightly further from its tip, is folding itself across the tip of the reed and the narrow slot which is the sole entry of the air into the mouthpiece. It is this second part of the tongue which really produces the attack in this method of tongueing, because it instantly arrests the movement of the reed, and the moment this happens the sound is stopped and the tip of the reed collapses on to the facing until the tongue is removed from it. This method can be used with a much thicker reed than can be tolerated with the first system of tongueing, so that a much richer variety of attack can be obtained.

Taken to its logical conclusion, this would indicate that the best attack upon a reed is not upon the reed itself, but upon the slot which separates it from the mouthpiece facing. Certainly this method is used by a great number of excellent players whose *staccato* is one of their best features; but it is not without its difficulties. To start with, the method cannot be used easily by a player with a naturally long tongue. He finds that to use it, he has to coil his tongue back in his mouth, snake-like, and in that tense position he has less control over it than he can command in its more relaxed 'forward' position.

Again, even with a shorter tongue, the 'clearance' between it and the tip of the reed is much less than the similar clearance from the blade in the 'vertical' method. This is a good thing in that it makes for more immediacy of attack, but it also requires more exact control, which takes time to acquire.

Whichever method is used, there seems to be little doubt that the part of the tongue to use is at the tip. Even in attacking the 'slot' the soft middle of the tongue gives a sloppy, soggy effect, in strong contrast with the more crisp attack of the tip. So the dictum must be, when possible, 'the tip of the tongue on the tip of the reed', but as usual there is a 'but' in this. The proviso this time arises from the question: 'But what do you mean by a *tongue?*' This query may at first seem to be a frivolous trouble-maker dragged in to cloud an issue which is crystal clear as stated. However, since the tongue is a muscle, and under conscious control, it can exist in many states of tension and relaxation. A moment's thought upon its incredible gymnastics during normal speech gives one an insight into its possibilities when using it to attack the clarinet reed. The tongue is so strong that it can be 'clenched' like a fist or a biceps muscle. Do this between the teeth of a half-open mouth and you will find that it resists most strongly the pressure of a finger which tries to push it back into the mouth. Relax the tongue and the finger wins instantly. It is this tension which must be used to transform the tongue into a rubbery hammer to strike the reed – and it must be achieved, not between the teeth, but much further back in the mouth, behind the point to which the reed and mouthpiece tip intrude. This requires concentration, and must be practised with the mouthpiece in the mouth. A conscious 'clenching' at this point is the real answer to a ready tongue, and this is a function of clarinet playing which is rarely appreciated. It is also a function which makes *staccato*, particularly fast *staccato*, more difficult on the clarinet than it is on the flute, the oboe, the trumpet or the recorder. All these instruments have little or nothing actually in the mouth, leaving the tongue in its 'forward' position and free to operate without the back-coiling necessary in the case of the clarinet. In fact a clarinettist is usually astonished at his skill when he tackles *staccato* on one of these instruments; suddenly the main obstacle to his production has been removed. This is a sad facet of clarinet-playing but one which cannot be removed. One simply has to live with it and, by listening to the other instruments, try to capture the best aspects of their *staccato*. The flute has an admirable light and incredibly swift attack, which the clarinet cannot easily emulate. The oboe by virtue of its tiny reed-aperture can produce a superb 'explosive' *staccato* – and this is an object lesson in that the only possible attack here is at the slot; emulate this, and it is possible to bring off that simplest and most difficult little interjection, in Beethoven's Fifth Symphony, without too much loss of face:

And here it should be said that, in spite of all this, when the obvious difficulties are overcome the clarinet has in fact something to offer in *staccato* effect which the other instruments cannot follow. It can echo the others in their chosen fields at least as well as they can each other; but no other instrument can produce the characteristic solid, 'meaty' and full-blooded effect that Mozart demands – and gets – from the clarinet in this variation from his great Quintet:

To be able to present such a passage as this with pride to any audience is worth a great deal of care and thought in the preparation of the right sort of clarinet *staccato*. The aim must be to have each note entirely separate from the rest, and to have it as a perfect note with a clean start and finish, without throat noises, tongue-slopping-sounds, or wet 'soggy' tongue noises. Each note should in fact be a gentle explosion, and its end should be so abrupt that one can sense the temporary vacuum which exists in the tube of the clarinet as the tongue cuts off the supply of air to the column in vibration inside the tube of the clarinet.

There are, of course, many passages which require a *staccato* entirely different from this Mozart variation. There is an excellent example in the last movement of Brahms's great Clarinet Quintet. Notice how Brahms does not leave the notes unadorned, but adds both dots and overall slurs to them. This double marking indicates the sort of note the French describe as *louré* – that is to say 'weighted'; the very name suggests the best method of approach to this sort of attack. The tongue, instead of being clenched and active, must be relaxed and lazy in its action. This is a sort of 'snowball' staccato where each note has a soft start and finish but a full sound for the rest of its duration:

This effect can be varied with considerable benefit by attacking the reed with the relaxed tongue either at the tip or further down the blade – say almost $\frac{1}{4}$in. from the tip. Obviously the tip-attack gives a more pronounced separation, the blade-attack a much more diffused effect.

These two types of attack are the extremes, and between them lies a world of gradation which it is necessary to explore. The degrees of attack are almost limitless, and all of them have a use in music-making. It is the job of the artist to differentiate and to be prepared at any time to use the gradation which is correct for the music he is playing as well as for the acoustic surroundings in which he finds himself.

The perfect legato

The question of attack usually leads one to think about degrees of *staccato* and their appropriate application. The subtle business of production of a perfect *legato* is, however, closely allied to this question, because it is a matter of having no attack at all – of avoiding it like the plague and making sure it does not intrude where it is not required. To be successful in obtaining this perfect legato, the player must overcome the inequalities of pressure between each note and the next, and must equalise them all in the progression from one to the other. In Chapter 3 we have considered these pressure areas and how to build up the weak ones so that they produce sounds of equal intensity and brightness. In solo legato playing all this must be instinctive or sub-conscious, and another factor must be taken into account. To achieve this smooth progress from one note to another – particularly another in a different register – it is essential to have in one's mind the image of the sound of the next note to be played, as well as to know the sort of pressure best applied to obtain the note. *Legato* is the art of *preparing* – of making sure the next note, be it a dull throat B flat or a bright clarinet register A, is given its correct support and projection. It must sound as if it comes from a similar note and goes to another similar one, smoothly and evenly, if true legato is to be achieved. Even when the interval to the second note is a wide one, a gentle push from the diaphragm is usually sufficient to overcome the difference of pressure between the two notes and so produce a fine *legato*. This is a factor worthy of careful attention, because it is the vocal 'heart' of the clarinet and has been the inspiration of all the great clarinet solos over the years it has been in general use. Another of these solos may be useful in indicating the problems of *legato* and how to solve them.

Here is part of Verdi's opera 'La Forza del Destino' – the great clarinet solo from the second act, which is so vital to the opera that it holds up the whole action for over two minutes. It is nothing less than a nostalgic aria, a most beautiful and florid tune which Verdi wrote for his much admired friend Cavallini. To appreciate the problems of playing this, the pressure indications are a guide. Dense and dull sounding notes are marked D, bright-sounding notes, B, weak and windy ones W.

See opposite.

All that remains is to equalise these; after that it is merely a question of keeping the whole solo in tune, obtaining the longest and best span of phrase, and of course adding a meaningful range of dynamic levels. No small feat; but finally the approach does become instinctive instead of studied, and the final touch is added when the capacity is developed to actually lead the conductor in the *nuances* of the solo, while tactfully appearing to follow him . . . This *can* be done, and it is a great conductor who can at such a moment add just a touch of his own which inspires the player to higher feats of expression than he had thought possible.

171

Six
Teaching the Clarinet

The second half of this century has produced a steady stream of young people who have a solid technique of playing the clarinet. There are good reasons for this. First is the fact that the mass-media have made the approach to the instrument more evident; the finest players can now be studied at close quarters. Then there is the fact that the world of education has now awakened to the fact that schools can be places of cultural interest as well as places of intense 'cramming' for public examinations; instrumental education is now often paid for by the State, and the fruits of this wise policy are all around us. Finally, the quality of teaching has improved tremendously; fine artists, who, a generation ago, would have been rewarded by a key post in an orchestra or as a chamber musician, now find that teaching has its own rewards, and give their skills to its service.

Theirs is a vital occupation. They teach what are described as the 'elementary stages' in wood-wind playing – a title which might suggest perhaps something simple and quick, something of scant importance and small effect. Nothing could be further from the truth. Given the correct foundation, the teacher at an advanced level has little to do but follow the student in his chosen path, correcting any faults he may develop and showing him the way to future success. Without these foundations there is no real hope of this success. It can often be too late to attempt to correct a habit ingrained with the very first experience of playing. It is easy to teach additional skills. How to attempt to instill the very first of these skills is a rare gift, and one which must be respected, fostered and emulated.

Laying the foundations

Anyone who wishes to learn from the work of these excellent new teachers must bear in mind some salient facts about the clarinet, and must bring them to his work with beginners.

The first and simplest of these facts is that there is no better teaching plan for the clarinet than that laid down by the history of the instrument. The clarinet started life as a chalumeau. The clarinettist must, even today, start life as a player of the chalumeau, and only the chalumeau. This register of the clarinet (the bottom twelve notes) is still an instrument in itself – a simple instrument, rewarding to play, and entirely innocent of the irregularities and wayward tendencies of the clarinet as described in Chapter 3.

The acoustics of the chalumeau register and of the clarinet are simple enough, and the key-arrangement sufficiently elementary for it to be mastered in a few weeks by an intelligent person. There is a lot of trouble to come later as a clarinettist; but in the early stages of the chalumeau – all is logical, predictable, and easy.

Learning the chalumeau: blowing. Obviously, the first thing to teach is how to blow the instrument. The very word 'blow' raises the eyebrows of some teachers, who know well enough that in fact the process is one of support for the air-column, and the 'blowing' is a misnomer. The beginner on the clarinet will never believe this. The very theory is a hindrance and a frustration to him. He wants to blow, and blow he will. So he must be presented with conditions of reed, mouthpiece and instrument which will ensure that he is in fact supporting the column and fulfilling all the correct necessary functions when he is sure he is simply blowing. These conditions are supplied by a fairly soft reed, a reasonably close mouthpiece facing and a perfectly padded clarinet. (The reed must not buzz; if it does, it is too thin and produces the sort of tone which must be avoided from the very start.) Given these conditions, the new player need not really blow, and finds instead that simple controlled exhalation produces the note he wants; but he still thinks he is blowing, and may think so for the rest of his life.

Fingering with the left hand. The note the beginner needs as a start is the 'open' G, and he can produce this with a reasonable sound quite easily if he is not told what to do with his tongue but simply allowed to 'blow'. He can then, with the careful addition of the fingers of the left hand, soon master such simple progressions as:

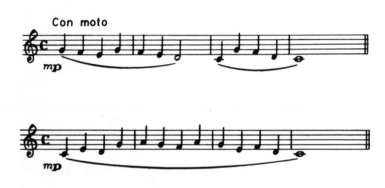

The slurs require special attention, and the attack of the first note is crucial. It is simply produced by breathing out and leaning the breath against the resistance of the reed.

It must be emphasised that these early exercises in the chalumeau register should involve the left hand only, and should be legato at all times. To ignore this is to involve the player in problems he is not yet ready to deal with. All too often one reads, at the start of a tutor, the instruction to place the tongue on the reed and withdraw it as the breath starts the note. This is almost impossible to do, even for an expert player, without producing an ugly 'quack' or a soggy, dull note. The theory is correct, the science provable. But it just doesn't work, because it doesn't feel like that. It is a complicated process, true in essence but false in feeling. In any case articulation is much better left until later. The best plan is to let the beginner feel the note build up as he increases the pressure in the tube of the clarinet. He need not be told this – only that the best way to get the first note is to say 'hoo-oo' and that he needs to do nothing but continue the 'oo' and move the correct finger to get the others. By simply doing this he can become a player of the chalumeau, or at least the upper part of it, in an hour or two. He can play it smoothly, too, because he is on safe and easy ground.

Adding the right-hand fingerings. Soon the pupil will want to complete the instrument by using his right hand, and this can easily be done one note at a time, as in these examples.

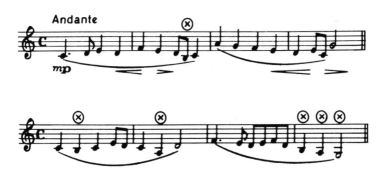

There is no need at this stage for any book from which to work, though there are one or two good ones which cover this ground. It is simple for the teacher to scribble out a few examples like those above. It is also impressive for the pupil, and restful for the teacher, to have different tunes played by various players. Monotony is fatal at all stages of learning. Hurrying at this point is also a mistake. The co-ordination between the two hands is the first really difficult thing a pupil has to tackle, and initially it must be expected that the moment the right hand moves it will disengage one or more fingers of the left from their holes – with sad results. A by-product of this is usually an almost spasmic tension of the left hand. At this stage the only thing to do is to stop, again learn the relaxed movement of the left hand and try the right hand once more.

Correct finger positions. This is the time to point out the correct relaxed position of the fingers, poised above the holes and keys, slightly bent and with relaxed wrists, avoiding any sort of tension or strain. There are some excellent pictures of this in many tutors. (See fig. **48**.)

When the two hands have been successfully co-ordinated the whole range of the chalumeau is available, and this is a flexible and melodically satisfying medium, since it embraces all the notes from bottom E natural to the 'throat' B flat – an octave and six semi-tones. At this point, before the exploration of the overblown 'clarinet' register, it is wise to extend the ability to play in, at any rate, three different key signatures – C, G and F. This involves only one change of fingering in each hand, and the use of the speaker-key as the upper B flat. There is no need yet to introduce this speaker-key as a means of extending the compass (its real function). The embouchure is usually not yet sufficiently mature for this, and some weeks of practice may be necessary to make it so. There is plenty to do meanwhile, because using the chalumeau register alone one can learn a lot about playing the clarinet. At first, the whole emphasis should be upon legato melodies, later with fairly big leaps but in conjunct motion at first:

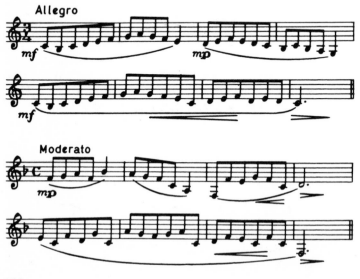

The chalumeau embouchure. The tone produced will usually be quite good, as this is an easy part of the instrument which requires scarcely any lip tension, but rather just a firm closure around reed and mouthpiece. Escape of air from the corners of the mouth is not serious at first, but should soon stop if attention is drawn to it.

Articulation: Tongueing. When a good legato has been obtained, articulation should be attempted. The best method of approach is certainly not the obvious one. The aim should not be to send single puffs of air down the tube of the clarinet by the method of tongue release mentioned above. This invariably results in a sloppy attack and poor tone, lacking crispness and clarity. The aim must be to take a single long note and cut it up into a series of short ones by attacking the reed with the tongue as near the tip as comfortably possible. This tongue movement happens while the note is being played – and while, incidentally, the air-pressure is being constantly maintained. It is of course true in scientific terms that the note starts as the tongue leaves the reed. In feeling and in effect it is produced by the actual impact of the tongue, so

that

The easiest note is again 'open' G, but the achievement as staccato is much simpler in the chalumeau than in other registers, so that the continuing use of that register alone is essential at this stage. It is probably best to limit the compass in this way until an exercise such as this can be accomplished with some style and ease:

Allegro molto

The overblown register

The exploration of the overblown register is now both possible and desirable. In practice, it is highly unlikely that this will be an entirely new experience, since any normally inquisitive person will surely have made attempts at it. It has, however, probably been tackled wrongly, and it must now be attempted in an orderly way, starting with the easiest twelfths to obtain. These are the G above chalumeau C and the A above D:

These should be 'thrown' continuously until the feel of the upper register is obtained and a sense of pitch developed. It is better not to move, as yet, to other intervals, as the flexibility of these two is a new experience. It is possible, even at this stage, to discover how the upper note can be sharpened or flattened by embouchure pressure alone. This is the essential difference between the registers, and the reason for the delay in the attempt to produce the upper twelfths. The upper register is much more variable, much less fixed; it needs more control and a greater awareness of support, pitch adjustment and tone control. It is in this register, right at the start, that the essence of good tone production is found. The beginner can feel it in his mouth, can 'taste' it, and influence the roundness and resonance of the sound by subtle variations in muscular tension of the cheeks, the position of the tongue, the position of the jaw and the many other variables of the embouchure. This is one of the great moments in learning to play the clarinet; it must not be hurried or passed over lightly. It is infact the start of clarinet, as opposed to chalumeau, playing. The other notes of the overblown register will be found to have separate characters of their own. Some are dull, like the D, others bright, like A; some tend to flatness (often the 'bell' B natural and the E natural).

This new register is a much more difficult instrument to learn to play than the chalumeau – but it has greater rewards, finer possibilities. It is, in fact, a clarinet; and contains all the mobility and expressive flexibility which makes the instrument great. It cannot be mastered in a couple of weeks, although the fingering is simple enough. The control of intonation, the balance of sound, and the equalization of tone are anything but simple. It should therefore, like the chalumeau before it, be practised alone and without interference at first from the other registers.

The teacher as a model
Next should come legato study as an imitation of the sound of the teacher, who can do more towards the production of good tone at this stage than at any other time. This aspect of study is dealt with at some length in Chapter 5, and the choice of resonance vowels and the actual aims must be the teacher's. He can try to explain what he aims at himself as he plays, but in fact his playing example is of crucial importance. He must play often and well, and act as a model for his student. It usually works; when it does not there is little hope for the student.

Simple tunes will be possible immediately, and echoed back and forth from teacher to pupil they quickly produce results. Two examples are shown on page 180.

This concentration upon the 'clarinet' register alone should be continued for possibly three weeks. There is little chance that the chalumeau will be forgotten in this time, and the muscular development which can be gained is startling. This is usually widest in a raising of the pitch, which is almost

always flat at the outset, to its correct level during this time. It is a great consolation that some of the finest melodies ever written lie completely within the compass of this register, and may be tackled, in all humility, not more than three months from the start of things (e.g. Mozart Adagio, page 181).

The introduction of expression. Here the question of expressive dynamics must be considered, and no teacher should be afraid to add them to works by the great masters to give the sort of effect he hopes to hear from his pupil.

Articulation in the clarinet register

So far it has been advisable, even necessary, to limit exercises to the use only of legato in the overblown register, even though articulation has been previously achieved in the chalumeau. There is a good reason for this: the use of the tongue is by no means as simple in the upper register, since the harmonic structure – the proportion of overtones in the sound and their reinforcement – is different, and is liable to be upset by the impact of the tongue, leading to 'quacks' and even squeaks. So staccato has to be approached with care. The essential advice here is to keep the embouchure firm, even at first rigid. The reason is two-fold. First, this tends to damp out the highest overtones – the ones which are in fact squeaks when unintentionally produced. Also, it prevents the clarinet from being actually pushed out of the mouth by the strong action of the tongue which is required. The movement may be fractional, but the loss of control caused by it is fatal. Given this firm and mature embouchure, the production of staccato notes is much the same as in the chalumeau register; but a larger oral cavity is necessary to resonate the notes, as they are much more dense. This is the reason for

tackling this particular problem so late. It is, frankly, difficult. Few but the finest clarinettists ever achieve a really perfect staccato in this register, particularly in *ppp*, which is why so many fail to satisfy Beethoven's demands in the Fifth Symphony for the tiny figure on page 182.

Most of these failures are due to having tackled this too early, with an immature embouchure, thus carrying over habits from the chalumeau which really do not apply. The time to master it is some weeks later, with such memorable phrases as:

This may seem to be over-cautious, but is in fact nothing of the sort. To be able to play such phrases as these within a few months of starting to learn the clarinet is fairly remarkable, even if only in isolation. The examples given are of course merely to illustrate the point to be gained for the pupil. There must be many more of them, similarly graded, either from established instruction books, and selected from these by the teacher as required, or better still invented by him.

Combining the registers

The next suggested stage is to renew acquaintance with the chalumeau, and alternate this with practice in the upper register – not combining the two at first, because separation makes clear the difference of support, control and resonation required for each.

Crossing the break. When this has become established for both the registers, and corrected carefully by the teacher, exercises combining the two registers should follow naturally and without any attention being called to that old bug-bear of clarinet technique – 'crossing the break'. This of course means the big jump from A natural to B natural, and obviously in the earliest examples of combination of the two registers it is best simply to avoid this:

The traditional way of learning to cross the break, that of playing the intervals A natural to B natural and B flat to B natural ad nauseam, should be avoided at all costs, as it is a saddening and frustrating task, which ensures that the student will have a deeply ingrained fear of these intervals. This problem can soon be solved as part of a general pattern, without undue emphasis, and failure to solve it can be treated as a source of fun. It is not a very serious matter, anyway, and probably will not trouble the student for long if he first meets it like this:

The Clarinet

The fingering aspect of the 'break'. At this point, and before leaving the important subject of the break in the registers, it is necessary to stress the fact that, here especially, adhering to the normal chart of clarinet fingerings is the worst possible method. To play A natural with the index finger of the left hand alone, as shown, and B natural with all the fingers and one thumb, is uneconomical, dangerous, unmusical and unintelligent. The crossing of the break from any note on the upper joint to any other on the lower joint should involve the use, when playing for instance A natural or B flat, of as many fingers of the right hand as are convenient for the second note, so that they are there and ready for the jump. This is quite independent of the fingerings dealt with in Chapter 5 as artistically necessary. It is a question of mechanics only at this stage, but it is a technique to be learnt at this point.

Consolidating the technique. From this point onwards the path is quite clear for the student and for the teacher. If all the questions of pitch resonance, control and support have been assimilated, it is possible to say that at any rate the major problems of clarinet playing have been posed.

There are many study books and published arrangements as well as quite a number of specially written original works which take over at this point to expand the world of musical possibilities of the moderately advanced student. I could wish for more specially written works, but there are signs which encourage me to think that soon this field will be well served. These should include the next and last part of the instrument to be explored: the third series of overtones, starting with the C sharp above the normal top C, and extending to the extreme top C above it.

The altissimo register. Caution is essential in making this extension. It should be made only a note at a time, and a feeling of control achieved for each before moving on to the next higher note. Not only that, but an acceptable sound must be achieved for each note as the student ascends, and without undue lip-fatigue. To this end fingerings in this register which produce sharper sounds are preferable to those producing a flatter-pitched note, because these require a less marked embouchure pressure and are less tiring.

Staccato in the altissimo register. The final extension of technique is staccato in the altissimo register. This must not be attempted until a high standard of tone-production, control and crispness of tongueing has been achieved in the other two registers. When this is so, production of altissimo staccato is the same as elsewhere but more so – it has all the difficulties, but in greater degree. At first it cannot be produced quietly, and this should not be demanded. Later it can be, if the student bears in mind the simple fact that it is helped by increased lip-pressure, diaphragm pressure and firmness of tongue – all *positive* factors, when the indications would seem to demand *negatives*.

Playing duets and in ensemble. It is at this point that the use of duets of graded difficulty by teacher and pupil is at its most useful.

The inclusion of a greater number of these in study-books would be an advantage. The less advanced player should take the lower part at first, but a well-conceived duet soon enables him to play the upper part, if it has been written with sufficient care. He should then be encouraged to join a clarinet choir, a wind ensemble (though not yet a classical wind octet, say for Mozart Serenades) and finally an orchestra, which should be the zenith of his achievement in the first main stage of his study – that of good amateur standard.

The advanced student

The groundwork I have described will ensure the student's continued interest, if this is in fact going to emerge. He is now at the cross-roads, and must decide whether or not he wishes to devote a great part of his time and energy to further mastery of the instrument. If he decides against this, nothing is lost, because he has a hobby and an interest which will stay with him always. If he decides that the clarinet is for him a thing very much of the foreground, he must enter the second stage of his study – a very different affair, but none-theless a continuation of what he has been doing. Now the serious attention of an advanced teacher is needed, and it must be remembered that the aims here are very different.

The advanced teacher. It must now be made plain that to play the clarinet simply for enjoyment limits its role. Many will wish to stop at this stage; others will, one hopes, always enjoy playing; but for those who move onward simple pleasure is a secondary consideration. The advanced teacher must soon make it obvious that the clarinet is by no means the simple thing it has so far appeared to be. To play it superbly, as opposed to reasonably well, requires a new slant upon its character. The important aspects of the artistic approach, as given in Chapter 5, must now be brought to bear upon the work of the student.

First, the advanced teacher must make it plain that the view of the clarinet as a producer of ready-made notes of varying quality is simply an elementary one, which must now be discarded. The effect of this realization upon a talented pupil can be startling, because it opens up an entirely new world of experiment for him, and can clear away, or at any rate indicate the way to remove, obstacles which have secretly plagued him for some time. The start of this process should be an examination of the acoustic phenomena of the instru-ment with particular reference to the pressure differences between various notes, the inherent intonation weaknesses, and the methods of helping these. At this point it must be made clear that the fingering-chart is to be forgotten now that it has been digested. It is a basic background only, and from this point onwards the method of fingering any note depends upon only one thing – the resultant sound. There are obviously many improved fingerings which are common to most clarinets, and which are of little use to a beginner because they are too complex at that stage. There are equally many improved fingerings which are not at all common to all clarinets, but can be invaluable in making the individual instrument into a viable musical vehicle of expression. Every clarinet has its own particular bag of tricks, which must be exploited and explored.

It must be a very great preoccupation of any clarinettist to be certain that he knows which way any given note on his clarinet must be 'bent' to make it play in tune. The usual way to correct a note, it must be stressed, is downwards, by relaxing the embouchure while continuing to resonate and support the sound by the oral cavity and the piston-action of the diaphragm. It can thus be seen that sharp fingerings are of much greater use than flat ones for any given notes, because they can be corrected. It is unfortunately almost impossible significantly to raise the pitch of a note in an upward direction by embouchure tightening, at any rate for any length of time. The results of attempting it are two-fold. First, the note is squeezed and damped almost out of existence. Secondly, the lower lip is almost bitten through in a very short time, and playing soon becomes impossible.

So a pupil must have at his command fingerings which resonate, fingerings which correct intonation, and embouchure corrections which go with both when supported correctly by the diaphragm. The permutations of these are quite endless and are what makes the clarinet the widely expressive instrument it is. This is the initial stage in advanced study of the clarinet, and the door to artistry is then open. The extremely complicated and detailed approach briefly dealt with in Chapter 5 is now within reach, and its benefits are there for the taking.

Finally, the advanced teacher must be a musical adviser and should also be a musical model if he is to be truly effective. It cannot be stressed too strongly that he should have really studied the works he is supposed to be teaching. This may seem a ridiculously obvious statement, but it is in fact one which seems to be necessary because it is so often disregarded. There will of course come the day when an adventurous pupil will bring along something he has found, and ask to have an opinion upon his playing of it. This is exactly what he should get, in these circumstances – a simple opinion given by an honestly uninformed but expert clarinettist. No pretence is necessary, because no teacher, however long in the tooth or experienced, can possibly have played everything. In any case pretence is useless, because ignorance shines out of every false sentence in such a case, even when no attempt is made to play the work concerned. The best plan, surely, is a sort of shared exploration of the work, with the teacher demonstrating how he breaks down an unfamiliar series of patterns, and overcomes the salient snags as they reveal themselves to him. This brings us to the vexed question – to play or not to play to one's pupils. . . . Incredibly, there is a division of opinion on this subject, as on most others concerning the clarinet. There are very few forms of human activity where it is possible to imagine a teacher who cannot or will not prove by demonstration that he can do what he is attempting to teach. The understanding teacher is the one who can pick up an instrument and on the instant give the spark which should communicate with the puzzled pupil. So much can be conveyed this way which cannot be put into words. To try to convey most aspects of sound without it is like trying to explain to a child what a spiral staircase is, without that all-revealing circling finger. One supposes that it can be done – but with what a waste of time and effort! A generation ago, when a now famous English oboist was in Belgium studying as a youth with the greatest of their players, the scale of charges varied widely. The fee for a lesson was one guinea – or its Belgian equivalent – if the great man talked; if he played at all, the fee rose instantly to five guineas! You paid your money and took your choice in that most pragmatic of schools, where there was no possible doubt as to the relative value of each type of lesson in the minds of either teacher or pupil.

One hears, also, horror-stories of secrecy, concealment and deliberate withholding of essential information in those past times. The case is often quoted of the teacher who, unable to stand the sound produced by his pupil, took his instrument from him, turned his back, adjusted the reed with a few well-practised strokes of his knife and handed it back to the astonished pupil in perfect playing condition; without a word of explanation and with the obvious intention of refusing to answer any questions on the subject. Happily, things are much more honest now, and it is astonishing but pleasing for any teacher to discover, within days, that a new and useful method he has only just started to employ himself comes back to him through a new pupil, having been passed on by one of that pupil's colleagues. This is a healthy attitude: shared knowledge of this sort can only do a power of good, and is one of the great virtues of clarinet 'clinics', woodwind 'workshops' and master classes of all sorts.

Two sorts of studies

To an advanced teacher there must come sooner or later the realization that so-called 'studies' are of tremendous importance at this stage. These are of two sorts – extracts from important works specially selected by experts in the field concerned, be it chamber music, opera or symphony, and special studies. The former type, if taken by a teacher whose experience is wide enough to enable him to give the atmospheric background as well as the correct tempo, can produce in the pupil the ability to tackle the works concerned with a great deal of insight. This is not 'study' in the usually accepted sense, because it does not aim at improving any particular point of technique. It is familiarization, and it may make all the difference to the future success of the pupil in the hard and most demanding world of music as it now exists. To play the first page of 'Boheme' at sight is one thing, to be able to stay with it at the tempo usually employed is quite another and can be a startling experience if it first happens actually in the pit. Thus it is the duty of any advanced teacher to make sure that his pupil knows the snags in any of the operas he is likely to meet, from the roulades of 'Rosenkavalier' to those incredibly difficult but simple-looking C clarinet parts of Verdi's 'Falstaff'. It should, for instance, be pointed out

that hardly anyone can transpose the note

up a tone, making it

without simply forcing himself to believe in it. It seems such a big gap, so much bigger than two semi-tones. These and other facts of life which are the stock in trade of the experienced player are the stuff of which advanced lessons are made.

The same applies to chamber music, where for instance the first movement of Brahms's Clarinet Quintet requires a careful re-marking of the solo part, with changed dynamics, in order to obtain a correct balance; this must be done with a close study of the score.

Finally the great symphonies must be tackled, and here it is usually better, if possible, to skip around the printed orchestral part rather than to depend upon extracts in studybooks. The pupil can then feel confident that he has had a chance to play every passage of importance in the work. Here again the subject of transposition must be stressed. It is surprising how many advanced pupils fall apart in those C clarinet scherzos of Beethoven's Ninth and Schubert's Great C major Symphonies.

The band-room approach

These and many, many other points must be explored so that the pupil can emerge, as now happily many seem to do, as the almost finished product. And it is not on his playing merely that training for this future must be concentrated. In addition he must learn a good band-room approach, so essential if he is to make his way easily and without hindrance into the profession he has chosen. This is something not generally understood nor are the underlying reasons for it the common knowledge they should be. Playing in a combination of musicians is not at all like working in an office or a factory so far as one's contact with one's colleagues is concerned. Relations are very much closer and more continuous than they can be in almost any other occupation. An office staff may meet and talk many times in the course of a day's work;

but when lunch time arrives they probably have quite a lot of experiences stored up of which their fellows can know nothing. They have had their private problems, their own little work-patterns and decisions to follow, so that they emerge to meet their colleagues with something to discover and discuss. With musicians this is demonstrably not so. For every second of the three-hour morning session they have been wrestling with the same problems at the same time, sharing the same experiences, pleasurable or the reverse, and to a great extent involved with the same emotions. Theirs, it is also pertinent to remember, is also an immensely competitive profession. Happily, at any rate in this country, dog rarely eats dog and it is sometimes quite remarkable to observe how well musicians seem to get along together, when one considers that the success and prosperity of one inevitably leads to a diminution of the living standard of others identically occupied. Dirty tricks are fairly rare, and seem to be generally frowned upon by the profession; but it is a confirmation of the need for more than physical refreshment that in many cases the members of the finest orchestras diverge dramatically like the fingers of an outspread hand as they emerge from a long and arduous session. They have thought too long together, and now they require either their own company, or that of someone not of their immediate circle.

It is thus obviously vital that a young artist should be temperamentally as well as musically equipped if he is to lead a happy and useful professional life. The picture of groups of players fighting like cat and dog during rehearsals but giving heaven-sent performances may be true on the surface, but certainly not in essence. For a string quartet to continue to thrive, as well as to produce worthwhile music, there must be a mutual respect and even admiration among its members. In the wind section very much the same sort of thing applies, for this is basically an octet within the orchestra, and it must work like one. Differences there must be, but not insoluble ones: a few seconds of re-focusing and then it's back to work again, as a unit or as solo voice, with perfect understanding or compromise, whichever is appropriate.

The Clarinet

It is scarcely necessary to remind a young player of the undesirability of 'preluding' his most brilliant orchestral solos at every opportunity just to show how it can be done. It is just possible his principal, or others, may not be able to do it quite like that. It is equally possible that it may underline what the player may not yet be able to do with it. In either case the effect is not to his advantage. It is the inevitable task of the advanced teacher to attempt to induce this attitude in his pupil – a task too often shirked.

The multi-instrumentalist

It is also important that at this stage the pupil should be introduced to the full range of possibilities a present-day job will offer and demand. He may have to play in a jazz style of one sort or another; he may need to consider becoming something of a multi-instrumentalist by 'doubling' or even 'trebling', though this may depend upon his geographical location – certainly scores from across the Atlantic seem to make the most remarkable demands of this sort. There are examples of players being required to play all four main members of the wood-wind family, as well as a variety of saxophones, and this as a routine matter, not as a special or freak effect. It is no part of our discussion here to look into the details of this, because we are concerned only with the clarinet; suffice it to say that it can be done, and with surprising success. The embouchure is an amazingly flexible affair, and with skill and practice it really does seem possible to produce a decent sound, reasonably controlled, on all these varied instruments. What is certain is that one of them will always remain the primary instrument, while the rest require modifications of this acquired technique; and in the case of the clarinet, observation suggests that the most successful results are achieved if the secondary instruments are introduced only after a considerable degree of efficiency has been attained. It is the task of the advanced teacher to decide when this moment has arrived, if in fact the pupil decides it is a course he wishes to follow. He must not suppress this ambition unduly or he will damage his pupil's future prospects; he must be certain that the foundations have been well and truly laid, and then stand aside and leave the additional work to individual specialist players with a silent prayer for the results. It is of very little use for a pupil who intends to be a multi-instrumentalist to try to learn all his skills from one player, however gifted; though the sheer act of multi-instrumental mentality should certainly be picked up by association with others who are similarly inclined.

One final word seems appropriate. It is of no use at all to tell a pupil that he will wreck his whole technique and musicianship by such a course. Manifestly this is untrue, and examples can be quoted to prove it. The finest bass-clarinettist in London of the generation now just past is also one of the greatest solo and orchestral saxophonists in the world. His clarinet playing is also no less than superb. It should only be pointed out to an aspiring multi-instrumentalist that energy spent in one direction is obviously lost to another, and that the clarinet, particularly nowadays, has such demands upon its performance that a lifetime is all too short for its full mastery.

Gaining experience

There remains only a consideration of the various fields of activity open to a fully trained player, and the necessary preparation for each of them. The first and most obvious of these is orchestral playing, an aspect of performance which has already been touched upon. The main fact to be remembered is that the only way to learn to play in an orchestra is – to play in one! Unhappily this is not always easy to manage, even at one of the major seats of musical learning. Even with three orchestras, there is no hope of inclusion for more than a dozen clarinettists of the inevitable thirty or so who are all aching to take part. Luckily the surplus is to some extent catered for by the great number of amateur and semi-amateur orchestras, especially in Great Britain, which are now busily engaged in preparing and presenting extremely ambitious concerts. Many of these are of an incredibly high star.dard of excellence and in addition are being well trained and conducted by younger professional conductors who are happy to have the opportunity to exercise their skills. This must therefore be the aim of the student clarinettist, who can learn not only a big repertoire in this way, but can also become familiar with points of intonation control, balance interpretation and transposition which will stand him in good stead. Nowadays he need rarely fear having to play with poor wind-players. The bulk of the strings are probably amateurs; the wind, almost to a man, are either future professionals or players who probably would have been if there had been more musical openings or indeed fewer 'plum' jobs to be found in their other fields.

Having gained some experience of transposition, a young player can greatly expand his chamber-music experience. This is one of the aspects of musical experience which can be an ever-increasing source of delight, and one which in any case will be with him for the rest of his life. For that reason it is essential that he should become a real chamber-musician; he should know all the great works in this realm, not merely those which involve the clarinet. As a clarinettist one is lucky, because some of the greatest chamber-music works ever written include and in some cases were inspired by the clarinet – such works as the Mozart Quintet and Trio, the Brahms pair of works in the same forms (though these of course use cello in place of viola), Schubert's great Octet, Beethoven's Septet and such later works as Messiaen's 'Quatuor pour la Fin du Temps'.

String quartets on the clarinet

To appreciate the stature of these fully, as well as judge the necessary approach, it is essential to know the rest of chamber music, from the superb quartets of Haydn through the delights of late Mozart and early Beethoven to the towering masterpieces of Beethoven's last great period, and such imperishable works as the Mozart and Schubert string quintets. One obvious way of finding out about these works is simply to listen to them in excellent performances, study the way in which the finest artists interpret them and apply these approaches to one's own performances. There is, however, a better way, a more practical and useful approach – to *play* them. This may seem ridiculous, impossible and even sacrilegious; but it is both possible, enjoyable, and certainly not a process which does violence to the great works involved. It is one of those activities which depend to a great extent upon the forces available. The obvious target is three friends who play string instruments – one each of violin, viola and cello. The approach must be tactful, particularly to the violinist, who naturally wants to lead the quartet, at any rate if he is good enough to be considered for the job one has in mind. He must of course be allowed to do this from time to time – but first let us consider those precious occasions when he is playing second fiddle, and the clarinettist has the seat of glory. At this moment there are three important factors to consider with great care. First, is the work in question one which can legitimately be expected to sound good when led by the clarinet? The key signature has an obvious bearing upon this, because this is where the long months of transposition study swing into action; usually the B flat clarinet will be employed, and in this case the obvious choice of keys is on the flat side of the chart – a series not too well represented in works written for strings with open-tuned E naturals and A naturals. But there are such works, by Haydn, Mozart, Beethoven and others, and to play them for the first time is a rare delight. At a more advanced level, the sharp key works can be taken in on the A clarinet, a process which greatly simplifies the key-signature but makes the actual transposition just a little more difficult. It is a general conclusion that such works probably sound less natural on the clarinet than the flat key quartets, because almost all composers take advantage of the natural sharp-key facility of the violin, writing double stopping and wide *arpeggiando* passages which cannot be brought off graciously on the clarinet. This is hardly surprising; what is really amazing is how perfectly some of the others suit a clarinet lead. Such works as Mozart's 'Hunt' Quartet (K. 458) can even sound better than in their original form. It is of course not suggested that performances should be aimed at with this changed scoring; but as a recreation, a study, and for pure enjoyment it is one of music's great delights.

The second thing to be considered, as the work is about to be tackled, is – can the clarinet actually manage the first violin part, or would it be wiser, quietly and graciously, to step down? If so, the player will gain a further experience in playing second violin, a part which is usually possible for him in such circumstances. The value of this experience is in learning to balance, to blend and to follow the lead given by the first violin. The compass of the part is rarely as extreme as that of the first violin, nor the writing so florid. As a result a much wider range of works becomes available for the clarinettist and so he becomes a more knowledgeable chamber music player, which is the aim of the whole exercise.

After this, all sorts of permutations become possible, according largely to the players available. Two clarinets can take the two violin parts with a viola and a cello. A missing viola can be replaced by the clarinet – a very interesting exercise, because the compass of the clarinet fits perfectly, and the transposition is extremely simple. In this case it is only necessary to read the alto clef as the bass clef (and of course, change the key by adding two sharps or taking away two flats):

This may look complicated but it is in fact the simplest of all transpositions. The one snag is that the lowest note of the viola, the C natural, is a tone below the compass of the B flat clarinet, so that it has to be played an octave higher than written. Lastly the case of the missing cellist has to be coped with, and obviously for this a bass clarinet is essential. Here again the transposition is not difficult, because in order to play the classical orchestral repertoire as a bass clarinettist it is essential to master the bass clef, and it is also part of any clarinettist's job to be entirely secure in transposing up one whole tone when reading C clarinet parts. A combination of these two exercises makes it possible to play cello parts on the bass clarinet quite effortlessly. Nor is there the same difficulty in obtaining the lowest note of the cello as there is in the case of playing viola parts on the B flat clarinet, because nowadays most bass clarinets are being constructed to descend to a concert B flat, a tone below the cello's lowest C; where this is not the case and the lowest note is a concert D flat, the extra semitone can be achieved either by the insertion of a short cardboard cylinder into the bell of the instrument, or, given average luck, by simply dropping the reed-cover into the bell.

All this seems quite makeshift in intention. In practice it actually works extremely well. It gives the player the opportunity to study the greatest chamber works from every possible angle – an exercise which will certainly make him a much more complete musician than he could otherwise be, and will inevitably give him a valuable insight into the great works which include the clarinet as normal practice. There is, an addition, the delight of hearing three clarinets and a bass clarinet, all of them transposing or not, as they wish, playing the works already discussed as a quartet. Here it must be remembered that there is always one player who has to be ready to take on the viola part, and who has therefore to be able to read the alto clef.

The clarinet choir

The sound of a quartet of clarinets is quite remarkably satisfying, and leads one naturally to the comparatively new delights of playing in even larger combinations of clarinets –

quintets, sextets or bigger aggregations, usually known as 'clarinet choirs'. Such choirs are capable of most beautiful and expressive effects, reminiscent of an organ but with infinitely more subtle shadings of expression. The best plan is to use one or more of all the members of the range of clarinets, comprising piccolo E flat, soprano B flat, alto E flat, bass B flat, and contrabass B flat, with possible substitution of contrabass E flat instead of B flat. Some people assert that the E flat contra instrument has a more readily blending tone than the B flat instrument, and its compass, which is a fifth below that of the bass clarinet, takes it down to the note a semitone below the lowest note of the string bass, a bottom E flat. The modern bass clarinet stops a fifth above this, on a B flat.

The repertoire of the clarinet choir is as yet far from complete, and such original music as has been written for it tends to be difficult to obtain. It is thus useful to be able to delve into the realms of the string orchestral repertoire, which can often be adapted with quite a small editing task rather than necessitating complete re-arrangement. There is no need here to go into the details of the essential re-arrangements, which obviously will be known to anyone who has reached the stage of branching out into this realm. Obviously the violin parts will be shared between the E flat and B flat clarinets as the *tessitura* of the music indicates – and no clarinet in a *cantabile* passage above approximately

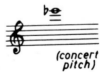

(concert pitch)

Incidentally, it is unnecessary to transpose the parts – they can be played *in situ*. This lowers the pitch of the work a tone, but is not serious.

Equally obviously, the alto clarinet is very much at home playing the viola part, because it is easily within its compass – it has in fact a minor third to spare, in case the arranger wishes to use it to help out the cellos. What is perhaps not so obvious is the simplicity of the transposition in this case. Taking middle C as our mean (and remembering that the B flat clarinets are not transposing) the actual sound to be

produced when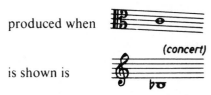

is shown is

On the alto clarinet, this sound is produced when the instrument plays

So all that remains, apart from the alteration of the key signature, is for the player to play one ledger line lower than written.

The cello parts, on the bass clarinet, are simply played as are bass clarinet parts in the bass clef in the orchestra – without any transposition. The same applies to the string bass parts on the B flat contrabass. With a little trial and error, perfect blend and balance can be at any rate approached. This massed clarinet experience must not in any way be equated with the much more familiar one of playing in a large military or concert-band, because in the latter every note is played, not only by many other clarinettists, but most often by many other instruments as well. This obviously requires a different approach from the players concerned – as different as is orchestral technique from chamber music technique in the case of a skilled violinist. In the clarinet choir, the general rule should be one player to one line of music, except in the case of the B flat instrument, where it is now found best to use three. Certainly in works written especially for the clarinet choir, where antiphony and contrapuntal effect are almost always the aim, the single clarinet voice should be the rule except in the case of the B flat. A list, albeit short, of such works, appears in our repertoire list. Before leaving the subject, one of its more qualities must be emphasized, because it is an attribute rarely used to the advantage it should be. More than almost any other combination, the clarinet choir can give a beautifully muted and comfortable support to any of the solo voices of its members. In most instrumental combinations the effect is obtained by the contrast of the timbre of the solo voice, which is of necessity a different instrument from its accompanying texture. In the case of the clarinet choir, such is the dynamic and tonal range of the instruments, the solo voice can stand out in an almost visible manner in front of the hushed whisper which is possible with even a dozen clarinets. It is an effect not to be overdone.

The soloist

The last and in some ways the most satisfactory stage of a clarinettist's experience is inevitably his gradual emergence and development as a solo recitalist. This is rarely an early blossoming, as it may well be with the violin, cello or piano. These instruments can give a really talented performer an obvious choice at a fairly early age. He may be an orchestral player; he may concentrate upon chamber orchestral work; he may found or join a quartet, or he may rely mainly upon concert performances for his reputation and his livelihood. Rarely indeed does he combine even two of these activities, hardly ever three. As a result of this state of affairs, if he is to devote his life to recitals of sonatas or the presentation of concertos, he is likely quite early to give both thought and energy to the development of a comfortable style and a really professional approach. He will set out, at undue financial sacrifice, with a recital at one of the famous recital rooms which specialize in just this sort of performance. If he is successful, the whole of a great repertoire is at his disposal, and he will be earmarked from that time forward as a solo performer by the various agencies who handle the type of work he wishes to make his aim in life. Many naturally fall by the wayside in such a race, but those who succeed have entered the field directly in the full knowledge of the requirements, and are likely to be much more sophisticated in style than are their wood-wind colleagues at a similar stage in their career. The majority of clarinettists who are destined to become famous as sonata-performers not only serve apprenticeships in the symphony orchestra or the opera-pit; they actually continue to occupy these surroundings for most or all of their recital lives. This almost invariably shows in their platform manner as soloists. Some of the greatest of them creep on and off like scared mice, trying their best to hide behind the music with which they are probably more familiar than almost anyone but the composer and giving the impression that this may not be the first recital they have ever given, but it is certainly the most difficult. At one of the major international competitions – Lucerne or Munich say, where the finest young players from all over the world come to compete, it is most noticeable that the professional recitalists are already in evidence even among the young. They are very rarely indeed wood-wind players, superb performers though many of these are.

So what must the aim of a young clarinettist be, if he wishes to be a recitalist? First, he must have in his mind's eye the sort of dedicated artistry and authoritative command of the situation that the greatest violinists inevitably seem to possess. It may be necessary to adjust the reed, fiddle about with the ligature, dog-ear the pages of the part and move the standard-lamp before starting. Let it be a *long* time before starting – either before the audience have taken their places, or out of their sight. Once he appears on the platform the audience should be aware of nothing other than the start of the music and its revelation by the performer. A tall order – but then, to be faced with a few hundred people whose whole evening's entertainment is one's responsibility, *is* a tall order; having accepted it, it must be discharged fully and honestly. The audience will almost always be friendly to an artist who seems to take them into his confidence – and that means that he must show confidence whether he feels it or not. All this assumes that the conditions in which he finds himself make it possible for a recital to be given at all. Plainly there are times when it might be kinder to tell the assembled enthusiasts that they must ask for their money to be returned, and quietly creep away into the night; for a clarinet recital, more than any other, can be rendered a travesty, a torment and an unmusical disaster, unless the pitch of the piano is right – and even an unduly hot hall combined with excessively dry acoustics can defeat the best of artists, for a fact which is not generally realized then comes into play – in order to give a musical performance, it is essential actually to enjoy the sound one is producing. Each note must be a sequel to the one before it, must add to its meaning and enhance its beauty. If it is not beautiful and meaningful to the player he has no foundation upon which to build, and is both frustrated and distressed.

This is why it is a shocking mistake to build sound studios as they are now almost invariably built. The theory seems to be that if there is little or no reverberation, the exact amount which is required to make the raw sound acceptable can be added by the talented engineer in control. This may be true, because often after the performer has played for a while in acute depression, he can scarcely believe the glossy and warm sound which greets him in the cubicle when his efforts are played back to him. This may give him cheer for the moment, but if he is to enjoy it for long he needs a very powerful imagination to translate mentally the starved and miserable sounds he hears himself producing into what he hopes they will be when polished and coloured by modern acoustic electronic magic. He will probably produce some very remarkable sounds in these surroundings. He is unlikely to achieve anything like a thoughtful or balanced performance, from an emotional standpoint.

This is, of course, by the way; but it does highlight the predicament of the artist when the tide seems to be running against him. Here he needs our sympathy – he can only grit his teeth and carry on, giving as good an account of himself as he can, trying to look unconcerned. To frown in these circumstances helps nobody. One hesitates to suggest that the performer should at such a time adopt the profession of actor in addition to that of musician, but it might help, and certainly would not hinder. Once the playing has started, it really doesn't matter much what sort of face you pull; some of the world's greatest concert personalities appear to be in agony most of the time, and several of them give the impression that they will strain themselves to death in a few years – an impression that time invariably proves to be unfounded. Before the performance, however, the man or woman can be seen and judged and a pessimistic and tentative personality does nothing to create the peace necessary for a receptive audience. There is certainly plenty to be pessimistic about; if one were to consider all the tiny springs, pads, corks, and gadgets upon which one has to rely for a performance, it would seem unlikely ever to take place. And of course – the reed! It is obviously impossible to play a difficult sonata perfectly without the perfect reed, or decently without a reasonable one. Yet the attempt must constantly be made to do so because it is always at the moment of starting an important work on a big occasion that one realizes that the piece of cane at one's disposal is no friend. This is the moment to put pessimism aside, and to find out just what this treacherous sound generator can really do. It is surprising; it will almost certainly leave the lower lip in a painful condition, and its dynamic response will probably be less than adequate. Nonetheless it can be made to give quite musical results in the emergency now to hand, and music is the whole reason for a recital. Happily, not even a skilled clarinettist usually knows whether his colleague is using a good or mediocre reed. A bad one, yes. But by the audience, even a bad reed can be undetected.

Having entered, then, and duly started the recital, what sort of performance should be the aim? Here there are as many answers as there are players. Some will aim at accuracy, some at a deep understanding of the composer's intentions, some at a glory of sound as their primary aim. The great player also uses his imagination. The experience of hearing, say, a Brahms sonata played by a clarinettist who uses his imagination in the way a great string player does is outside the realm of what one would normally call clarinet playing. The instrument becomes a vehicle of expression to such an extent that it almost seems to cease to exist. Indeed until he can forget that he has a clarinet in his hands, and actually sing the work with the medium of the clarinet as his voice, the clarinettist has not conquered the task of becoming a recitalist. He must use every technique of the singer and the fine string-soloist, combine the two, and add to it his own conception of clarinet sound, phrasing, style and utterance. And here we come to the most thorny of all problems, the most controversial of all aspects in considering the clarinet. To use or not to use vibrato? The advanced teacher can only advise, not decide.

Vibrato

On the face of it, this might seem to be not only a trivial, but a ridiculous question. To give a flute recital without vibrato would in most people's opinion be quite unthinkable. It goes without saying that no violinist would dream of playing one of the Brahms sonatas *senza vibrato*. Yet there are many thousands of clarinettists who would share a recital with such a player, and solemnly plod their dead-pan path through the E flat sonata immediately after the audience had heard a luscious *con amore* interpretation of the F minor on its incorrect instrument, the viola. The same certainly cannot be said of oboists, who use vibrato or not as they feel the music requires it, or of bassoonists. What, then, is the real underlying cause of this rise in temperature, this lack of tolerance, this shutting off of logical consideration of what seems to be a reasonable suggestion for giving enjoyment as a performer? The probable causes would seem to be twofold. First, more than any other instrument, the clarinet can depict the sort of cool, flawless beauty of a marble statue or a piece of perfectly polished wood. The pure sound has a fascination which makes one think at times that the slightest dimple on its surface would be a blemish. This is one of the finest aspects of the instrument, and one must respect the feelings of those who think that it must be protected at all costs. Certainly great performances have been, and are, presented with just this sound in all its purity. But is life really like that *all* the time? The second reason for this back-turning upon the clarinet vibrato is that in fact it has been for long done so very *badly*. Not badly for its own purpose, which was jazz, and which responds well to the much more reedy, louder, more 'edgy' sound of the small-interior mouthpiece together with a vibrato produced usually by a chewing action of the lower jaw – an action which causes pulsations in the air column by compressing the reed intermittently, damping its vibration, and pressing the reed closer to the facing so that very little air can enter until the tension is released, when it enters with a rush. This vibrato is simply an addition to the tone, not part of it, and as it is usually applied to a tone very different from the polished and perfect affair described above, it commands little respect among thinking musicians.

But – need it be like this at all? There are two additional types of vibrato – three, if one includes the 'nanny-goat' dither of the intensity vibrato which is often given the blessing of extremely sophisticated clarinettists, but is clearly an abomination. The first of these is a gentle pulsation of the lips, and impels the air as does the jaw vibrato but without disturbance of the mirror surface of the tone. Like the jaw-vibrato it also results in a slight raising and lowering of the pitch, exactly as does a well-produced string vibrato. This is a very shallow vibrato, and must never be just a 'wobble', as it is when too slow, or a 'dither', as it can be if too fast. The second is the purely diaphragmatic vibrato, which produces pulsations of the same sort in the air column of the instrument, but by controlled impulses from the diaphragm exactly as practised by singers. This is the most difficult sort of vibrato, but in some ways the best. It has, however, the decided disadvantage of being extremely tiring, even after it has been fully mastered, and for this reason many excellent players use a combination of the lip and diaphragm vibrato.

Whichever method is used, one thing seems certain – it should not be used all the time, nor should it be switched on and off like the *vox humana* stop of an organ. In fact, although it must be very much under the control of the player, in the end it should be so much a part of his technique that he is not aware of playing with vibrato or not. The choice should in fact not be his, but dictated by the music, out of which it must grow naturally, or not at all. The player himself, in these days of electronic marvels, may be surprised at the absence or presence of vibrato in the recording he has just made, because he was thinking only of the music as he played. He would be wise to ponder before making a decision to alter his first impulse, because such studied decisions can sound what they are – the result of cogitation rather than instinct.

Another point worthy of consideration is that the use of vibrato can be used to cover faults of intonation. This is not really the sin it may appear at first statement. No player, living or dead, has ever been able to play the clarinet *perfectly* in tune, even at a pitch which is comfortable and in acoustic conditions which are kind. He can, however, do so well enough in most surroundings to be able to build his smooth marble statues to our delight when that seems indicated by the music. If things are impossible, is it correct for him to be fearlessly honest and just play out of tune when even his finger corrections and his embouchure prove insufficient to take the strain? One may admire his courage, appreciate his integrity – but probably never forgive the suffering he is inflicting. At such a moment, even when the music might dictate otherwise, he may possibly gently coax the intonation by a trace of vibrato, and so correct his tuning relatively undetected with no real need for forgiveness. He is certainly not alone in his need. It is possible to hear a superb string section play the first half of Stravinsky's 'Rake's Progress' – and then wilt with horror to hear their tuning in the *senza vibrato* graveyard scene. They *must* resist the temptation to vibrate, but rarely manage to do so. It is for this sort of desperate position that the thoughtful performer will reserve his corrective, as opposed to his expressive, vibrato. He must be sure that he has done everything he can to make it unnecessary – all the subtleties of mouthpiece and reed preparation and an instrument as perfectly balanced as skilled tuning can make it; a flexible embouchure, coupled with a properly resonated air column aided by finger-corrections which aim not only to strengthen but to perfect the pitch. He must never be lazy in his use of vibrato in this way – but he can be effective and artistic at the same time.

It seems a shame that what is manifestly a useful addition to the armoury of expressive capabilities of the clarinet should have been the victim of the fact that it first appeared in an abused and somewhat sinister form. Or was the use of vibrato in jazz in fact its first manifestation? It seems scarcely likely that, for over two hundred years, clarinettists should have failed to respond to, and at least to attempt to answer the shapes of phrases and the style of playing which they must have heard around them, both instrumentally and vocally. As one can observe from a glance at the early historical section of this book, most of these early players were very bright individuals indeed, too slick for even Mozart and Beethoven to guide with any success. A reminiscence of no less a player than Mühlfeld himself seems to suggest that the use of vibrato may have fallen out of fashion temporarily after his day, to return after about thirty years. Just before World War II a question was put to a very old viola-player, sometime conductor of the Duke of Devonshire's Orchestra, about the playing of Mühlfeld. The old man had occasionally been called in by Joachim to play in his quartet, and on several occasions had played the Brahms Quintet with the great Mühlfeld. Of the clarinettist's playing he was most enthusiastic, saying that three things mainly stuck in his memory. 'He used two clarinets, A and B flat, for the slow movement, to simplify the gypsy section; he had a fiery technique with a warm tone – and a big vibrato.' Asked again by a startled questioner if he didn't mean to say '*rubato*' the old man looked puzzled. 'No,' he said, 'vibrato – much more than Joachim, and as much as the cellist.' (It will be recalled that Joachim was reputed to play with little or no vibrato.) This account, while of no authority, does at least give one food for thought; it could be that the achievements of exceptional players (and Mühlfeld was certainly that) do not always take root in the years that follow their finest period. There is sometimes, indeed, a reaction in the opposite direction. This has certainly happened twice in living memory in Britain, and probably to a lesser extent elsewhere; but in general it is to be at least hoped that the movement is in a forward direction. If so, it is legitimate to pose the question: 'Where next?'

Clarinets to come

The plain fact is that, though there have been improvements both in playing and in making the clarinet in the hundred years now past, these have not been radical changes, but gradual, almost imperceptible evolutionary developments. This is in quite startling contrast with the century and a half which preceded this. With the work of Klosé we come to an instrument much as we find it today, and the decades which followed his work showed only a slow acceptance of the realization of the great worth of his instrument. Yet each decade which preceded his work can be said to have contributed something new to the clarinet, to have solved some inherent problem and given a spur to the imagination of composers anxious to write for it. Whether further mechanical improvement is altogether desirable, let alone possible, is a moot point. There are many who feel that there are already too many holes in the tube of the instrument; and certainly it is a joy to play a few of the good notes on the simple system clarinet, with their direct, clear sound and a resonance which feels unhampered by the wind-resistance of hole-edges and undamped by the sheer weight of the mechanism above them. But it is difficult to imagine what could be done to achieve the equality of the Klosé clarinet without employing a large number of holes.

Possibly the field of experiment might be the careful shaping of these holes to disturb the air column to a minimum extent when they are not in use. In other words, the holes should open at the bottom, where they join the bore, instead of at the top. An impossible task? No – merely a difficult one. It is certainly not the function of this book to give hints to inventors, but surely a camera-shutter does something very like this, and is a remarkably efficient piece of mechanism when properly made. Using this type of closure, the bore would be smooth and even to the point of termination for any given note or series of notes. In theory this should be a great improvement, and unless in practice it altered the clarinet tone out of recognition it would revolutionize the instrument. Obviously the present-day pad, efficient though it is as a seal, is a dismal loss of efficiency where resonance is concerned. If it cannot be eradicated, it must certainly be modified so that it reflects in the way the bore of the instrument would if there were no hole present. In addition, there is no doubt that the clarinet is burdened with mechanism that is almost incredibly clumsy and overweighted. Compare it with the slender, artistically designed keywork of the oboe, let alone the superbly simple and silent lay-out of the flute, and it looks like a very primitive piece of machinery indeed. One wonders what the real reason can be for this. There is no doubt that it works well enough, and it is both strong and durable. Possibly the use of the instrument as the mainstay of the music of the armies of most of the world accounts for this. It has to be knocked about, played in sunshine or rain, frost or snow. One sometimes wonders if maybe the sheer inert mass, with its resistance to the player's demands, may not at times spur him on to efforts he would otherwise never make, and that the reflected tension of this is what gives the clarinet its deep throated and personal utterance. One has a right to wonder what the result might be if this weight were to be taken away and replaced by resonance in every part of the instrument – with perfect bore for every note, corrected acoustics by further ingenious mechanisms which would perfect all the overblown notes, and so allow the chalumeau register to be tuned as a perfect fundamental scale; with light, silent and perfectly balanced mechanism to make the true *legato*, already the glory of the clarinet, even more silky and cat-like. This might give us an instrument quite unlike the clarinet we know, and in fact unacceptable for that reason. But that seems hardly likely, for with all the improvements which have been made in clarinets since Denner first gave it to a grateful world, the instrument is still recognizably what it then was. History has given us a rare treasure – we can build upon it if we will.

The Clarinet Repertoire

To select and discuss any list of works which can be regarded as complete or exhaustive is an obvious impossibility. There may very well be a large number of important and interesting works omitted from the list below. Certainly there is a great deal of music one must ignore in a list of this length which is both useful and amusing; the player can discover this for himself by browsing through publishers' lists and his local lending libraries. All the works included here are known to the author either personally as a player or a listener, or by hearsay from the accounts of others whose opinions he respects. Short comments which may be helpful are added where pertinent. The list obviously most difficult to delineate is that of chamber music: where does the chamber combination stop and orchestra begin? Where, for instance, does one place Stravinsky's Dumbarton Oaks Concerto, for fifteen players, one of whom must play the clarinet? Probably not in the chamber music list, which is for more centrally-oriented clarinet involvement.

Works included may be taken as having the approval of the compiler, and works which are unobtainable are excluded unless there is a reasonable chance that they may soon appear. It must be stressed that this is a short list only, and such books as those by Kroll and Rendell included in the Bibliography may be relied upon to fill out the remainder.

The author and publishers have endeavoured to ensure that the information in this section is complete but some omissions are unavoidable.

Clarinet and Piano

1. d'Alessandro, Faraele (1911–59). Sonata. Cologne Sidmten Verlag, 1956. A modern, lightweight suite of dances.
2. Alwyn, William (1905–). Sonata in E flat. Boosey & Hawkes, 1963. Tuneful and fairly simple.
3. Arne, Thomas (1710–78). Sonata in B flat, arr Craxton. O.U.P., 1950. Two contrasted movements from a harpsichord sonata. Works well.
4. Arnold, Malcolm (1921–). Sonatina Op. 29. Lengnick, 1951. Light, tuneful, short, with some diverting rhythmic tricks. A winner with audiences, like everything else by this composer.
5. Babin, Victor (1908–). 'Hillandale Waltzes'. Boosey & Hawkes, 1947. A set of tuneful variations which look trite but are subtle.
6. Bach, J. S. (1685–1750). Sonata in C, arr Harry Gee from a flute sonata. Southern Music, 1969. Useful.
7. Bärmann, H. (1784–1847). Adagio (previously thought to have been by Wagner). Breitkopf & Härtel. A lovely melody, and perfect for the clarinet.
8. Bartók, Bela (1881–1945). Sonatina, arr Gyorgy Balassa from piano movements on Transylvanian themes. Zenemukiado, Vallalot, 1958. Difficult on the B flat clarinet. A good show piece.
9. Bax, Arnold (1883–1953). Sonata. Murdoch, 1935. A work which the composer used to enjoy hearing, and the more romantic the approach the better. The second of the two movements is difficult and requires a clarinet in the peak of mechanical condition.
10. Berg, Alban (1885–1935). Four pieces, Op. 5. Schlesinger, 1920. One of the most rewarding works of the past half-century, it explores not only the rhythmic possibilities of the medium but its immense tonal variety. It requires a really fine piano and should not be attempted in unknown conditions.
11. Bernstein, Leonard (1918–). Sonata. Wetmark, New York, 1943. Early, but interesting. Short and with much

rhythmic interest. Possibly better to play than to hear, but makes its mark with audiences.

12. Blavet, Michel (1700–68). Sonatina in F minor, arr Loosen from a three-movement violin sonata. Wormerveer. Helps to fill out the absent period of clarinet repertoire in a quite pleasant way.

13. Blok, Vladimir (1932–). Sonatina. Moscow State Publishing House, 1965. Modern in harmony. Rhythmically not difficult, but requires good finger technique.

14. Bowen, York (1884–1961). Sonata. Unfortunately in manuscript. A work which should have been published long ago. Lyrical and brilliant in parts, it will find a ready public when this is rectified.

15. Bozza, E. (1905–). Fantaisie Italienne. Leduc. In typically brilliant French style, and with a good sense of line.

16. Brahms, Johannes (1833–97). Sonata Op. 120 No. 1 in F minor and Op. 120 No. 2 in E flat. Published by Simrock, 1895, and by many others since. Little needs to be said about these two masterpieces except that they do belong to the clarinet and not to the viola. The greatest ever.

17. Busch, Adolf (1891–1952). Sonata Op. 54. Not published but obtainable from the Swiss Music Archives. A fine work, long but well constructed.

18. Busoni, F. (1866–1924). Élégie. Breitkopf & Härtel, 1921. Simple, tuneful and effective.

19. Byrne, Andrew (1925–). Suite (three movements). Hinrichsen, 1961. Simple and effective. Good concert music for the smaller occasions. Can split into encore pieces.

20. Cardew, Philip. Scherzo. Boosey & Hawkes, 1954. Tricky and technically difficult, but a worthwhile challenge.

21. Carter, Elliott (1908–). Pastorale. Universal Editions. A pleasant and simple programme piece.

22. Cooke, Arnold (1906–). Sonata. Novello, 1962. A pleasant modern work, with something of Hindemith in it, but a lot of Cooke. A good scherzo and a tarantella finale.

23. Danzi, Franz (1763–1826). Sonata in B flat. Simrock. A good study sonata, not too difficult but not too dull.

24. Debussy, Claude (1862–1918). Première Rhapsodie. Durand, 1910. Composed as a test-piece for the Paris Conservatoire. Difficult but rewarding. Requires stamina and imagination. The piano version is the original, though the last bars show clearly that the composer was thinking in orchestral terms, with horns.

25. Duncan, Clyde (1920–). Sonatina. E. H. Morris, New York, 1955. A modern work, not too difficult. Effective and fluent.

26. Dunhill, Thomas (1877–1946). Fantasy Suite, Op. 9. Boosey & Hawkes, 1941. Light music, but none the worse for that. Well contrasted movements, most of which will stand alone, particularly Nos. 3 and 5.

27. Finzi, Gerald (1901–56). Five Bagatelles. Boosey & Hawkes, 1945. A charming work by an English composer whose early death robbed us of much great music. The movements may be used separately, but the final Fughetta – a little masterpiece of craftsmanship – must never be missed.

28. Freimann, Witold (1889–). Sonata. Polskie Wydawn, Cracow. Interesting and original. A lyrical slow movement and a lively Polish dance finale.

29. Fulton, Norman (1909–). Three Movements. Augener, 1955. Pleasant music, and well written. Not difficult.

30. Gade, N. V. (1817–90). Fantasy Pieces, Op. 43. Breitkopf & Härtel, 1864. Romantic and easy for both player and listener.

31. Gál, Hans (1890–). Sonata Op. 84. Hinrichsen, 1965. A romantic work, but with some modern spice. Moderately difficult.

32. Garlic, Antony (1927–). Sonata for E flat clarinet and piano. Seesaw Music, New York, 1970. Modern, not difficult, and (dare one say?) highly flavoured.

33. Gibbs, Armstrong (1889–1960). Three Pieces. O.U.P., 1957. Very simple, but with a final Caprice which is an excellent encore piece.

34. Grechaninov, Alexander (1864–1956). Sonata Op. 172. Moscow State Publishing House, 1949. A very pleasant sonata, possibly over-long but well written and very playable.

35. Hamilton, Iain (1922–). Sonata Op. 22. Schott, 1955. Well written for the instrument. Quite difficult, as is his Concerto.

36. Heiden, Bernard (1910–). Sonatina. Associated, New York, 1935. Written forty years ago, this is a fairly simple piece but has charm and style.

37. Hindemith, Paul (1895–1963). Sonata. Schott, 1940. A masterpiece in Hindemith's best vein. Ranks with everything else ever written for the combination, apart from the Brahms sonatas.

38. Hoddinott, Alun (1929–). Sonata. O.U.P., 1968. Later than the Concerto and more difficult, ending with a *moto perpetuo* which is a great test of ensemble. A challenge.

39. Hoffmeister, Franz (1754–1812). Sonata. Musica Rara. A very early clarinet sonata, apparently in its original form, and pleasant.

40. Honegger, Arthur (1892–1955). Sonata. Rouant-Lerolle, 1925. A period piece, but interesting. The finale is in the jazz idiom of its day, and comes off very well.

41. Hook, James (1746–1827). English Sonata, arr Joosen. Wormerveer. Probably for recorder in the original, but successful on the clarinet. Four contrasted baroque movements.

42. Horovitz, Joseph (1926–). Three Majorcan Pieces. Mills, 1958. Excellent representation of the traditional rhythms of the area. Not difficult. Good concert pieces, but essentially for entertainment.

43. Horovitz, Joseph. Three Nocturnes Op. 6. Schott, 1951. Earlier, but also well written.

44. Howells, Herbert (1892–). Sonata. Boosey & Hawkes, 1954. A great work. Very difficult. Should really be played on the A clarinet as it was for its premiere, with Frederick Thurston. Possible as written for the B flat, but worth the trouble to re-write.

45. Hoyer, Karl (1891–1936). Sonata Op. 55. Porteus, 1934. More romantic than the date would suggest. Pleasant to play.

46. Hurlstone, William 1876–1906. Four Characteristic Pieces. Novello, 1909. Written by a young English composer

who would have become very important, but died young. They have charm, and use the clarinet with great understanding of its more recent lyrical qualities. There are at any rate two encore pieces here.

47. Ireland, John (1879–1962). Fantasy Sonata. Boosey & Hawkes, 1945. Has a difficult but arresting start and some very testing arabesque passages. Ensemble problems make this a work for advanced players only. In one movement.

48. Jacob, Gordon (1895–). Sonatina. Novello, 1949. A fairly mature work by this distinguished English composer.

49. Jettel, Rudolph (1905–). Sonata. Hoffmeister, 1953. A large-scale work in the post-romantic style which characterizes all his works. Well written, as befits a composition by a master-clarinettist who is also a gifted composer.

50. Juon, Paul (1872–1940). Sonata Op. 82. Schlesinger, 1925. Short, but interesting and melodic.

51. Karg-Elert, S. (1877–1933). Sonata Op. 139. Zimmermann, 1924. Modern, difficult and stimulating.

52. Kelly, Brian (1934–). Two Concert Pieces. Novello, 1967. Light, well contrasted. The Adagio is lyrical, the Allegro aggressive.

53. Laderman, Ezra (1924–). Sonata. O.U.P., 1970. Reputedly well written, modern and original.

54. Lefèvre, J. Xavier (1763–1829). Sonata in B flat. O.U.P. 1973. Written by the clarinettist who first added the sixth key, a pupil at the Paris Conservatoire. Realized by Georgina Debree, it is virtuoso, rather over-long, but with a rollicking last movement that can stand alone.

55. Liadov, Anatol (1855–1914). Prelude Op. 46. Moscow State Publishing House. First published in 1899. Simple and tuneful.

56. Lutoslawski, W. (1913–). Prelude, 1954. Polish State Publishing House. A piece of excellent music by Poland's leading contemporary composer. Not difficult, and effective.

57. Lutyens, Elizabeth (1906–). Valediction. Mills, 1953. A piece written in memory of Dylan Thomas. Requires a feeling for modern music, but no very advanced technique other than flexibility between registers and control *in altissimo*.

58. McCabe, John (1939–). Three Pieces. Novello, 1964. Modern in conception, but with a feeling for melody which is most welcome. The rhythms are complex, but not for the sake of complexity. Contains a fine bossa nova, in five-four time.

59. Martinu, B. (1890–1959). Sonatine. Leduc, 1957. A good work, sometimes uneven but holding interest.

60. Mendelssohn, F. (1809–47). Sonata. Leeds Music, 1941. Not the best of music by this great composer, but useful as an opening gambit in sonata-playing.

61. Mihalovici, Marcel (1894–). Sonata Op. 78. Huegel, 1959. Not easy, but reflects a thoroughly workmanlike approach. Good ensemble training.

62. Milhaud, Darius (1892–1974). Sonatina for clarinet, 1927. Witty, dissonant and full of rhythmic quirks. It also has charm.

63. Parrott, Ian (1916–). Aquarelle. Chester, 1952. Requires great flexibility; abrupt changes of register as well as some rhythmic patterns which need care. Many changes of mood in this five-minute piece, which is very effective if well played.

64. Pierné, Gabriel (1863–1937). Canzonetta Op. 19. Leduc. A charming and lively programme piece. Excellent *arpeggio* study.

65. Pierné, Gabriel. Serenade, Op. 7. Leduc. Simpler, and extremely pleasant.

66. Pitfield, Thomas (1903–). Sonata. Elgin, 1966. Melodic, but with some amusing rhythmic experiments. Not difficult.

67. Pitfield, Thomas. Four Conversation Pieces, with piano or string accompaniment. Simpler, and well written.

68. Poulenc, F. (1899–1963). Sonata. Chester, 1963. One of the finest of modern sonatas. Contains the best of Poulenc's characteristics and may be said to sum up his output.

69. Prout, E. (1835–1909). Sonata Op. 26. Augener, 1886. Speaks with a now out-moded voice, but has charm and is brilliant in parts. Worth exploration.

70. Rakov, Nicolai (1908–). Sonata. Moscow State Publishing House, 1956. In the modestly modern Russian style, with a bright second movement.

71. Reger, Max (1873–1916). Sonatas Op. 49 Nos. 1 and 2.

For clarinet in A – a rather rare event. Fine music which somehow misses the mark with audiences, at any rate in Britain. Well worth study, especially the difficult piano part.

72. Reger, Max. Romance in G. Pleasant but unremarkable.

73. Reinecke, Carl (1824–1910). Undine sonata, Op. 167. International Music, New York. Reputed to be romantic and pleasing.

74. Richardson, Alan (1904–). Roundelay. O.U.P., 1936. A charming movement which uses the lyrical quality of the clarinet perfectly. A good programme piece.

75. Richardson, Alan. Three Pieces. Augener. Slightly later, and less immediately attractive, but well written – and extremely satisfying from the playing angle.

76. Ridout, Alan (1934–). Sonatina. Schott, 1968. Simple, but with interesting changes of time and rhythm which make it a good study to approach more modern pieces.

77. Ries, Ferdinand (1784–1838). Sonata in E flat, Op. 169. Barenreiter, 1970. Written by a great flautist who was associated with Beethoven for some years. An easy work, it goes surprisingly well on clarinet.

78. Rossini, G. (1792–1868). Fantaisie. Schott, 1828. Possibly merely founded on a Rossini theme and developed by an expert in clarinet technique. Brilliant and amusing.

79. Saint-Saens, Camille (1835–1921). Sonata Op. 167. Durand, 1924. Not as easy as it looks, especially the finale. Slow movement is weak, but the third is a very attractive scherzo which can stand alone.

80. Salowski, A. (1907–). . . . Omega, New York, 1948. One of the brightest of contemporary works, and easy to listen to. A brilliant finale which sounds more difficult than it is.

81. Schmidek, K. Sonatine Op. 30. Doblinger, Vienna, 1963. Reputedly a well written and melodious work.

82. Schumann, Robert (1810–56). Fantasy Pieces Op. 73. Peters. For A clarinet. Excellent music, difficult to play well, but rewarding. Should never be attempted on the B flat clarinet. For the intimate recital only.

83. Searle, Humphrey (1915–). 'Cat Variations' for clarinet in A and piano. Faber 1974. Inspired by the 'cat' theme in Prokofiev's 'Peter and the Wolf'. Six minutes of pleasant fun, not so difficult as the original, and immediately intelligible to the audience.

84. Seiber, Mátyás (1905–60). Andantino Pastorale. Schott. An excellent and deeply-felt little piece of atmosphere music. Quite simple, but not easy to| play perfectly. Short and effective.

85. Shaw, Christopher (1924–). Sonata. Novello, 1948. The *tessitura* of the clarinet part is rather high for comfort, but this sonata is notable for a good scherzo. The finale is difficult to read because of tied notes, which should be dotted. Lively, and excellent study.

86. Stanford, C. V. (1852–1924). Sonata Op. 129. Stainer & Bell, 1918. A fine work which is not presented as often as it should be. Audiences enjoy it. It is pleasant and absorbing to play, and the slow movement, a 'caoine' or Irish lament, can stand alone.

87. Tartini, G. (1692–1770). Concertino, arr Gordon Jacob. Boosey & Hawkes, 1946. Arrangements of violin sonata movements, equally effective with piano accompaniment or strings. Perfectly fills the gap in the repertoire left by the paucity of classical works.

88. Telemann, G. F. (1681–1767). Sonata. International, New York, 1960. Suits the purpose of the Tartini above. Transcribed from a flute sonata.

89. Templeton, Alec (1909–53). Pocket Sized Sonatas Nos. 1 and 2. Leeds Music, New York, 1949. Most entertaining pieces using the harmonic and stylistic elements of the jazz of the thirties. An excellent concert piece. Should not be attempted without a proper knowledge of the idiom; otherwise it is embarrassing.

90. Tomasi, H. (1901–). Three pieces: (a) Introduction et Danse; (b) Complaint du jeune Indien; (c) Chant Corse. Leduc, 1949. Entertaining and useful.

91. Tuthill, Burnet C. (1888–). Fantasy Sonata Op. 3. Carl Fischer, New York, 1936. A fairly difficult single move-

ment work by a well-known American clarinettist, composer and musicologist.

92. Vinter, Gilbert (1909–68). Concertino. Boosey & Hawkes. Piquant but no great weight, by a well-known bassoonist conductor whose knowledge of wood-wind was always evident.

93. Weber, C. M. (1786–1826). Grand Duo Concertante, Op. 48. (Various publishers.) The finest of all show pieces for the medium, with a slow movement almost completely operatic in inspiration. Requires first-class playing from both partners.

94. Weinberger, J. (1896–1928). Sonatine. Carl Fischer, New York, 1940. A simple piece, valuable because of its *cantabile* character and the interest in the ensemble. Good experience.

95. Whettam, Graham (1927–). Sonatina. Leeds, 1967. Short and pithy, with some finger-twisters in the third (and last) movement.

96. Wildgans, F. (1913–). Sonatina in B minor. Doblinger, Vienna, 1963. A short work of some charm, with economy of utterance and style.

Concertos and works with orchestra

1. Arnold, Malcolm (1921–). Concerto for Clarinet and Strings. Lengnick, 1952. A fairly easy work by this always stimulating composer. Not as original as his Sonatina, but worth exploration. Well written for the instrument. There is talk of a new concerto, for Benny Goodman.

2. Bärmann, Heinrich (1784–1847). Adagio, with strings. Breitkopf & Härtel. Formerly thought to be by Wagner. See clarinet and piano section.

3. Bärmann, Karl (1811–85). Concerto Militaire. Schott, 1875. Not to be confused with his father Heinrich, whose melodic gifts were superior. A work of some technical brilliance, useful for study leading to Spohr and Weber.

4. Ben-Heim, Paul (1897–). Pastoral Varié, with strings and harp. (No publisher known, but photostat copies in many

libraries.) A pleasant short work of unusual melodic beauty in parts.

5. Bozza, E. (1905–). Concerto in B flat. Leduc, 1952. Fluent and full of problems, but with musical interest.

6. Bruns, V. (1904–). Concerto Op. 26. Hoffmeister, 1952. A tricky work, but worth study. A modern sound.

7. Bush, Geoffrey (1920–). Rhapsody with strings. Elkin, 1953. An effective concert piece in the older style, also useful with piano. For A clarinet, and sometimes high in *tessitura*.

8. Busoni, F. (1866–1924). Concertino Op. 48. Breitkopf & Härtel, 1919. An unusual-sounding work with Busoni's characteristic melodic side-slips. Marred only by some string-inspired arpeggios which should be edited by the player to assist breathing.

9. Cimarosa, D. (1749–1801). Concerto with strings, arr Arthur Benjamin. Boosey & Hawkes, 1942. First played on the oboe, but equally valid on clarinet, since the original was for piano.

10. Copland, Aaron (1900–). Concerto. Boosey & Hawkes, 1950. After a slow introduction a jazzy cadenza leads to a lively final movement which is both playable and listenable. Very effective writing and good concert-technique.

11. Cruft, Adrian (1921–). Concertino with strings. Joseph Williams, 1956. A work which deserves more notice than it has had so far. It is modern-romantic and musical, and not over difficult. Piano reduction available.

12. Crusell, Bernhard (1775–1838). Three Concertos. Not published, but in several libraries (e.g. B.B.C., London). That in B flat is an interesting work and of considerable technical freedom.

13. Debussy, Claude (1862–1918). Première Rhapsodie. Durand, 1910. The finest work of its kind, even more colourful with orchestra than with piano, though more difficult to balance, except microphonically.

14. Dello Joio, Norman (1915–). Concerto. Carl Fischer, 1955. An excellent work, which makes an immediate impression on the public. Easier to balance as a recording or broadcast than as a concert piece, but always effective.

15. Dubois, Pierre Max (1930–). Beaugency Concerto. Leduc, 1969. That rare creation, an uncomplicated modern French concerto. With strings, and neo-classical in effect.

16. Finzi, Gerald (1901–56). Concerto, with strings. Boosey & Hawkes, 1951. One of the very best works of this century. Not difficult ,very melodic, but modern in a piquant manner. The slow movement rather over-balances the other two in length and intensity.

17. Françaix, Jean (1912–). Concerto. Éditions Musicales Transatlantiques, 1963. A work for the future, possibly, when the instrument has developed further or the human hand has changed. At present, its roulades in the key of B major are beyond almost any player; but the work is a worthwhile challenge, and the A clarinet would probably provide the answer.

18. Grovlez, G. (1879–1944). Concertino. Callet & Fils, 1940. Light and melodic, like all his music. It has more the character of a suite in three movements, finishing as it does with a march.

19. Hamilton, Iain (1922–). Concerto Op. 7. Schott, 1950, London (available on hire only). A large-scale work commissioned by the Royal Philharmonic Society about 1950, it now sounds much less modern but is still a fearsome task for the soloist. Trombones in the score indicate the sort of balance problem to be faced. An interesting work.

20. Handel, G. F. (1685–1759). Concerto, with strings, arr J. Barbirolli. O.U.P., 1952. A good baroque selection of four movements which fit well together. Fills out the classical repertoire.

21. Hindemith, Paul (1895–1963). Concerto. Schott, 1950. In the late Hindemith manner. A fine work, but not as memorable as the Sonata. Difficult but effective. The orchestra must be kept at bay.

22. Hoddinott, Alun (1929–). Concerto, with strings. O.U.P., 1955. Started out in life as a concerto for the B flat clarinet. The composer wisely accepted this writer's own A clarinet edition, including some revisions in the finale. A useful work as it now stands, and a good display piece.

23. Holbrooke, Josef (1878–1958). Double concerto, 'Tamerlane', with bassoon. Modern Music, London. A romantic piece, and a good display piece for both players.

24. Horovitz, J. (1926–). Concertante with strings. Chester, 1953. Fairly difficult, but effective.

25. Hummel, J. F. (1841–1919). Concerto No. 2. Breitkopf & Härtel, 1932. A Weberish work, and brilliant.

26. Jettel, R. (1903–). Concertino. Eulenberg, 1969. Apparently only in piano accompaniment form at present. A good work in two contrasted sections, which it is hoped this fine clarinettist-composer will orchestrate.

27. Jongen, J. (1873–1953). Concertino. Gervan, Brussels, 1947. A brilliant, showy piece.

28. Keys, Ivor (1919–). Concerto, with strings. Novello, 1959. For A clarinet. Has had some successful performances. Makes a pleasant impression. Not difficult.

29. Kleinsinger, G. (1914–). 'Street Corner Concerto.' Chappell, 1953. As the title suggests, not a serious work. Jazzy in style. Pleasant and easy.

30. Krenek, Ernst (1900–). Suite with strings (or piano). Rongwen, New York, 1956. A strangely atonal work, but one which makes a good impression. Better with strings.

31. Krommer, F. (Kramar) (1759–1831). Concerto in E flat. Musica Antiqua Bohemica, 1953. A charming Weberish work which has had a considerable vogue through two recordings in recent years. Should be played more often.

32. Krommer, F. Concerto for two clarinets. Offenbach, 1962. Less successful, but one of the few worthwhile works in this form.

33. Macdonald, Malcolm (1916–). Cuban Rondo, with small orchestra. Ricordi, 1960. Idiomatic and well written. Better with a large percussion section.

34. Malko, Nicolai (1888–). Concerto. Belaieff, 1955. (Boosey & Hawkes.) Easy and melodic, and quite short. A useful second work for any programme.

35. Maurer, L. (1789–1878). Concerto. Hoffmeister, 1900. The same period as Weber and Spohr. Reputed to be a worthwhile work.

36. Milhaud, Darius (1892–1974). Concerto. Elkan-Vogel, 1942. Like the Françaix, this work may have to wait. At present it is too tiring for any performer to play with comfort. It is attractive and worthy of attention as a challenge.

37. Molique, Bernhard (1802–69). Concertino in F minor. Barenreiter, 1824. By a German violinist and one-time professor in London at the Royal Academy of Music. Graceful music, virtuoso without vulgarity. Moderately difficult. Should be heard more often.

38. Molter, J. M. (1695–1765). Four concertos, for clarinet in D. Breitkopf & Härtel, 1957. Brilliant and remarkable. Probably the very first clarinet concertos. Scarcely any use of the chalumeau, pointing to the fact that the new clarinet was tuned for its overblown register only.

39. Mozart, W. A. (1756–91). Concerto in A. Many publishers. Comment is superfluous. Simply the greatest clarinet concerto, almost certainly the greatest wind concerto, and one of the finest concertos in any form.

40. Musgrave, Thea (1928–). Concerto. (Should soon be published in London). A most amusing work, theatrical as well as brilliantly virtuoso. The soloist conducts various 'rebel' groups in turn, superimposing these on the main orchestral palette. It comes off, and has had many hectic and hilarious performances in London and Central Europe.

41. Nielsen, Carl (1865–1931). Concerto. Dania, 1946. A modern classic, dating from 1926 and sketching the character (volatile) of the soloist Oxenvaad. Brilliant, difficult and rewarding, it has also moments of real beauty.

42. Patatich, Ivan (1922–). Concertino. Musica Budapest, 1970. Three pieces in Bulgarian style. Rhythmically interesting and stylish. Difficult but rewarding.

43. Piston, Walter (1894–). Concerto. Associated Music Publishers, 1968. Reputed to be difficult, intelligent and rhythmically interesting.

44. Rawsthorne, Alan (1905–71). Concerto, with strings. O.U.P., 1936. A work which has somehow been overlooked, possibly because there is no piano reduction – nor would one be playable. Not too difficult. An important work.

45. Reiter, A. Concerto. Doblinger, 1968. An agreeable and un-modern work which will give pleasure to many. Not difficult.

46. Rimsky-Korsakov, N. A. (1844–1908). Concerto, with military band. Omega, 1949. As written, quite trite and unoriginal. It can be edited and embellished to be effective and showy. Needs imagination.

47. Rossini, G. (1792–1868). Introduction, theme and variations. Sikorski. Brilliant. Probably not by Rossini. Brought to London by the late Karl Haas some years before this publication. The original manuscript has at the start 'Andante di Rossini', indicating that he wrote the tune rather than the variations. A fine show piece which badly needs a long cadenza to end it.

48. Sarkozy, Istvan. Sinfonia Concertante, with strings. Budapest Music, 1970. Florid, rhapsodic and brillaint. Difficult.

49. Seiber, Mátyás (1905–60). Concertino, with strings. Schott, 1953. A work of complex tonality but simple and attractive structure and moderate difficulty. Some good tunes.

50. Siegmeister, Elie (1909–). . . Sam Fox, 1962. One of the very best works in the jazz idiom, being more up-to-date than most. Quite difficult, but pleasant to play and well orchestrated. Requires a soloist well versed in jazz, as well as experienced in concertos.

51. Sikorski, K. (1910–). Concerto. Polish State Publishing House, 1959. In romantic style, but never dull. Difficult to play, but not to listen to.

52. Spohr, L. (1784–1859). Concertos Nos. 1, 2, 3 and 4. Peters, Breitkopf. All four are fine works and technically brilliant. Well worth careful study. The slow movements of all of them are very rewarding.

53. Stamitz, Johann (1717–57). Concerto, with strings. Leeds, 1953. Good writing by the elder Stamitz, this work was unpublished for over two hundred years. Not easy, but worth playing.

54. Stamitz, Karl (1745–1801). Concerto No. 1 in E flat. Hoffmeister, 1956. Less in stature than his father's work, but

notable for the use of the chalumeau register. Easy to play. Eleven of his concertos are listed by Burnet Tuthill, as being of varying value.

55. Stamitz, Karl. Concerto for two clarinets and orchestra. Budapest Music, 1969. Excellent baroque music, well written for the soloists and always well balanced.

56. Stanford, C. V. (1852–1924). Concerto Op. 80. Manuscript. Not generally available, but possibly to be published soon. Both clarinets (A and B flat) are used, which somewhat complicates performance, but it is an enjoyable work to play. It has a good audience reaction.

57. Strauss, Richard (1864–1949). Double concerto, with bassoon, strings and harp. Boosey & Hawkes, 1949. Late Strauss, and good in its florid way. Deserves more attention than it has had.

58. Stravinsky, I. (1882–1971). Ebony Concerto. Charling, 1946. Scored for jazz orchestra. Not really a clarinet concerto at all, but fairly interesting as a work for reed players generally.

59. Tartini, G. (1692–1770). Concertino, with strings, arr Gordon Jacob. Boosey & Hawkes, 1945. A most useful work compounded from movements from Tartini's violin sonatas; it comes off perfectly as clarinet music, and is sufficiently brief to use as a second work in a programme. Not difficult.

60. Veale, John (1922–). Concerto. O.U.P., 1955. For A clarinet. A romantic work using a fairly large orchestra. Enjoyable and moderately difficult.

61. Vinter, Gilbert (1909–68). Concertino. Boosey & Hawkes, 1955. A lightweight work by an expert on woodwind technique. Not important, but pleasant and well written.

62. Weber, C. M. (1786–1826). Concertino, Concertos Nos. 1 and 2. Many publishers. All superb in their own way, and posing problems of technique. Showy and rewarding. They are in the repertoire of all clarinettists, and much enjoyed.

63. Whettam, Graham (1927–). Concerto Op. 40. Manuscript 1959. Probably to be published soon. A well written work by a knowledgable composer. It has had many successful per-

formances and good reviews. A notable feature is the cadenza, which shows much originality. Quite difficult.

64. Wilson, Ken. Concerto, with strings, Manuscript (*c.* 1960). A romantic sounding work of moderate difficulty which has been very well performed by this most able New Zealand clarinettist. Requires good musicianship. Deserves publication.

Works for Solo Clarinet Alone

1. Baur, J. (1918–). Six Bagatelles. Breitkopf & Härtel. Listed by Kroll.
2. Camilleri, Charles (1931–). 'Three Visions for an Imaginary Dancer'. Fairfield, 1968. Well written music by a Maltese composer. Good concert pieces, especially the second piece, a lively waltz.
3. Cavallini, E. (1807–74). Caprices, Hofmeister. Of varying difficulty and value. Lively and useful, probably as separate pieces rather than complete.
4. Chagrin, Francis (1905–72). Improvisation and Toccatina. Augener. Brilliantly effective, but fiendishly difficult. Certainly among the finest display pieces, and standing up well to public performance before knowledgeable audiences. For experts only.
5. Hummel, Berthold (1925–). Suite, Simrock, 1965. Five movements. Well contrasted. The last two, a grotesque march and a tarantella, make good encore or concert pieces.
6. Jacob, Gordon (1895–). Five Pieces. O.U.P., 1974 Charming, easy and effective. Good concert pieces, ending with a brisk scherzo and including a 'Homage to J. S. Bach' which is in a well-calculated style.
7. Kardos, Istvan. Solo Sonata. General Music Publishers, 1970. Eleven minutes of well contrasted and well written music with lots of rhythmic excitement.
8. Karg-Elert, S. (1877–1933). Sonata Op. 110. Grahl & Necklar. Modern sounding and rather stark. Good for study or for special purposes.

9. Krenek, Ernst (1900–). Monolog. Barenreiter. Has its own melodic shape, redolent of this composer's harmonies. Effective.

10. Lang, Istvan (1933–). Monodia. Budapest Music, 1918. A fairly long piece, full of challenge. Not a good concert material. Difficult.

11. Lehmann, Hans (1937–). Mosaic. Schott. Listed by Rendell.

12. Levy, Ernst (1895–) . . . Manuscript from Swiss Archives. Listed by Kroll.

13. Martino, D. (1931–). 'A set for clarinet.' McGinnes & Marx, 1957. Fairly simple and effective. Could be used in part.

14. Mayer, John (1929–). Raga Music. Lengnick, 1958. Nine pieces written by an expert Indian violinist in correct Raga technique. Require study for appreciation and performance. Difficult.

15. Pinkham, Daniel. Etude. Ione Press, 1963. Short, difficult and challenging.

16. Rychlik, Jan (d. 1964). Burleskni Suite. Panton. Bratislava, 1964. Very much gypsy in style, with a finale full of rhythmic twists.

17. Saucier, Gene . . . Schirmer, 1966. Good exercise in rhythmic patterns. No bar lines, but the music reveals itself easily ehough. Difficult.

18. Stravinsky, Igor (1882–1971). Three Pieces. Chester,1919. The best-known of all solo pieces for the clarinet. They display the character of the instrument well and are good Stravinsky. Difficult to play well. The last one is not really jazz, but rather Stravinsky's impression of it.

19. Sutermeister, A. (1910–). Capriccio. Schott. Lively and effective.

20. Wellesz, Egon (1885–1974). Suite Op. 74. Peters. Inclined to be cerebral and remote, but good study.

Duets with various instruments

1. Beethoven, L. van (1770–1827). Three Duos Op. 147

(with bassoon). Various publishers. The best known duos for the combination. Quite good Beethoven. Difficult to sustain.

2. Berg, Alban (1885–1935). Duets (with violin). D.F.M., 1947. Listed by Kroll.

3. Crusell, Bernhard (1775–1838). Duos for two clarinets. Peters, 1820. Good classic style. Florid and interesting.

4. Frank, Alan (1910–). Suite for two clarinets, O.U.P.,1934. Amusing and simple.

5. Hindemith, Paul (1895–1963). Duets (with violin). Schott, 1932. Solid and well constructed with well contrasted instrumental styles.

6. Koechlin, Charles (1867–1950). Idyll for two clarinets. Chant du Monde. Short but pleasant. A good programme piece.

7. Krenek, Ernst (1900–). Sonatina, with flute. Barenreiter. Listed by Kroll.

8. Lefèvre, J. (1763–1829). Six Duos Concertantes Op. 9, 10, 11. Naderman, 1810. Unusually well balanced for the period.

9. Poulenc, Francis (1899–1963). Duo for two clarinets. Chester, 1924. B flat and A clarinets. Highly original and characteristic. Effective. Difficult to control, but rewarding.

10. Poulenc, Francis. Duo (with bassoon). Chester, 1922. Equal to the duos above, and equally rewarding.

11. Pranzer, J. Three Duos Concertantes for two clarinets. Transatlantique, 1967. Surprisingly, an original work by a pupil of Haydn. Excellent classical style and obvious knowledge of the clarinet.

12. Reizenstein, Franz (1911–68). Duo (with oboe). Galliard, 1965. Plenty of contrapuntal and melodic interest. Simple.

13. Riegger, W. (1885–1961). Duet Op. 35 (with flute). Universal. Modern and atonal. Good introduction to modern duo playing.

14. Salowski, A. (1907–). Duet (with flute). Omega, 1948. Florid and lively.

15. Schuller, Gunther (1925–). Duo (with bass clarinet). Peters. Listed by Kroll.

16. Tate, Phyllis (1911–). Sonata (with cello). O.U.P., 1949.

A good work, too rarely performed. Not difficult for either instrument.

Trios

(a) Trios with piano and another instrument

1. Bach, C. P. E. (1714–88). Six sonatas (with bassoon). E.M.B., Budapest. Formal, but lively.

2. Bartók, B. (1881–1945). Contrasts (with violin). Boosey & Hawkes, 1942. A most effective and satisfying work. Originally for A and B flat clarinets, and commissioned by Benny Goodman. B flat version available, to avoid change of clarinet in the finale. Difficult.

3. Beethoven, L. van (1770–1827). Trio Op. 11 (with cello). Breitkopf & Härtel. An early work, written before Beethoven fully understood the clarinet. Fine music, which has to be mae to sound as good as it is.

4. Brahms, J. (1833–97). Trio Op. 114 (with cello). Simrock, 1892. A great masterpiece. For A clarinet. It requires fluent technique and excellent musicianship. Very satisfying.

5. Bruch, Max (1838–1920). Trio (with viola): Eight Pieces Op. 83. Simrock, 1910. Rather dated in style and lacking in drama, but pleasant and worthy of attention.

6. D'Indy, V. (1851–1931). Trio (with cello) Op. 20. Hamelle, 1887. Somewhat dated in style, but good music and craftsmanship.

7. Glinka, M. (1804–57). Trio Pathétique (with bassoon). Musica Rara. An unusual sound, and a work worthy of attention.

8. Ives, Charles (1874–1954). Largo (with violin). Southern Music Co. Short, meandering and characteristic. A study in leaps to the altissimo.

9. Khachaturian, A. (1903–). Trio (with violin). Anglo-Soviet, 1932. An unusual-sounding work in which the clarinet takes on an Eastern character. Excellent study in *legato* chromatic movement.

10. Mendelssohn, F. (1809–47). Two Concert Pieces (with

basset horn). Breitkopf & Härtel. Fascinating works, and surprisingly effective even today. The basset horn parts require great facility in the lowest register. Ensemble problems abound.

11. Milhaud, D. (1892–1974). Suite (with violin). Senart, 1937. Spiky and humorous. Requires perfect balance and attack. Comes off well in performance.

12. Mozart, W. A. (1756–91). Trio K 498 (with viola). Breitkopf & Härtel. The greatest work for this combination. Said to have been written between games in a skittle-alley, it shows no signs of haste or aberration. A masterpiece.

13. Reinecke, C. (1824–1910). Trio Op. 264 (with viola). Simrock. Not a masterpiece like the Mozart, but acceptable music and good craftsmanship.

14. Reizenstein, F. (1911–68). Trio (with flute and bassoon). Modern and dissonant, but easily understood. Quite difficult, but never unplyable.

15. Saint-Saens, C. (1835–1921). Trio-Serenade (with flute). Durand. Charming, and fairly simple.

16. Schumann, R. (1810–56). Fairy Pieces Op. 132. Breitkopf & Härtel. Good light pieces.

17. Stravinsky, I. (1882–1971). 'L'Histoire du Soldat.' Chester, 1920. Composer's own trio version (with violin). Surprisingly effective. Difficult. Requires either a low E flat on the A clarinet or an elastic embouchure to produce this note.

18. Tate, Phyllis (1911–). Trio (with violin): Air & Variations. O.U.P., 1959. Pleasant music, and not difficult.

(b) Trios for three clarinets
1. Cooke, Arnold (1906–). Suite. O.U.P., 1962. Well written and with contrapuntal interest.

2. Picket, F. Legend and Jollity. Omega. Amusing and piquant.

(c) Trios with flute and bassoon
1. Koechlin, Charles (1867–1950). Trio Op. 92 in G. Senart, 1928. A pleasant romantic work with modern touches.

2. Lorenzo, L. de (1875–   ). Trio Eccentrico, Op. 26. Peters. Listed by Kroll as important.

3. Pijper, Willem (1894–1947). Trio. Peters. Written by a craftsman who understands the difficult balance of the combination.

(*d*) *Trios with flute and oboe*

1. Arnold, Malcolm (1921–). Divertimento Op. 37. Patterson, 1952. Witting and amusing both to play and to hear. Not difficult, but tricky.

2. Bennet, Richard Rodney (1936–). Trio. Universal. A quite serious work in modern guise. Difficult, but a challenge many will welcome.

3. Shostakovich, D. (1906–75). Preludes, Musicus, New York. Listed by Kroll.

(*e*) *Other combinations*

1. Handel, G. F. (1685–1759). Overture (two clarinets and horn). Schott, 1952. A surprising composition, believed to be original; first introduced to London by the late Karl Haas. Of historic rather than musical importance.

2. Mozart, W. A. (1756–91). Canonic Adagio (two basset horns and bassoon). Breitkopf & Härtel. Excellent music, and satisfying to play. Short.

3. Mozart, W. A. Five Divertimenti (two clarinets and bassoon). Breitkopf & Härtel. Probably originally for three basset horns; sounds even finer in this form. Always popular.

4. Stravinsky, I. (1882–1971). Epitaph (flute, clarinet and harp). Boosey & Hawkes, 1959. One of the strangest and certainly the shortest of pieces. Five bars in length, only three of which include the wind. A curiosity.

(*f*) *Reed trios* (*oboe, clarinet, bassoon*)

By far the most numerous. The following is a very short list of the best works.

1. Barraud H. (1900–). Trio. Oiseau Lyre, 1938. Florid and lively.

2. Bozza, E. (1905–). Suite Brève Op. 67. Leduc, 1947. Easier than most of his music, and very listenable.

3. Constant, Marius (1925–). Trio. Chester, 1949. Moderately difficult, pleasant.

4. Ferroud, P. O. (1900–36). Trio. Durand, 1934. For A clarinet. Florid.

5. Françaix, Jean (1912–). Divertissement. Schott. Witty.

6. Ibert, J. (1890–1962). Five Trio Pieces. Oiseau Lyre. One of the famous ones. Tricky, but excellent.

7. Lutoslawski, W. (1913–). Trio. Polish State Publishing House. Listed by Kroll.

8. Milhaud, D. (1892–1974). Suite d'après Corrette. Oiseau Lyre, 1938.

9. Milhaud, D. Suite Pastorale. Senart. Both in the neoclassical style rather than in Milhaud's normal language. Well balanced and clear voiced.

10. Pierrie, P. Bucolique Variée. Costallat, 1947. A good programme piece.

11. Poulenc, F. (1899–1963). Trio Hansen. Not the greatest Poulenc, but with much of his usual charm.

12. Schulhoff, Erwin (1894–1942). Divertissement. Schott, 1928. Stimulating. Not easy, but a good sound.

13. Villa-Lobos, Heitor (1887–1959). Trio. Eschig, Schott, 1921. One of the most fascinating works for the combination. Very difficult, and the difficulty not helped by the material normally provided. The score seems to be unobtainable and the parts are not only inaccurate but badly transposed, including one notable patch in the bass clef. The result is nonetheless worth the trouble.

14. Walthew, Richard (1872–1951). Triolet. Boosey & Hawkes, 1934. Simple and pleasant.

Quartets

(a) Quartets with piano
1. Françaix, J. (1912–). Quartet (flute, oboe, clarinet and piano). Andraud. Witty and well written.

2. Hindemith, P. (1895–1963). Quartet (clarinet, violin, cello and piano). Schott, 1938. One of the two finest works for this combination. Good to play and to hear.

3. Honegger, A. (1892–1955). Rhapsodie (two flutes, clarinet and piano). Salabent. A strange work, and sad; but worth playing.

4. Messiaen, Olivier (1908–). Quatuor pour la Fin du Temps (clarinet, violin, cello and piano). Durand, 1942. The finest work for the combination; one of the great chamber works of this century. Individual, modern, difficult and rewarding.

5. Milhaud, D. (1892–1974). Sonate (flute, oboe, clarinet and piano). Durand, 1923. Much earlier than the trio, and less individual; but interesting.

6. Saint-Saens, C. (1835–1921). Caprice Op. 79 (flute, oboe, clarinet and piano). Durand. Listed by Kroll.

(b) *Quartets with strings* (*violin, viola, cello*)

1. Crusell, Bernhard (1775–1838). Three Quartets, Op. 2, 4, 7. Peters. Historic curiosities, not easy to locate, but amusing.

2. Hindemith, P. (1895–1963). 'Aus Plöner Musiktag.' Schott. Listed by Rendall.

3. Hummel, J. H. (1778–1837). Quartet. Musica Rara, 1958. Straightforward and simple.

4. Rawsthorne, Alan (1905–71). Quartet. O.U.P., 1950. A work of major importance. Original, rhapsodic and with a lively finale owning something to jazz in spite of its triple rhythm. Difficult.

5. Stamitz, Karl (1745–1801). Quartets. Sieber and others. Many quartets, but none of outstanding merit. They make good secondary material for a programme.

(c) *Wind quartets* (*flute, oboe, clarinet and bassoon*)

1. Bozza, E. (1905–). Three Pieces (Serenade). Leduc. Pleasant and well constructed.

2. Bridge, Frank (1879–1941). Divertimenti. Boosey & Hawkes, 1940. As the title suggests, diverting music. Two of

the four movements are duets, and surprisingly effective.

3. Françaix, Jean (1912–). Quintet. Schott. Short and pithy.

4. Kabalevski, D. (1904–). Kindersuite Op. 27. Spratt. Listed by Kroll. Can be used effectively as illustrative material,

5. Kay, Norman (1929–). Miniature Quartet. O.U.P., 1959. An attractive little work which has proved popular. Records well.

(d) Wind quartets of mixed combinations

1. Butt, James (1929–). 'Winsome's Folly' (with oboe, horn and bassoon). Boosey & Hawkes, 1957. In neo-baroque style, well written and simple.

2. Cruft, Adrian (1921–). Dance Movement (with flute, oboe and horn). Elkin. Simple and effective.

3. Goepfart, Karl. Quartet (with flute, oboe and bassoon). Rudall Carte. Simple and pleasant to play. A good scherzo.

4. Ibert, J. (1890–1962). Two Movements (with two flutes and bassoon). Leduc, 1923. A light-sounding work which requires delicate handling.

5. Mozart, W. A. (1756–91). Cassation (with oboe, horn and bassoon). Andraud. Not great Mozart, but good music.

6. Rossini, G. A. (1792–1868). Six Quartets (with flute, horn and bassoon). Schott, 1935. Works of great dharm and varying difficulty. Require superb technique for telling performance.

7. Stamitz, Karl (1745–1801). Quartet Op. 8 in E flat (with oboe, horn and bassoon). Denkmaler, Munich. Listed by Kroll.

8. Sutermeister, H. (1910–). Serenade (with second clarinet, trumpet and bassoon). Schott. An unusual work, and surprisingly effective for such a combination.

Quintets

(a) Quintets with piano

1. Beethoven, L. van (1770–1827). Quintet Op. 16 (with oboe,

horn and bassoon). Various editions. A great work which combines a virtuoso piano part with excellent wind writing. The opening is difficult for ensemble and the horn needs great agility.

2. Danzi, Franz (1763–1826). Quintet Op. 41. Benjamin. A rather staid work, but of interest.

3. Dunhill, T. (1877–1946). Quintet (with horn, violin and cello). Rudall Carte, 1913. An early work of this English composer. Melodic and pleasant.

4. Hindemith, P. (1895–1963). Three Pieces Op. 35 (with trumpet, violin and double bass). Schott. Listed by Kroll and Rendell.

5. Mozart, W. A. (1756–91). Quintet K 452. Various editions. A great and mature work, witty as well as of great beauty. Not easy.

6. Rawsthorne, Alan (1905–71). Quintet (with oboe, horn and bassoon). O.U.P., 1964. A good work by this first-class composer. Too rarely performed.

7. Spohr, L. (1784–1859). Quintet Op. 52 (with flute, horn and bassoon). Peters. Listed by Kroll and Rendell.

(*b*) *Quintets with string quartet*

1. Bliss, Sir Arthur (1891–1975). Quintet. Novello, 1933. For A clarinet. Certainly one of the really significant works for this combination. A fine appreciation of the possibilities of modern clarinet technique, allied to a real sense of balance and rhythmic possibilities.

2. Brahms, J. (1833–97). Quintet. Composed 1892; many editions. Possibly the greatest of them all. A work of breathtaking insight into clarinet requirements and possibilities.

3. Cooke, Arnold (1906–). Quintet. Boosey & Hawkes. Well written and all playable. Well worth care and attention.

4. Hindemith, Paul (1895–1963). Quintet Op. 30. Schott, 1922. An originally constructed work, too rarely played. Requires an E flat clarinet for the Ländler movement, and ends with a palindromic movement of great difficulty. Interesting.

5. Jacob, Gordon (1895–). Quintet. Novello, 1946. Fluent and well written, as well as easily digested by audiences.

6. Mozart, W. A. (1756–91). Quintet. Many editions. Scarcely requires mention, since it is the foundation-stone of every piece ever written in this form. Magnificent.

7. Mozart, W. A. Allegro in B flat, completed by Robert D. Lewin. Barenreiter. Interesting and playable.

8. Reger, Max (1873–1916). Quintet Op. 146. Peters, 1916. For A clarinet. Depends for its success upon a player who really knows this composer's music. Perfect craftsmanship and good musical content.

9. Weber, C. M. (1786–1826). Quintet Op. 34. Various publishers.

10. Weber, C. M. Introduction, Theme and Variations. Works in the best Weber style. Showy, effective, challenging and always amusing and enjoyable. The second work suffers from a surfeit of B flat major.

(*c*) *Wind quintets* (*flute, oboe, clarinet, bassoon and horn*).
A very short list of selected works. There is much rubbish in this medium.

1. Barber, Samuel (1910–). 'Summer Music.' Schirmer, 1957. Charming and rhythmically original.

2. Birtwistle, Harrison (1934–). Refrains and Choruses. Universal. One of this composer's best works. Modern, but not impossibly so.

3. Damase, J. M. (1928–). Seventeen Variations Op. 22. Leduc, 1952. Charming, amusing and original. Difficult.

4. Danzi, Franz (1763–1826). Five Quintets Op. 56 to 68. Various publishers. Foundation-stones of quintet writing. Good, but dull.

5. Françaix, Jean (1912–). Quintet. Schott, 1951. Bright and amusing. Difficult.

6. Fricker, Peter Racine (1920–). Quintet Op. 5. Schott, 1951. An early work, and a good one. The last movement is in almost unplayable rhythm, simplified in a later edition. Should be played often.

7 Henze, A. W. (1926–). Quintet. Schott, 1953. One of his

best works; easy to understand, and effective.

8. Hindemith, Paul (1895–1963). Kleine Kammermusik Op. 24. Schott, 1922. Possibly the finest wind quintet so far written. Original, effective, moderately difficult. Above all, successful.

9. Holbrooke, Josef (1878–1958). Quintet Op. 27. Blenheim Press. Old-fashioned, but charming and well written.

10. Ibert, Jacques (1890–1962). Trois Pièces Brèves. Leduc, 1930. Charming, easy (apart from the clarinet part of the third piece) and perfect programme material.

11. Jacob, Gordon (1895–). Quintet. Boosey & Hawkes, Effective and well written.

12. Milhaud, D. (1892–1974). 'La Cheminée du Roi René'. Andraud, 1939. Fills the need for baroque quintet music. Antique in sound, and charming.

13. Nielsen, Carl (1865–1931). Quintet Op. 43. Hansen, 1923. After Hindemith, the finest. Like the clarinet and flute concertos, the quintet has echoes of the personalities of the players for whom it was written. Amusing and effective.

14. Pijper, Willem (1894–1947). Quintet. Donemus. Well written and elegant.

15. Reicha, A. (1770–1836). Many quintets from Op. 88 to Op. 100. All well written, but best if taken in small doses. Several separate movements are real gems.

16. Schoenberg, A. (1874–1951). Quintet Op. 26. Universal, 1924. A turning point in his career, since it was his first great experiment in serial form. A great work, requiring long rehearsal for success; can be done without a conductor, but is a major feat.

17. Tomasi, H. (1901–). Quintet. Lemoine, 1952. Conservative in style, but good programme material.

18. Vinter, Gilbert (1909–68). Two Miniatures. Breitkopf & Härtel. Slight but pleasant. Encore material.

19. Zafred, Mario (1922–). Quintet. Ricordi, 1952. Lively and original.

(*d*) *Other quintets*

1. Bach, J. C. (1735–82). (a) Four quintets. (b) Wind sym-

phonies. For two clarinets, two horns and bassoon. Surprisingly florid for the period. The symphonies, written in London for concerts in Vauxhall Gardens, are excellent programme material and show real understanding of the clarinet.

2. Mozart, W. A. (1756–91). Adagio (two clarinets, three basset horns). Superbly written. Sombre.

3. Rawsthorne, Alan (1905–71). Quintet for piano, oboe, clarinet, horn and bassoon. O.U.P., 1964. Typically approachable and enjoyable.

4. Nielsen, Carl (1865–1931). 'Serenata in vano' (clarinet, bassoon, horn, cello and bass). Pleasant music, and easy apart from the bass cadenza, which can lead to bathos.

Sextets

(a) *Piano, and wind quintet*

1. Holbrooke, Josef (1878–1958). Sextet Op. 33a. Chester, 1906.

2. Jacob, Gordon (1895–). Sextet. Benjamin.

3. Pijper, Willem (1894–1947). Sextet. Donemus, 1923.

4. Poulenc, F. (1899–1964). Sextet. Chester, 1932. Brilliant and amusing.

5. Roussel, A. (1869–1937). Divertissement Op. 6. Rouant, 1905.

(b) *Other sextets with piano*

1. Copland, Aaron (1900–). Sextet (clarinet, piano, string quartet). Difficult, and in places needlessly so, but effective.

2. Dankworth, John (1927–). Sextet (clarinet, piano, string quartet). Manuscript. Effective and interesting.

3. Falla, Manuel de (1876–1946). Concerto da Camera (flute, oboe, clarinet, violin, cello and harpsichord). The best harpsichord concerto in chamber form.

4. Onslow, George (1784–1853). Sextet (flute, clarinet, bassoon, horn, bass and piano). Breitkopf & Härtel.

5. Prokofiev, S. (1891–1953). Overture on Jewish Themes Op. 34. Breitkopf & Härtel. A florid clarinet part, worth study.

(c) *Sextets for wind alone*

1. Beethoven, L. van (1770–1927). Sextet for two clarinets, two bassoons and two horns. Breitkopf & Härtel. A great work with a lovely slow movement and a brilliant finale with superb clarinet writing.

2. Danzi, Franz (1763–1826). Sextet in E flat. Sikorski. Dull beside the Beethoven, but well written.

3. Janacek, L. (1854–1928), 'Mladi' (for flute, oboe, clarinet, bass clarinet, bassoon and horn). A great work, both difficult and rewarding.

4. Mozart, W. A. (1756–91). Serenade in E flat, K 375. Musica Rara. The original form of the great work usually played as an octet. Contains an extra trio to one of the minuet movements. Well worth attention. Exhausting in this form.

5. Seiber, Mátyás (1905–60). Serenade for two clarinets, two bassoons and two horns. Hansen, Original and appealing.

(d) *Other sextets without piano*

1. Addison, John (1920–). Serenade for flute, oboe, clarinet, bassoon, horn and harpsichord. O.U.P., 1958.

2. Bärmann, H. (1784–1847). Adagio (clarinet, string quartet, bass). Usually attributed to Wagner. A lovely tune, perfectly suited to the clarinet. Sad.

3. Ibert, Jacques (1890–1962). 'Garden of Samos' (for flute, clarinet, trumpet, violin, cello and percussion). Heugel, 1935.

4. Jettel, R. (1903–). Sextet (flute, oboe, two clarinets, bassoon and horn). Doblinger. Workmanlike and playable.

5. Spohr, L. (1784–1859). Fantasy and Variations Op. 81 (clarinet, string quartet and bass). Schmitt.

Septets

1. Bach, C. P. E. (1714–88). Six Sonatas (two flutes, two clarinets, bassoon, two horns). Musica Rara. Early effective ise of clarinets.
2. Beethoven, L. van (1770–1827). Septet Op. 20 (clarinet, horn, bassoon and string quartet). The greatest septet of them all. A wonderful slow movement which is one of the finest ever written. Difficult.
3. Hindemith, Paul (1895–1963). Septet (flute, oboe, clarinet, bass clarinet, bassoon, horn and trumpet). Schott, 1949. A most original score for a very unusual combination.
4. Ravel, Maurice (1875–1937). Introduction and allegro for flute, clarinet, strings and harp. Durand, 1906. One of the loveliest sounds in all music. Really a harp concerto, but involving great intonation and ensemble problems for all.
5. Spohr, L. (1784–1859). Septet Op. 147 (flute, clarinet, bassoon, horn, violin, cello and piano). Heavy going in parts, but good music.
6. Stravinsky, I. (1882–1971). Septet. Breitkopf & Härtel, 1953. Brittle, agile music. Original and worthy.
7. Stravinsky, I. 'Histoire du Soldat' (for violin, clarinet, bassoon, trumpet, trombone, bass and percussion). A famous work, full of complex rhythms and unusual effects. A haunting score.
8. Villa-Lobos, Heitor (1887–1959). Choros No. 7 (flute, oboe, clarinet, alto saxophone, bassoon, violin and cello). Eschig, 1928. Not as fine as the trio but good music.

Octets

(a) *Two oboes, two clarinets, two bassoons, two horns*
1. Beethoven, L. Van (1770–1827). Octet Op. 103. Various publishers. A great work, and brilliant. Also: Rondino, which contains some inspired writing for horns.
2. Haydn, J. (1732–1809). Octet in F. International Music,

1901. Listed by Kroll, An interesting item.

3. Jacob, Gordon (1895–). Divertimento.
A good work, containing virtuoso horn parts.

4. Mozart W. A. (1756–91). Serenade in E flat, K 375; Serenade in C minor, K 388; Divertimento in E flat, K 196c; Divertimento in B flat, K 196t. Musica Rara. Great works, all of them. The greatest is the C minor ,which is among Mozart's most poignant utterances.

It is worth noting that there a great many 'lost' octets by Mozart: these are sometimes listed as 'spurious' when discovered, but recent research by Daniel N. Leeson and David Whitwell tends to suggest that most of them are original, and it is to be hoped that many may soon be available. Among them there may be several 'operas for winds', the most celebrated of which is 'Il Seraglio', in Mozart's own arrangement, not those by Sedlak or Wendt.

(b) *Octets for other combinations*

1. Bach, C. P. E. (1714–88). Six Sonatas (two flutes, two clarinets, two bassoons, two horns). Breitkopf & Härtel.

2. Ferguson, Howard (1908–). Octet (clarinet, bassoon, horn, string quartet, bass). Breitkopf & Härtel, 1934. Melodic and pleasant.

3. Jacob, Gordon (1895–). Serenade (two flutes, two oboes, two horns, two bassoons). Breitkopf & Härtel.

4. Schubert, Franz (1797–1828). Octet Op. 166 (clarinet, bassoon, horn, strings and bass). The greatest octet of any – and especially for the clarinet.

5. Spohr, L. (1784–1859). Octet Op. 32 (clarinet, two horns and string quintet). An interesting work, with virtuoso horn parts.

6. Stravinsky, I. (1882–1971). Octet (flute, clarinet, two bassoons, two trumpets, two trombones). 1924. Good middle-period Stravinsky.

Nonets

1. Goossens, E. (1893–1962). Fantasy Nonet Op. 40 (flute, oboe, two clarinets, two bassoons, two horns, trumpet). Curwen, 1924. Wears well and should be played.
2. Gounod, C. (1818–93). Petite Symphonie (flute and normal wind octet). A fine work, with charm and style. The parts are so badly arranged that two sets are needed.
3. Spohr, L. (1784–1859). Nonet Op. 31 (for wind quintet and strings). Possibly the best known of all nonets, and not without reason. A memorable work.
4. Krommer, F. (1759–1831). Wind octet with contra-fagotto, Op. 79. Hoffmeister. Attractive, like all his music. Should be better known.

A few selected and valuable works for larger combinations.

1. Dvořak, A. (1841–1904). Serenade Op. 44 (eleven instruments). Simrock, 1879.
2. Mozart, W. A. (1756–91). Serenade in B flat for thirteen wind instruments, K 361.
3. Rawsthorne, Alan (1905–71). Concerto for ten instruments. O.U.P., 1962.
4. Schoenberg, A. (1874–1951). Chamber symphony Op. 9 (fifteen instruments). Universal, 1906.
5. Stockhausen, K. (1928–). Kontrapunkte (for ten instruments). Universal.
6. Strauss, Richard (1864–1949). Serenade Op. 7; Suite Op. 4 (both for thirteen instruments). Universal, 1884.

Works including basset horns

1. Birtwistle, Harrison (1934–). 'The World is Discovered.' For two flutes, oboe, cor anglais, clarinet, basset horn, two bassoons and two horns. Universal.

2. Mendelssohn, F. (1809–47). Two Concert Pieces Op. 113, 114, for clarinet, basset horn and piano. International. Really fine music, and effective. Difficult for the basset horn.

3. Mozart, W. A. (1756–91). Twelve Duets for basset horns, K 487; Canonic Adagio for two basset horns and bassoon, K 410; Adagio for two clarinets and three basset horns, K 411.

Graham Melville Mason of Edinburgh is making a collection of basset horn music which should be complete and authoritative. The International Clarinet Society of Denver, Colorado, has also published a list of twenty-five chamber works including basset horn which are of great interest to players. It is thought that this subject is outside the scope of this book.

Works for several clarinets

1. Fleming, Robert. Two piece suite (two clarinets and bass clarinet). Manuscript.

2. Agostini, Lucio. Trio Québécpis (three clarinets), Manuscript.

3. Weinzweig, John (1913–). Quartet (three clarinets and bass clarinet). Manuscript.

The three above works recommended and recorded by Avrahm Galper of Toronto.

4. Harvey, Paul (1935–). Four Easy Trios for three clarinets. Schott.

5. Harvey, Paul. Quartet for three clarinets and bass clarinet. Schott.

6. Wilson, Ken. Variations on a Teheme by Paginini. Boosey & Hawkes, 1968. An amusing and well written set of variations, by a New Zealand composer, on the most familiar of Paganini's themes.

7. Jacob, Gordon (1895–). Quartet for four clarinets (E flat, B flat, alto, bass). A transcription of an interesting saxophone quartet published by Emerson Music of York, England.

There is a large catalogue of excellent arrangements for three or four clarinets by various composer-arrangers also published by Emerson Music. The most important part of their output is in the field of the clarinet choir, listed blow.

Clarinet choir

1. Barat, J. Piece en sol mineur (clarinet with choir accompaniment). Leblanc.
2. Caillet, Lucien (1891–). 'Carnaval'; 'Clarinet Poem'; 'Caprice Sentimentale' (solo with choir). Leblanc.
3. Gates, Everett (1914–). 'Seasonal Sketches.' Leblanc.
4. Grundman, Clare (1913–). 'Caprice.' Boosey & Hawkes, 1961.
5. Harvey, Paul (1935–). Fantasia in one movement; Sinfonia for clarinet choir; Quartet for two clarinets, bass clarinet and contrabass clarinet; Quartet for E flat, B flat clarinets, basset horn and contrabass clarinet; Concertino for soprano saxophone and clarinet. choir. Manuscript.
Four easy trios for 3 clarinets. Schotts.
Quartet for 3 clarinets, bass clarinet. Schotts.
6. Sacci, Frank, and others. Arrangements of Mozart, Tschaikovsky, Handel, Bach, Pachabel, Palestrina and Klauss (contemporary). At State College of Fredonia (Dr William C. Willett). Recorded.
7. Troon, Vivian (London). Arrangements of pieces by Lambert, Milhaud, Bach, Schumann and others. Manuscript.
8. Holden, Roy (London). Similar arrangements. Recorded by his own clarinet choir.
9. Many arrangements of popular pieces published by Emerson Music of York.

Book-list for suggested further reading

Baines, Anthony, *Woodwind Instruments and Their History*. London 1957.

Carse, Adam, *The Orchestra from Beethoven to Berlioz*. Cambridge 1948.

Chatwin, R. B., 'Handel and the Clarinets' in *Galpin Society Journal* 1950.

Gabucci, A., *Origins of the Clarinet*. Milan 1937.

Grove, Sir George, *Dictionary of Music and Musicians* (various editions).

Klosé, Hyacinthe E., *Clarinet Method*. Paris 1843.

Kroll, Oskar, 'Das Chalumeau' in *Zeitschrift für Musikwissenschaft* May 1933.

Kroll, Oskar, *The Clarinet*. In German, Kassel 1965. In English (trans. Hilda Morres, ed. Anthony Baines), London 1968.

Landon, H. C. Robbins, *The Symphonies of Joseph Haydn*. London 1955.

Lazarus, H., *New and Modern Method*. London 1881.

Opperman, K., *Repertory of the Clarinet*. New York 1960.

Rendall, F. C., *The Clarinet*. London 1957.

Rendall, F. C., articles in Grove's *Dictionary*.

Richmond, Stanley, *Clarinet and Saxophone Experience*.

Sachs, Curt, *The History of Musical Instruments*. New York 1940.

Siegel, Alan, *The Twentieth Century Clarinettist*. Colombo.

Street, Oscar, *The Clarinet and Its Music*. London 1916.

Stubbins, William, *The Art of Clarinetistry*. Ann Arbor.

Weber, M. M., *Carl Maria von Weber*. Leipzig 1866.

The Clarinet

Weston, Pamela, *Clarinet Virtuosi of the Past*. London.
Whewell, Michael, 'Mozart's Basset Horn Trios' in *Musical Times* 1962.
Also: *Journals* of the International Clarinet Society of Denver, Colorado.

Discography

The following is a tolerably complete list of recordings that are or have been available in the United States and Europe. European pressings are followed by an asterisk (*). If a record is available in both the United States and Europe, the asterisk is enclosed in parentheses. A few 78 RPM recordings are listed, when they contain particularly good performances, or works not otherwise recorded. They are marked with a dagger †.

BARTÓK, Bela (1881–1945)
  Contrasts (1938)

Brymer, Grinke, Parry	Argo 89
de Peyer, Hurwitz, Crowson	EMI HQS-1306(*)
Drucker, Mann, Hambro	Bartok BRS-916
Goodman, Szigeti, Bartók	Columbia LOX-485-6†
	Odyssey 32160220(*)
International Soloists Chamber Ens.	Mace S-9055
Kell, Ritter, Rosen	Decca DL-9740
Kovács, Pauk, Frankl	Dover 7275
Lemser, Lautenbacher, Kontarsky	Turnabout 34480
Prinz, Gertler, Farnadi	Westminster 17074

BAX, Arnold (1883–1953)
  Sonata (1934)

Drucker, Hambro	Odyssey Y-30492(*)

BEETHOVEN, Ludwig Van (1770–1827)
  Duos (3) for Clarinet and Bassoon, G. 147 (WoO. 27)

Lancelot, Hogne	Turnabout 30476
	Vox SVBX-580
Zukovsky, Breidenthal	Avant 1011

  Trio in B♭, Op. 11 (1798)

de Peyer, du Pre, Barenboim	EMI SLS-789(*)

249

Discography

Trio in B♭, Op. 11 (1798) (cont.)
  D. Glazer, Soyer, F. Glazer   Turnabout TV-34108(*)
                                       Vox SVBX-580
  Hoogland, Honigh, Bylsma   Das Alte Werke SAWT-9547*
                                     Telefunken 641251
  Kell, Miller, Horszowski   Decca DL-9543
                         Columbia DX-1164-66(*)†
  Leister, Fournier, Kempff   DG 2530408
  McGinnis, Conable, Platt   Coronet 3032
  Montagnana Trio   Everest 3262

Trio in E♭, Op. 38 (arr. from Septet, Op. 20)
  Leister, Boettcher, Besch   DG ARC-2533 118(*)

BENJAMIN, Arthur (1893–1960)
  Le Tombeau de Ravel
    de Peyer, Preedy   Oiseau Lyre SOL-60028(*)

BERG, Alban (1885–1935)
  4 Pieces, Op. 5 (1913)
    Campbell, York   Crystal 331
    de Peyer, Crowson   Oiseau Lyre S-282(*)
    Stolzman, P. Serkin   Orion 73125

BERNSTEIN, Leonard (1918–   )
  Sonata (1941)
    Drucker, Hambro   Odyssey Y-30492(*)
    Willett, Staples   Mark 32638(*)

BLISS, Arthur (1891–1975)
  Quintet (1931)
    de Peyer, Melos Ens.   EMI HQS-1299(*)
                             Everest 3135
                             Everest 6135

BRAHMS, Johannes (1833–1897)
  Quintet in b, Op. 115 (1891)
    Berlin Phil. Octet   Philips 6500453*
    Boksovsky, Vienna Octet   Decca SXL-2297*
                                  London 9301
                                  London 6234
    Brymer, Prometheus Ens.   Pye TPLS-13004*
    de Peyer, Melos Ens.   EMI ASD-620(*)
                                  Angel S-36280
    Draper, Lener Quartet   Columbia L-2228-32(*)†
    Ettlinger, Tel-Aviv Quartet   Oiseau Lyre 146
    Geuser, Drolc Quartet   Mace S-9029
    Kell, Busch Quartet   HMV DB-3383-86(*)†

Kell, Fine Arts Quartet	Brunswick AXTL-1008*
	Decca DL-9532
	Concert Disc 1202
	Concert Disc 202
Leister, Amadeus Quartet	DG SLMP-139354
Michaels, Endres Quartet	Vox DL-560
	Vox STPL-516.200
	Vox SVBX-578
Oppenheim, Budapest Quartet	Columbia ML-5626
	Columbia MS-6226
Puddy, Gabrieli Quartet	Monitor S-2142
Sorokin, Oistrakh Quartet	Bruno 14062
Stolzman, Cleveland Quartet	RCA ARL 1-1993
Wlach, Vienna Konzerthaus Quartet	Westminster 18442
	Westminster 9016

Sonata No. 1 in f, Op. 120, #1 (1894)
Sonata No. 2 in E♭, Op. 120, #2 (1894)

de Peyer, Barenboim	EMI ASD-1436(*)
D. Glazer, F. Glazer	Vox SVBX-578
	Vox STDL-501210
Goodman, Rosenberg (#2)	CBS 71813-5 (Set M-629)(*)†
Kell, Horszowski	Mercury MG-10016*
Kell, Rosen	Decca DL-9639
Lancelot, d'Arco	Oiséau Lyre 50030
Leister, Demus	DG 104987(*)
M. Lurie, L. Lurie	Crystal S-301
Michaels, Kraus (#1)	CMS/Oryx 3C-325
Thurston, Foggin (#2)	Decca X-171-3*†
Wlach, Demus	Westminster XWN-18446
	Westminster 9023

Trio in a, Op. 114 (1891)

Forrest, Greenhouse, Balogh	Lyrichord 9
Geuser, Troester, Hansen	Mace S-9038
D. Glazer, Soyer, F. Glazer	Turnabout TV-34108(*)
	Vox SVBX-578
Kell, Miller, Horszowski	Decca DL-9732
Kell, Pini, Kentner	Columbia DX-1007-9†
Leister, Donderer, Eschenbach	DG SLPM-139398(*)
McGinnis, Conable, Platt	Coronet 3023
McLane, Hunkins, Kaye	Grenadilla Soc. GS-1002
Michaels, Storck, Kraus	CMS/Oryx 3C325
Montagnana Trio	Everest 3262
Wlach, Kwarda, Holetschek	Westminster 18449
	Westminster W-9017

BRUCH, Max (1838–1920)
  Concerto for Clarinet, Viola, and Orch., Op. 88
    Irmisch, Orch.   Grenodilla Soc. 1005

Discography

BUSONI, Ferruccio (1866–1924)
  Concertino, Op. 48 (1919)
    Triebskorn, Bunte/Berlin Sym.

Vox STGBY-616*
Candide 31003

CAGE, John (1912–)
  Sonata for Clarinet Solo (1930)
    Rehfeldt

Advance FGR-4

COPLAND, Aaron (1900–)
  Concerto (1948)
    de Peyer, Jacob/London Mozart Players
    Drushler, Gibson (piano)
    Goodman, Copland/Columbia Sym.

Unicorn RHS-314*
Mark 3344
Columbia ML-4421
Columbia ML-5897
Columbia MS-6497
Columbia MS-6805

  **Sextet for clarinet, piano, and string quartet
    (arr. from Short Sym.)** (1933)
    Wright, Copland, Julliard Quartet

Columbia M-30376

CRUSSELL, Bernhard Henrik (1775–1838)
  Grand Concerto in f, Op. 5
    de Peyer, Jacob/London Mozart Players

Unicorn RHS-314*

  Quartet, Op. 2
    Dössekker, Zürcher Quartet

Rimaphon LP-30-283*

  Quartet No. 2 in c, Op. 4
    Hacker, Music Party

Oiseau Lyre DSLO-501(*)

DEBUSSY, Claude (1962–1918)
  Petite Pièce (1910)
    de Peyer, Preedy
    Drucker, Hambro

Oiseau Lyre DSLO-501(*)
Odyssey Y-30492

  Première Rhapsodie (1909–1910)
    Boutard, Baudo/Czech. Phil.
    Brymer, Prohaska/Vienna State Opera Orch.

Supraphon SUAST-50874*

Vanguard VSL-11006*
Vanguard 71167

    Dangain, Froment/Luxembourg Radio

Vox STGBY0679*
Candide 31069

    Dangain, Martinon/ORTF Orch.

EMI SLS-893*
Angel S-37065

    de Peyer, Boulez/New Philharmonia

CBS 72785*
Columbia M-30483

    Deplus, Constant/ORTF Orch.
    Drucker, Bernstein/N.Y. Phil.

Erato STU-70719*
CBS 72453
Columbia MS-6659

252

Drushler, Lee (piano)	Mark 3344
Gigliotti, Ormandy/Philadelphia Orch.	Columbia MS-6977
Goodman, Barbirolli/N.Y. Phil.	Columbia LOX-521*†
Gugholtz, Ansermet, Suisse Romande	Decca SXL-6167*
	London 6437
Hamelin, Coppola/Sym. Orch.	HMV DB-4809†
	Grenadilla Soc. 1006
Kell, Rosen (piano)	Decca DL-9570
	Decca DL-9744

DIAMOND, Arline
Composition for Clarinet (1963)
    Rehfeldt   Advance FGR-4

FRANÇAIX, Jean (1912–)
Concerto
    Lancelot, Male/Orch. de Chambre de Nice
                                Inédites ORTF 995 019(*)

GLINKA, Mikhail (1803–1957)
Trio Pathétique (1826–1827)
    G. Feigin, V. Feigin, Zhukov   Angel S-40165(*)

HERRMANN, Bernard (1911–)
Quintet for Clarinet and Strings
    Hill, Ariel Quartet   Unicorn RHS-332

HINDEMITH, Paul (1895–1963)
Concerto (1950)
    Cahuzac, Hindemith/Philharmonia Orch.   Angel 35490
                            Columbia 33CX1553*
Sonata (1940)
    Forrest, Tupas   Lyrichord 15
    Kell, Rosen   Decca DL-9570(*)

HODDINOTT, Alun (1929–)
Concerto, Op. 3 (1954)
    de Peyer, Atherton/London Sym. Orch.   Decca SXL-6513*

HOFFMEISTER, Franz (1754–1812)
Concerto in b
    Concerto Amsterdam   BASF BAC-3049*

HOLBROOKE, Josef (1878–1958)
Quintet No. 2 in G., Op. 27, "Legeia" (after Poe)
    Kell, Willoughby Quartet   Columbia LX-814-6†

Discography

HONEGGER, Arthur (1892–1955)
  Sonatina (1922)
    Cahuzac, Jensen   Columbia LDX-3†
                                        Grenadilla Soc. GS-1006
    Drucker, Hambro   Odyssey Y-30492(*)

HUMMEL, Johann Nepomuk (1778–1837)
  Quartet in E♭
    Glazer, Kohon Quartet   Vox DL-960
    Hacker, Music Party   Oiseau Lyre DSLO-501

IVES, Charles (1874–1954)
  Largo for Clarinet, Violin, and Piano
    D'Antonio, Sandler, Stevens   Laurel LR-103

KHACHATURIAN, Aram (1903–   )
  Trio (1932)
    Bellison, B. Urban, V. Urban   Grenadilla GS-1003
    D'Antonio, Candler, Stevens   Laurel LR-103
    de Peyer, Hurwitz, Crowson   EMI SQS-1306(*)

KRENEK, Ernst (1900–   )
  Monologue (1956)
    Rehfeldt   Advance FGR-4
  Trio for Clarinet, Violin, and Piano (1946)
    D'Antonio, Sandler, Stevens   Laurel LR-103

KROMMER (KRAMAR), Frantisek (1759–1831)
  Concerto in E♭ Op. 36
    Brymer, Prohaska/Vienna State Opera Orch.
                                        Vanguard VSL-11006*
                                            Vanguard 71176
    Riha, Smetacek/Prague Sym.   Supraphon SUA-19039*

LESEMANN, Frederick (1936–   )
  Sonata for Clarinet and Percussion
    Lurie, Ervin   Crystal S-641

MANEVICH, Alexander (1908–   )
  Concerto
    Roginsky, Rabinovich/Leningrad Phil.   Monitor MC-2030

MARTINO, Donald (1931–   )
  B-a-b-b-i-t-t for Clarinet
    Rehfeldt   Advance FGR-17
  A Set for Clarinet (1954)
    Rehfeldt   Advance FGR-4

254

MARTINU, Bohuslav (1890–1959)
  Sonatina (1957)
    de Peyer, Preedy   Oiseau Lyre SOL-60028

MESSIAEN, Olivier (1908–)
  Quatour pour la fin du temps
    de Peyer, Gruenberg, Pleeth, Beroff   Angel S-36587
    Rabbai, Cohen, Eddy, Levin   Candide 31050
    Stoltzman, Kavafian, Sherry, P. Serkin   RCA ARL1-1567

MILHAUD, Darius (1892–1974)
  Sonatina (1927)
    Drucker, Hambro   Odyssey Y-30492(*)
  Suite (1936)
    Compinsky Ens.   Sheffield S-3
    Dangain, Boussinot, Boury   EMI CO65-12526(*)
    Delecluse, Parrenin, Hass-Hamburger   Period 563
    de Peyer, Hurwitz, Crowson   EMI HQS-1306(*)
    Kell, Ritter, Rosen   Decca DL-9740

MOLTER, Johann (1695–1765)
  Concerto in A
    Lancelot, Beaucamp/Rouen Chamber Orch.
      World Series PHC-9078
  Concerto in D
    Lancelot, Beaucamp/Rouen Chamber Orch.
      World Series PHC-9078
  Concerto No. 3 in G
    Michaels, Stadlmair/Munich Chamber Orch.
      DG Archive 198 415(*)

MOORE, Douglas (1893–1969)
  Quintet for Clarinet and Strings (1946)
    Oppenheim, New Music Quartet   Desto 6425

MOZART, Wolfgang Amadeus (1756–1791)
  Concerto in A, K. 622 (1791)
    Brymer, Beecham/Royal Phil.   EMI ALP-1768(*)
      EMI ASD-344(*)
      Seraphim S-60193
      Capitol SG-7201
    Brymer, Davis/London Sym.   Philips SAL-3535(*)
    Brymer, Marriner/Acad. of St.-Martin-in-the Fields
      Philips 6500 378(*)
    Cahuzac, Haydn Soc. Orch.   Haydn Soc. HSL-1047
    de Peyer, Collins/London Sym.   Decca Eclipse ECS-567*
      London 9118

Discography

Concerto in A, K. 622 (1791) (cont.)

de Peyer, Maag/London Sym.	Decca SXL-2238*
	London 6178
	London 9247
de Wilde, van Beinum/Concertgebouw Orch.	
	Philips ABL-3217(*)
	Epic LC-3456
Dienzer (basset-clar.), Collegium Areum	BASF BAC-3001(*)
Dörr, Leitner/Bamberg Sym.	Nonesuch 71074
Etienne, Hewitt/Orch.	Haydn Soc. 9049
Fadle, Ger. Phil.	CMS/Oryx 17
Geuser, Fricsay/Berlin State Radio Sym.	
	Heliodor H/HS-25017
	DG 17 159/19 130
Gigliotti, Ormandy/Philadelphia Orch.	CBS 61657*
	Columbia M2L-284(5851/2)
	Columbia M2S-684(6451/2)
	Columbia MS-6452
Goodman, Munch/Boston Sym.	RCA RB-16013*
	RCA VICS-1402(*)
	RCA LM-2073
Kell, Sargent, London Phil.	HMV C-3167-70†
Kell, Zimbler/Zimbler Sinfonietta	Brunswick AXL-2002*
	Brunswick AXTL-1071*
	Decca DL-7500
	Decca DL 9732
Lancelot, Froment/Oiseau Lyre Orch.	Oiseau Lyre 50006
Lancelot, Paillard/Paillard Ens.	Westminster 18859
	Westminster 14068
	Music Guild S-136
Leister, Karajan/Berlin Phil.	EMI ASD-2916(*)
	Angel S-3783
Leister, Kubelik/Berlin Phil.	DG SLPEM 136 550(*)
McCaw, Leppard/New Philharmonia	Unicorn UNS-239(*)
Marcellus, Szell/Cleveland Orch.	Columbia MS-6968
	Columbia D3M-33261
	Epic LC-3841
	Epic BC-1241
Michaels, Reichert/Westphalian Sym.	
	Vox STGBY 511.110(*)
	Vox 11110
	Turnabout 34188/91
Prinz, Böhm, Vienna Phil.	DG 2530 411(*)
Prinz, Münchinger, Vienna Phil.	Decca SDD-115*
	London STS-15071
	London 6351
	London 9351

Walton, Karajan/Philharmonia Orch.

Columbia 33CX-1361*
Angel 35323

Wlach, Rodzinski/Vienna State Opera Orch.

Westminster 18287

Divertimenti for 2 Clarinets and Bassoon, K.A. 229,
#2–5 (1783)

Wlach, Bartosek, Oehlinger — Westminster W-9058

Quintet in A, K. 581 (1789)

Bellison, Roth Quartet	Grenadilla Soc. GS-1003
A. Boskovsky, Vienna Octet	Decca LXT-5032*
	London 2403
	London 6379
	London 9121
	London 9379
Brymer, Allegri Quartet	Philips 6500 073(*)
Deplus, Danish Quartet	Telefunken 5635017
de Bavier, New Italian Quartet	Decca LXT-5032*
de Peyer, Melos Ens.	EMI ASD605(*)
	Angel S-36241
Draper, Lener Quartet	Columbia L-2252-5†
Etienne, Vegh Quartet	Haydn Soc. 9049
Forrest, Galimir Quartet	Lyrichord 67
Gärtner, Kussmaul Quartet	CMS/Oryx 7
Geuser, Drolc Quartet	Mace S-9028
Goodman, Boston Sym. Quartet	RCA RB-16013*
	RCA ML-2073
	RCA VICS-1402(*)
Goodman, Budapest Quartet	HMV 5683-6†
	HMV DB-3576-9†
Kell, Fine Arts Quartet	Brunswick AXTL-1007*
	Concert Disc 203
	Concert Disc 1203
	Decca DL-9600
Kell, Philharmonia Quartet	Columbia DX-1187-90†
King, Aeolian Quartet	Saga STXID-5291*
Leister, Berlin Phil. Quartet	DG 138 996(*)
Oppenheim, Budapest Quartet	Columbia MS-6127
	Columbia ML-5455
Pieterson, Grumiaux Quartet	Philips 6500 924
	Philips 7300 414
Puddy, Gabrieli Quartet	Classics for Pleasure CFP-121*
Michaels, Endres Quartet	Vox STPL 511.110
	Vox 11110
	Vox SVBX-548
Simenauer, Pascal Quartet	Monitor S-2115
Wlach, Vienna Konzerthaus Quartet	Westminster 18269

Discography

Quintet in A, K. 581 (1789) (cont.)
Wright, Schneider Quartet Columbia MS-7447
Columbia D3M-3300

Trio in Eb, K. 498 (1786)
A. Boskovsky, Vienna Octet Decca LXT-5293*
London 9181
London STS-15059

Brymer, Ireland, Bishop Philips 6500 073(*)
de Peyer, Melos Ens. Oiseau Lyre 50190
Oiseau Lyre 60020(*)
EMI ASD-605
Angel S-36241

Forrest, Cooley, Balogh Lyrichord 9
Kell, Fuchs, Horszowski Brunswick AXTL-1011*
Decca DL-9543

Kell, Riddle, Kentner Columbia DX-998-1000†
Klocker, Consortium Classicum CMS/Oryx 43
Triebskorn, Endres Quartet Turnabout TV-34035(*)
Vox SVBX-548
Vox SVBX-568

Weber, Mester, Hancock Cambridge CRM-817

MUSGRAVE, Thea (1928–   )
Concerto
de Peyer, del Mar/London Sym. Argo ZRG-726(*)

NIELSEN, Carl (1865–1931)
Concerto, Op. 57 (1928)
Cahuzac, Orch. Columbia ML-2219
Deak, Maga/Philharmonia Hungarica

Turnabout TV-34261(*)
Drucker, Bernstein, N.Y. Phil. CBS 72639*
Columbia MS-7028
Eriksson, Wöldike/Danish Radio Orch. Decca LXT-2979*
Decca ACL-292*
London LL-1142
Goodman, Gould/Chicago Sym. RCA SB-6701*
RCA LSC-2920
McCaw, Leppard/New Philharmonia Unicorn UNS-239(*)
Stevensson, Blomstedt/Danish Radio Orch. EMI SLS-5027(*)

PIERNE, Gabriel (1863–1937)
Canzonetta in Eb, Op. 19 (1888)
Cahuzac, Jensen Columbia LDX-3†
Grenadilla Soc. GS-1006

Sérénade, Op. 7 (1875), arr.
Délécluse, d'Arco Sel SA-11†

258

POKORNY, Franz (1729–1770)
  Concerto in B♭
    Lancelot, Beaucamp/Douen Chamber Orch.
                             World Series PHC-9078

POULENC, Francis (1899–1963)
  Sonata (1962)

Boutard, Fevrier	Nonesuch 71033(*)
Campbell, York	Crystal 331
Drushler, Lee	Mark 3344
Portal, Fevrier	EMI EMSP-553*

  Sonata for Clarinet and Bassoon (1922, rev. 1945)

de Peyer, Waterhouse	EMI ASD-2506
	Angel S-4076
Gigliotti, Garfield	Golden Crest 4115
Listokin, Popkin	Golden Crest S-4076
Portal, Wallez	EMI EMSP-553

  Sonata for 2 Clarinets (1918)

Portal, Gabai	EMI EMSP-553

RAWTHORNE, Alan (1905–1971)
  Quartet (1948)

King, Aeolian Quartet	Argo ZRG-660(*)

REGER, Max (1873–1916)
  Quintet in A, Op. 146 (1915)

Bell' Arte Ens.	Vox SVBX-586
de Peyer, Melos Ens. (2d mvt.)	EMI ASD-620*
Gall, Keller Quartet	Mur 22*
Leister, Drolc Quartet	DG 2530 303(*)

  Sonatas in A♭, Op. 49, #1; in B♭, Op. 107

H. Tichman, R. Tichman	Mark 3366

REICHA, Anton (1770–1836)
  Quintet in B♭

Dössekker, Zürcher Quartet	Rimaphon LP-30-283*

RIMSKY-KORSAKOV, Nikolai (1844–1908)
  Concertstück in E♭ for Clarinet and Military Band (1878)
    Mikhailov, Dunsev/USSR Ministry of Defense Symphonic
      Band   EMI ASD-3107(*)
                           Melodiya/Angel S-40108

ROSSINI, Gioaccino (1792–1868)
  Introduction and Variations in C (1809)
    de Peyer, Frübeck de Burgos/New Philharmonia
                             Angel S-36589

Discography

SAINT-SAËNS, Camille (1835–1921)
Sonata in Eb, Op. 167 (1921)
    Kell, Smith   Decca DL-9941

SCAVARDA, Donald (1928–)
Matrix for Clarinetist (1962)
    Rehfeldt   Advance FGR-4

SCHMITT, Florent (1870–1958)
Andantino (1920)
    de Peyer, Preedy   Oiseau Lyre SOL-60028(*)

SCHUMANN, Robert (1810–1856)
Fantasiestücke, Op. 73 (1849)
    Campbell, York   Crystal 331
    de Peyer, Melos Ens.   EMI ASD-2374(*)
    Kell, Moore   HMV C-3170†
                                    HMV C-3228†
    Kell, Rosen   Decca DL-9744
    Weber, Wingreen   Lyrichord 7193(*)
    Wright, Goldsmith   RCA VICS1621

SPOHR, Ludwig (1784–1895)
Concerto #1 in c, Op. 26
    de Peyer, Davis/London Sym.   Oiseau Lyre 50204
                               Oiseau Lyre 60035(*)
Concerto #2 in Eb, Op. 57 (1810)
    Denman, Vivienne/Sadlers Wells Orch.   Oryx 1828(*)

STAMITZ, Johann Wenzel Anton (1717–1757)
Concerto in Bb
    Hacker, Hogwood/Academy of Ancient Music
                          Oiseau Lyre DSLO-505(*)
    Lancelot, Beaucamp/Rouen Chamber Orch.
                          World Series PHC-9078
    Michaels, Munich Chamber Orch.   DG ARC-3092

STAMITZ, Karl (1749–1801)
Concerto #3 in Bb (1785)
    Denman, Vivienne/Sadlers Wells Orch.   Oryx 1821(*)
    Glazer, Wagner/Innsbruck Orch.   Vox 1130
                           Turnabout TV-34093(*)
    Klein, Müller-Brühl/Cologne Soloists Ens.
                        Nonesuch H-71148

STEVENS, Halsey (1908–)
Concerto for Clarinet and String Orch. (1969)
    Lurie, Endo/Crystal Chamber Orch.   Crystal S-851

260

STRAUSS, Richard (1864–1949)
  Duet Concertino for Cl., Bsn., Strings, and Harp (1947)
    Michallik, Buttkewitz, Rögner/Berlin Radio Sym.
                                         EMI ASD-2320(*)

STRAVINSKY, Igor (1882–1971)
  L'Histoire du Soldat, arr. for Clarinet, Violin, and Piano (1918)
    D'Antonio, Sandler, Stevens   Laurel LR-103
  Three Pieces for Clarinet Solo (1918)
    Deplus   Everest 3184
    Kell   Decca DL-9570

SZALOWSKI, Antoni (1907–　)
  Sonatina (1948)
    Kell, Smith   Decca DL-9941
    Willett, Staples   Mark 32638

TEMPLETON, Alec (1909–1953)
  Pocket Size Sonata #1 (1942)
    Kell, Smith   Decca DL-9941

UHL, Alfred (1909–　)
  Symphonie Concertante (1944)
    Drapal, Orch.   Grenadilla Soc. 1005

VAUGHAN WILLIAMS, Ralph (1872–1958)
  Six Studies in English Folk-Song (1927)
    Campbell, York   Crystal 331
    Kell, Smith   Decca DL-9941

WAGNER, Richard (1813–1883)
  Adagio
    Boskovsky, Vienna Octet   London 6234
                                     London 9301
    Brymer, Marriner/Acad. of St.-Martin-in-the Fields
                               Vanguard 71167
    Brymer, Prohaska/Vienna State Opera Orch.
                       Vanguard VSL-11006(*)
                              Argo ZRG-604

WEBER, Carl Maria von (1786–1826)
  Concertino in c, Op. 26 (1811)
    Brymer, Prohaska/Vienna State Opera Orch.
                             Vanguard 709/10
                       Vanguard VSL-11006(*)
                           Vanguard 71167
    de Peyer, Frübeck de Burgos/New Philharmonia   ASD 2455*
                                Angel S-36589

Discography

Concertino in c, Op. 26 (1811) (cont.)
Gigliotti, Ormandy/Philadelphia Orch.   Columbia 91A02033
Columbia ML-4629
Glazer, Wagner/Innsbruck Sym.   Turnabout TV-34151(*)
Hite, Dambrans (piano)   Coronet 1142

Concerto #1 in f, Op. 73 (J. 114) (1811)
de Peyer, Frübeck de Burgos/New Philharmonia
EMI ASD-2455*
Angel S-36589
Glazer, Wagner/Innsbruck Sym.   Turnabout TV-34151(*)
Goodman, Martinon/Chicago Sym.   RCA SB-6805*
RCA LSC-3052
Heine, Walter/Salzburg Mozarteum Orch.   Period 529
Dover 5246
Leister, Kubelik/Berlin Phil.   DG 136 550(*)
DG 2530 087
Lancelot, Buschlbauer/Bamberg Sym.   Erato STU-70517

Concerto #2 in E♭, Op. 74 (1811)
de Peyer, Davis/London Sym.   Oiseau Lyre 50204
Oiseau Lyre 60035
Goodman, Martinon/Chicago Sym.   RCA SB-6805*
RCA LSC-3052
Heine, Walter/Salzburg Mozarteum Orch.   Period 529
Dover 5246
Pacewicz, Cathcart/Lambeth Orch.   Lor 1001

Grand Duo Concertante, Op. 33 (1816)
de Peyer, Preedy   Oiseau Lyre SOL-60028(*)
Kell, Rosen   Decca DL-9744
Schulze, Jackson   Amphion CL-2149

WHITTENBERG, Charles (1927–)
Three Pieces for Clarinet Solo (1963)
Rehfeldt   Advance FGR-4

WINTER, Peter von (1754–1825)
Concertino for Clarinet, Cello, and Orch.
Michaels, Güdel, Ristenpart/Chamber Orch. of the Saar
Nonesuch H-71041

Index

Clarinet